The
Church
A Believing Fellowship

John H. Leith

John Knox Press
ATLANTA

Library of Congress Cataloging in Publication Data

Leith, John H
    The church, a believing fellowship.

    Bibliography: p.
    1. Presbyterian Church—Doctrinal and controversial works—Presbyterian authors. 2. Church. I. Title.
BX9175.2.L44   230'.5133   80-82192
ISBN 0-8042-0518-2

© Marshall C. Dendy 1965
© copyright 1981 John Knox Press
10 9 8 7 6 5 4 3 2 1
Printed in the United States of America
John Knox Press
Atlanta, Georgia 30365

Preface

This book originated in the communicant classes which the author taught at the First Presbyterian Church, Auburn, Alabama during the years 1948–1959. In 1965 it was published as a textbook for church school classes, grades 7–9 (ages 12–14), in the Covenant Life Curriculum. It has been widely used as a text for communicant classes for senior high and college students and also for officer training and the introduction of new church members to the Presbyterian Church.

Eighteen years have passed since this text was written for publication, allowing for continuity and development in the writer's own understanding. The book, however, has proved useful in its present form, and it has been allowed to remain substantially as it was written. This new edition has made possible numerous revisions and some enlargement, which should enhance its usefulness.

The literature in the areas covered by this text is enormous. A highly selected and annotated list of supplementary readings is included as an appendix. The author's *Introduction to the Reformed Tradition* complements this text on many themes.

The usefulness of this text will be greatly enhanced if it is combined with the mastery of certain basic Scripture passages, creeds, and hymns. The Protestant reformers took over the medieval practice of basing communicant instruction on the basic texts of the law, the creed, and the prayer along with a knowledge of the sacraments and practices of piety. This instruction enabled believers to participate intelligibly in the worship of the church, and it gave to them a knowledge of the basic elements and practices of Christian piety.

The life of the church today is impoverished by a loss of a Christian memory. This loss of memory is related to the decline in the old practice of committing important texts to memory. "Memory work" has been increasingly dropped from the teaching ministry of the church, sometimes for pedagogical reasons which are controversial and sometimes as a result of the corroding influences of a secular and pluralistic society. Yet it is difficult to see how the church can tradition itself and how the faith can be renewed from generation to generation without the committing to memory of certain basic materials. This memory work is the responsibility not only of the home but also and primarily of the church. The writer's own experience as a pastor for fourteen years and as a teacher of the communicants' classes in which this text first developed established the conviction that real familiarity, if not the memorization of certain basic material, is essential for the life of the congregation and for personal piety. In any case familiarity with the following texts will greatly enhance the value of this book in incorporating members into the life of the church. This incorporation of members into the church is the pastoral as well as the teaching responsibility of the church.

The Bible
> The books of the Bible in order
> The Ten Commandments, Exodus 20:1–17
> Psalm 23
> The Beatitudes, Matthew 5:3–12
> The Lord's Prayer, Matthew 6:9–13
> The Great Commandment, Matthew 22:37–40
> Matthew 6:25–34
> John 3:16
> John 14:1–7
> Romans 8:28–39
> 1 Corinthians 13

Creeds
> The Apostles' Creed
> The Nicene Creed

Hymns
> All People That on Earth Do Dwell
> A Mighty Fortress Is Our God

Prayers (See Appendix of Chapter VII for texts of some of the great prayers of the church.)

In the original edition this study was accompanied by a guide that assumed the student would keep a notebook and do written assignments. Some of the questions that presupposed this guide remain in the questions and projects suggested at the conclusion of each chapter.

Eleanor Godfrey of Media Resources, Union Theological Seminary in Virginia, very generously helped to update the resources available to supplement the text. My friend and colleague Charles Swezey has been very helpful in revisions of Chapter VI.

John H. Leith

Dedication

For those friends whose participation
in communicant and seminary classes
made teaching a joy
and whose subsequent living, teaching, and preaching
of the Reformed and Christian faith
have made teachings eminently worthwhile

Contents

CHAPTER I

The Church in the Bible

This book is a study in the meaning of the church. It will seek to answer two questions: (1) What is the church? and (2) How does the church live and express itself in the world? These questions are personal, for you and I are the church. For this reason we need to state them another way. First, who am I as a member of God's people? Second, how do I live as a member of the people of God?

We have to identify ourselves. Have you tried telling a stranger who you are? How do you do it? One of the most frequent ways by which we tell who we are is by pointing out our relation to other people. We tell who we are by giving the name of our father or mother or brother or sister. We say who we are by telling of the groups to which we belong. We say we attend such and such a school, or live in such and such a community. We tell who we are by naming the people with whom we live.

Christians are likewise identified by the people to whom they belong. A Christian is a member of the people of God, the church. Once we are identified as members of the church, we have to identify ourselves further within the church. Our first task in this part of our study is to answer the question, Who am I as a Christian, as a member of the church? Once we have answered this question, we can then move to the second question: How do we as members of the church live?

Creation and Covenant

THE CREATION OF ADAM AND EVE(GENESIS 1:1–24)

Have you ever asked the question, When did the church begin? The answer depends partly upon what we mean by the question. But the basic answer is that the church began with the creation of man. The old Scots Confession declared, "We most surely believe that God preserved, instructed, multiplied, honoured, adorned, and called from death to life His Kirk (Church) in all ages since Adam. . . ."[1] As long as there has existed a believing fellowship who have worshiped God, so long has the church existed.

God created human beings to live in fellowship with himself. He created them to be responsible; that is, to respond to his revelation of himself and his will. This was God's intention. This was God's purpose for humans, for they are not machines that run mechanically. They are not simply animals who live by instinct and impulse. Human beings are created in God's image. This means that they have a freedom which machines and animals do not have. A person can set goals for life and can deny instincts to fulfill those goals. For example, human beings may be hungry and food may be available, but they have the freedom and ability to refuse to eat in order to do something else. An animal does not so clearly have this freedom. If an animal is hungry and if food is available, the animal eats. Human freedom gives the capacity for love, for trust, for loyalty, for courage, for friendship. So far as we know, animals do not have this power, nor do machines.

God created Adam and Eve with ability for friendship and loyalty. The great purpose of every human life is fellowship with and obedience and loyalty to God. This is God's intention for every human being.

THE FALL (GENESIS 3—11)

God's intention for Adam and Eve was not to be fulfilled. They refused to live in loyalty and trust and rebelled against God. The story of their fall is told in Genesis 3.

It would be wrong for us to see this simply as a story of something which happened long ago. It did happen long ago. But it has continued to happen ever since. It has happened in our own lives.

The consequences of Adam and Eve's refusal to live according to God's intention for their lives were disastrous. Adam and Eve became ashamed and hid (Gen. 3:10). They became afraid (Gen. 3:10). Adam began to accuse Eve (Gen. 3:12) and to excuse himself. Their lives became disorganized and painful.

The consequences of Adam and Eve's refusal did not end with them. People now began to have difficulty living with one another. In Genesis 4 we learn that Cain became jealous of his brother Abel and slew him. When human beings refuse to live according to God's intention for their lives, they also have difficulty living in fellowship with one another.

Human beings have the freedom to rebel against God, but they must suffer the consequences. They cannot live as they please and get away with it. The refusal to live according to God's intention had disastrous consequences for humanity and for human relationships, as we have seen. But this is not the end of God's judgment. In the story of the flood (Gen. 6), we are told clearly that individuals cannot get away with rebellion. Read Genesis 6:5–8. God sets limits to our rebellion.

Yet even the flood did not convince people that God's judgment stood over them. They still thought they could do as they pleased and get away with it. They said, "We shall build a tower which reaches to heaven. The floods will not reach us now." The Tower of Babel was an attempt to make life safe for rebellion (Gen. 11:1–9). Again, this is not simply a story of something which happened a long time ago. We are always trying to build towers which reach to heaven.

But the Tower of Babel did not succeed. God confused the builders so that they did not understand one another. They were scattered, and the tower, of course, did not reach heaven. This, too, is the story of every human effort to escape God's judgment, and of

every effort of human beings to live life as they please. When we
ebel against God, we end up being unable to talk to one another
and to get along with one another.

The first eleven chapters of Genesis tell us the great and wonderful news that God created man for fellowship with himself. They
also tell us the terrible news that men and women refused to accept
God's intention for human life. They rebelled against God and
sought to live their lives as they pleased. The consequences of this
rebellion were disaster. Individuals became dissatisfied with themselves and their neighbors. They even became murderers.

Yet as Augustine said centuries ago, humanity's rebellion did
not take God by surprise. He had a remedy at hand. He called out a
people who would be his people. Through this people, the church,
God would fulfill his purpose in creation.

THE CALL OF ABRAHAM (GENESIS 12:1–3)

A clear promise that God did not intend to leave human beings
in their plight is found in the story of Noah. God limited the expression of his judgment upon human sin. His flood did not blot out
man from the face of the earth. God provided a way for Noah to
escape with his family. God's purpose for his people could still be
fulfilled.

But the deliverance of Noah did not solve the problem. People
continued to sin. If God's purposes for human beings were to be
fulfilled, something else had to be done.

How would God now create a people for himself? The answer is
found in Genesis 12:1–3. Here God meets the problem of human
rebellion by calling Abram and promising to use his family as a
means of blessing all the nations of the earth. God would use one
man and his seed (his family or descendants) as a means of accom-
plishing his purpose for all people.

God's call to Abraham was a call to faith, loyalty, and trust: "Go
from your country and your kindred and your father's house to the
land that I will show you. And I will make of you a great nation, and
I will bless you, and make your name great so that you will be a
blessing. I will bless those who bless you, and him who curses you I

will curse; and by you all the families of the earth shall bless themselves" (Gen. 12:1b—3).

Read carefully the words of God's call. Note their demand for
trust and loyalty. The answer of Abraham to this call has ever since
been regarded as an example of faith. Read Hebrews 11:8. If you
had asked ancient Hebrews about the meaning of faith, they would
have answered by telling the story of Abraham. Theology, what we
believe about God, can be stated in a short creed such as the
Apostles' Creed. It can also be expressed in the story of a person's
life. One way of learning the meaning of faith is to recall the story of
Abraham.

Our concern here is not simply with Abraham's response to
God's call. Rather, the focus of our attention is on God's purpose to
use the faith of Abraham and his family as a means of blessing and
cursing. Those who bless Abraham will be blessed and those who
curse him will be cursed. God's intention is to use Abraham and his
seed as a means of establishing his people. But there is nothing automatic in God's work with his people. For this reason the very
means which God intends to use to bless them can be their curse if
they reject this means. So it is with Abraham and his family. Read
carefully Deuteronomy 11:26—32.

THE COVENANT AT SINAI (EXODUS 19—24)

The people of God who had their beginning with Abram were
established anew with the exodus and the giving of the law at Sinai.
In the background of this new covenant was God's deliverance of
the children of Israel from slavery in Egypt. You are familiar with
the story. The Hebrews had gone to Egypt in time of famine. In the
course of time they became slaves, and their plight became desperate. In the face of the people's need, God called Moses, and under
his leadership delivered his people.

This was no small accomplishment. First, Pharaoh had to be per-
suaded to let the people go. Then when Pharaoh changed his mind,
a miraculous deliverance saved them from Pharaoh's clutch at the
Red Sea. The important point is the conviction of the Hebrews that
this deliverance was something which God had done for them. In

this deliverance God made himself known to them. "I am the Lord your God, who brought you out of the land of Egypt, out of the house of bondage" (Exod. 20:2). The Hebrews knew that they could not have delivered themselves. They were a weak and desperate people. But God had delivered them.

God delivered Israel for a purpose. This purpose was the same as his purpose in calling Abraham. By delivering Israel he would establish his people and bless all the people of the earth. He would do this by means of the covenant at Sinai.

A covenant is a contract or a pact between two or more people. It is a bond uniting a people. In the Bible the covenant is one of the ways the relationship between God and his people is established. We call the people of God the covenant people, a people united with God through a compact.

God's covenant with his people is both like and unlike the covenants which human beings have with one another. In Exodus 19— 24 you may discover the following characteristics of God's covenant at Sinai:

1. God establishes the covenant. The covenant is not between equals. Abraham had never thought of God's calling him. The Hebrews in Egypt were a poor and desperate people. They did not decide that they should make a covenant with God. No! God called Abraham. God chose the Hebrews in Egypt to be his people, and he delivered them from slavery. God elected his people before they ever thought about him.

In addition, God is creator. He made humanity. We belong to him and exist because God wills for us to exist. We depend upon God so totally for life that we cannot find any adequate illustrations of this dependence. No created thing depends upon any other created thing in the same way that all created things depend upon the creator. God is the creator of man and the chooser of his people.

This is the first and greatest difference between the covenant of God with his people and all other covenants.

2. The covenant depends upon decision. The covenant with God is not established by natural ties such as those of race and blood and birth. It is established by a free decision. God chooses us.

We respond to God by answering Yes to God's call upon us. Our decisions are expressed in many ways: in faith, in loyalty, in trust, in obedience. The most important point to note is that the covenant is not automatic. It is personal, moral, historical.

3. When human beings accept God's call, they commit themselves to serve and obey God. God gives to his people the law as the constitution. This law is quite clear and specific. It is set forth in Exodus 19—24 and again in Deuteronomy. The Ten Commandments are a clear summary of it.

The law is not a discipline which is harshly imposed upon people. It is rather, first of all, a description of the way the people of God live. The Ten Commandments can be translated, "You are a people who have no other gods before me," or "You do not steal."

Furthermore, the law is an expression of the intention God had for man from the beginning. The law describes the way man was created to live. It indicates the true nature of life. When human beings do not live according to law, they are violating their own nature.

Here then is a new stage in the life of the church, the people of God. God calls a people into being by delivering them from Egypt and giving them his law. The people obligate themselves to be God's people. They will live in obedience to God's will. Through his people, God will fulfill his purpose to bless all nations.

THE COVENANT WITH DAVID (2 SAMUEL 7)

In addition to giving the covenant to the people at Sinai, God also gave to Israel a king. Read 1 Samuel 8—9. The king was God's anointed, God's elect, just as the people were chosen by God. His appointment was accompanied by a covenant, again just as in the case of the people. God would grant power and endurance to the king, and the king would serve God. The purpose of the king was to rule for God and to establish God's rule on earth. The king was to be one of the means by which God would establish his people and by which the descendants of Abraham would be a blessing to all the peoples of earth.

Saul, the first king of God's people, did not prove to be a good king. God renewed the covenant with David, his successor. In 2 Samuel 7 we learn that David the king was concerned that he had not built a house for God. Nathan the prophet advised him to do this. But God revealed himself to Nathan and told him that this was not God's will. "I have not dwelt in a house since the day I brought up the people of Israel from Egypt to this day," he declared. God is not confined to a house. God is wherever his people are. (Read 2 Samuel 7.)

It is in this connection that God renewed his covenant with David. God did not need David to build him a house, but God would build David's house. He would establish David's kingdom. (Read 2 Samuel 7:14-16.)

This word of God to David was to be fulfilled in a way far beyond David's power to imagine. Through David's seed there would come a king who would bless all people, as David could not have hoped to bless them. This king would be Jesus Christ. He would rule not by a sword but by his word and spirit.

For the moment let us note that God gave Israel a king to be his representative and to establish his kingdom. In this way he offered a remedy for human sin and rebellion.

The Suffering Servant and Jesus Christ

THE SUFFERING SERVANT (ISAIAH 53)

The people failed. The history of Israel is a history of rebellion against God. The king failed. Many of David's successors did not walk in his footsteps. Neither the people nor the kings kept their covenant with God. The old problem rose again.

After the people and the kings fail, God sends his Suffering Servant, who suffers for the people. He bears their punishment. He takes as his own the guilt of all. (Read Isaiah 53:4-6.)

The Suffering Servant does two things. First, he offers forgiveness for sin. He bears the guilt incurred by sin and pays its price. We get some glimpse of the meaning of this in human relations. A father or mother accepts the guilt of a child and forgives. A boy forgives a real wrong done him by a friend simply by taking a blow and not returning it. This is a new kind of suffering. It is undeserved suffering which one voluntarily chooses to accept. It is suffering which one person bears freely for another.

The great hope of Israel was in the understanding that God himself was revealed in the Suffering Servant. God himself bears our guilt and forgives our sin. Here in the Suffering Servant we have a still greater revelation of the God who had earlier revealed his nature as he delivered his poeple from Egypt and gave to them the law.

The second work of the Suffering Servant is to establish a people who will be servants. God's covenant people are the servant people. The work of God's people is the work of the servant, a work to be done in obedience and humility. They too must bear the guilt of the world. They too must suffer for the sins of others.

JESUS CHRIST (MATTHEW, MARK, LUKE, AND JOHN)

God's answer to human rebellion comes to its fulfillment with the coming of Jesus Christ. Jesus did not end the history of Israel. He did not cancel it. He completed it and fulfilled it. By completing and fulfilling what God had been doing through the centuries, he renewed and reestablished the people of God.

How did Jesus Christ renew the people of God?

First of all, he renewed the ancient people of God through his baptism. (Read Mark 1:9–11.)

In his baptism Jesus identified himself with the people of God. More than this, he identified himself with what God had been doing for his people. Mark tells us that Jesus heard a heavenly voice saying, "Thou art my beloved Son; with thee I am well pleased" (1:11). This word combines two important statements from the Old Testament. "Thou art my beloved Son" was a formula to be used at the time of crowning of the Messianic king of Israel. "With thee I am well pleased" has to do with the setting apart of Isaiah's Suffering Servant for his task. Here Jesus deliberately takes upon himself the work of the Messianic king (as promised to David) who is to establish God's kingly rule on earth. He also takes upon himself the work of the Suffering Servant which has been so well described in Isaiah

53. The means which God used to establish his Kingdom in the Old Testament are fulfilled and completed. In a way far beyond what Israel could have imagined, Jesus is the king who will establish the Kingdom of God. He is the servant of God who will redeem the people of God.

Secondly, Jesus chose disciples who were to be the nucleus of the new Israel. The prophets had cherished the hope that Israel would be renewed by a small group who would be faithful, loyal, and obedient. That group, called a remnant, is what was to be left when the judgment has passed over. It was to be both a saved remnant and a saving remnant. Through that small group the whole people would be renewed.

By his deeds and by his teaching Jesus left no doubt that he chose disciples to be the continuation of the old Israel and the means for the renewal of a new Israel. By choosing and training disciples, Jesus renewed the people of God.

A third way in which Jesus strengthened the New Israel was by his teachings. Matthew's Gospel emphasizes this work of Jesus. Jesus is the teacher and the giver of a new law. He tells people about God, and he tells them how they are to live in obedience to God. (See pages 112–116.)

One of the first names given to Christians in New Testament times was "people of the Way." They were set apart from other people by their manner of life. It was through teaching about the nature and will of God and about obedience to him that Jesus established anew God's people.

In the fourth place Jesus established the people of God through his death and resurrection. The death of Jesus made a great impression upon the disciples. A large portion of each Gospel is devoted to telling the story of it. The most remarkable thing about the death of Jesus is that the disciples saw in it a revelation of the love of God.

They could have seen many other things in the death of Jesus. It could have been a sign that God did not care or that he could not do anything about the people who put Jesus to death. Why did the disciples see in the death of Jesus the love of God? Isn't it because they had seen Jesus voluntarily accept the work of the Suffering Servant? In his death Jesus as the servant of God bore and forgave sin. On the cross he prayed, "Father, forgive them; for they know not what they do" (Luke 23:24). The cross is a revelation of the love of God, who bears and forgives the sins of his people.

The resurrection of Jesus was more than the revival of a dead man. It was also the undoing of what wicked men had done in the crucifixion of Jesus. God did not leave Jesus in the grave. He raised him from the dead.

In these four ways Jesus renewed the people of God. In these ways he completed and fulfilled what God had been doing through all the centuries.

CHECK YOUR UNDERSTANDING

1. How does the Suffering Servant do the work of God?
2. In what ways was Christ both a Messianic King and a Suffering Servant?
3. How did Jesus bring new life to the people of God?
4. Consider questions 5–8 under "For Discussion" on page 18.

The Church in the First Century

PENTECOST—THE GIVING OF THE SPIRIT (ACTS 2)

The giving of the Spirit at Pentecost has frequently been called the birthday of the church. This is not true if it means that the church had not existed before. As we have seen, the church has existed since the beginning of human history. It is true that Pentecost ushered in a new stage in the life of the church. What is this new stage in the life of the church? What new quality did Pentecost bring to the life of the people of God?

Let us begin our answer to this question with a careful reading of Acts 2. Pentecost was one of three great Hebrew festivals. It was a harvest festival, and all Jews were required to attend. The disciples had participated in this festival. They were all together in one place. In the New Testament "all together" is sometimes a synonym for worship. We can imagine that they remembered the experiences which they had shared with Jesus. They recalled his appearances to them after his crucifixion. As they recalled what Jesus had said and done they received the gift of the Spirit.

The gift of the Spirit was described in this quite extraordinary language. (Read Acts 2:2–3.)

Today we cannot tell exactly what happened. But note the vividness of the language used to describe it. The Spirit is like the wind. His coming is sudden and unexpected. Like the wind he is mighty and powerful to move men. The Spirit is also like fire, which is recognized as a symbol of the Divine Presence. Fire destroys chaff and cleanses impurities away.

The Spirit filled all who were there in the upper room. That is, he became a part of them. He entered their personalities. One consequence was that he enabled them to speak so that strangers could understand them. Again, we do not know exactly what took place. We do know that those who received the Spirit found it easy to talk with one another. The contrast between the disciples' experience on Pentecost and the experience of those who built the Tower of Babel is striking in this respect. At the Tower of Babel men were rebelling against God and trying to build a tower which would rise above any flood he would send. They found that they could not talk with one another. They could not understand one another. Rebellion against God always leads to this problem. But at Pentecost those who received the Spirit found that they could be understood even by those who spoke another language.

Now why is this event so important in the life of the church?

1. The coming of the Spirit answered the question of the presence of Jesus Christ. Where was Jesus Christ? The disciples knew that Jesus was the revelation of God. They waited for him to return. But where was he?

Jesus himself had said to his disciples, "it is to your advantage that I go away, for if I do not go away, the Counselor will not come to you; but if I go, I will send him to you" (John 16:7). Now at first this seems strange. We would have expected Jesus to say, "I am sorry that I shall go away. But you will be able to get along without me." But this is not what Jesus said.

Jesus knew that the disciples had come to depend upon his physical presence. He knew this was not good enough. When he could not be physically present, they would become discouraged and go back to their fishing boats. They needed to come to depend upon another kind of presence. Consider this illustration: If a boy depends upon his father's physical presence to help him to do something, he may utterly fail when his father is not with him.

We call the new presence of God the Holy Spirit. Christ is no longer present physically, but he is present in the Spirit. He is present even within our lives. Paul could say that Christ so lived within him that he did what he did through the power of the Spirit. (See Galatians 2:20.)

We cannot fully understand this. But we see countless illustrations of this truth in human relations. One person can so influence another person that this person lives in a sense in him. Sometimes we see a girl acting like a woman whom she admires, and we say, "There goes Sally Brown all over again." You can live so close to another person that this person in a real sense begins to live in you.

So in our faith: We can live so close to Jesus Christ that he lives in us through his Spirit. Pentecost is called the birthday of the church because it answers the question of how Jesus Christ is now present among his people.

2. Pentecost is a great date in the life of the church because those who received the Spirit on that day had a new sense of power. They had seen remarkable things happen in the life of Jesus. They had known his resurrection from the dead. They had experienced a wonderful change in their own lives. They were convinced that God was near. They lived in the expectancy that God would continue to do wonderful things in their lives and in the lives of his people.

As a consequence of this new sense of power, the disciples dared to do unheard-of things. They dared to oppose rulers and mobs. They declared that they must obey God rather than men (Acts 5:29). Peter, who on the eve of Christ's crucifixion had been afraid of a servant girl, now stood up boldly before the people. The Apostles spoke with great power. Many people were won to the new faith (Acts 2:14f). They set forth on long and arduous missionary journeys to tell all people the good news which God had made known unto them. It is surprising that they believed that anyone would listen to them. But they had seen such remarkable evidence of God's power that they were moved to declare, "We cannot but speak of what we have seen and heard" (Acts 4:20).

Johannes Weiss, a German church historian, declared, "The proud sense of belonging to the few elect, to the little flock is morally possible only when it is combined with a feeling of obligation to fulfill extraordinary duties." The members of the New Testament church surely had this proud sense.

Paul gives in Galatians 5:16-24 a description of the new life in the Spirit as he contrasts it with the old life in the flesh.

By "flesh" Paul does not mean the physical body. Flesh stands for the opposite of life in the Spirit of Christ. Many of the works of the flesh may be quite spiritual, that is, personal, but they are not Christlike.

3. The gift of the Spirit united the disciples in a common life. In the Spirit, they became one body, members one of another. In somewhat the same way, a group of young people belong together because they share the spirit of a school. On a much deeper level, Christians belong together because they share a common life in the Spirit of God.

4. The gift of the Spirit sent the disciples forth to claim the world for God by preaching the gospel. This, you will notice, is the immediate consequence of what happened on the day of Pentecost. (See Acts 2.) Peter began preaching to the multitudes, and thousands were converted.

We have been studying about the gift of the Spirit. Now we come to the crucial question, Have I received the gift of the Spirit? What evidence of the Spirit's presence should I expect to find? One evidence is my own awareness of the Spirit. Have I felt the Spirit's presence? This is one test, but it is not the safest test. Does the paragraph from Paul's letter provide us other tests? John Calvin once said that the truest test of one's faith is love of neighbor. Do you agree? Another test is the poise and dignity that trust in God and confidence that this world is our Father's home gives one.

There is a second question: How can I receive the gift of the Spirit? How can I become more and more aware of the Spirit's pres-

ence? There is nothing automatic about the gift o
cannot receive the Spirit at will, as we take a do
There is nothing magic about Christian faith. The
God's gift.

There are, however, some things which we can do
receive the gift of the Spirit. And if we do these thi   ., very
likely indeed that we shall receive this gift. We can resolve to think
each day about Jesus Christ, about what he said and did. We can
spend some part of each day in prayer. We can seek to live according to the teachings of Jesus Christ. We can associate with those
who have received the gift of the Spirit.

The disciples would not likely have received the gift of the Spirit
at Pentecost if they had not been together, if they had not been in
prayer, if they had not been seeking to do the will of God. Neither
are we likely to receive the gift of the Spirit if we are not doing these
things.

THE LIFE OF THE CHURCH IN THE NEW TESTAMENT

Luke has given us a description of the life of the church in the
first century. We know from many passages in the New Testament
that the church in the New Testament was not perfect. There were
troublemakers in it (1 Cor. 1:10–17). There were liars in the church
(Acts 5). At least one man even went to sleep during a sermon (Acts
20:7–12). Some parents didn't discipline their children (Eph.
6:1–4). But in Acts 2:41–47 Luke gives us a picture of the church as
it ought to be and as the church in the New Testament tried to be.

Study this passage, asking, What does it tell about the life of the
people of God in our time?

1. *They devoted themselves to the Apostle's teaching and fellowship,
to the breaking of bread and prayers.* The early church was a teaching
church. Jesus himself, as Matthew emphasizes in his Gospel, was a
teacher. Disciples are learners, and in our faith learning is important. It is not enough to "feel" one's religion. It is not enough to
have good intentions. It is not even enough to do good deeds. It is
important to know who God is and what he requires of his people,
for what a person knows about God and God's law will sooner or
later affect feelings and actions.

2. *Fear came upon every soul.* Fear does not necessarily involve being scared or frightened as one may be frightened by the shot of a gun or by an enraged animal. "Fear" here means wonder, awe, reverence. It is awareness of the holy, of the sacred. It is the kind of feeling which young people may have when they hesitate to go into the pulpit of their church. It is the feeling of mystery, of wonder, of awe which many of us have known at some great and solemn occasion, perhaps at a time of a death of a friend or loved one.

The disciples had witnessed and experienced the power of God's presence. They knew that God was their creator and that their lives depended upon him. They knew that he was at work in the world and in their lives. In his presence they were filled with awe and fear.

Perhaps we can illustrate this feeling of the disciples by our experience with other human beings. Perhaps you have felt awe as you have stood in the presence of a great person. You would be solemn, quiet, respectful in the presence of the President of the United States. You would be mindful of the office which the President holds.

In the presence of God do you have the awe which the early church felt? Have you seen children playing in the pulpit of the church or on the communion table or running up and down the aisles of the church as if it were a recreation center? Of course a church building is much like any other building. But it is the place where people gather for prayer and for reading and hearing the Word of God; as such, it is different from any other place.

3. *And all who believed were together and had all things in common.* This word "together" is frequently used of the early Christians. At times it is almost a synonym for worship. It underlines the very close fellowship which existed among the followers of Jesus.

They had all things in common. That is, they shared all their material possessions with one another. Read Acts 4:34-37. This is an indication of the willingness of early Christians to share. Barnabas, who was later to become a great missionary, sold a field and gave the money for those who were in need. We are told that no needy persons were neglected.

Christian faith does not encourage a person to be lazy. New Testament Christians are commanded to work. (See 2 Thessalonians 3:10.) The early church later established rules that visitors were to be given free meals only for three days. If they stayed longer, they had to go to work. But the early church also taught that Christians must be ready to share what they possess with those in need.

4. *Attending the Temple.* The Christian church had not completely separated from the traditional worship of God. The disciples faithfully worshiped God in the Temple. To this worship they added the new knowledge of God which had come to them through Jesus Christ. The early church was a worshiping church.

5. *Breaking bread in their homes, they partook of food with glad and generous hearts, praising God and having favor with all the people.* The breaking of bread was an important part of the life of the early church. Jesus had appeared to his disciples as they were eating on several occasions after his resurrection. Probably for this reason the time of "breaking of bread" was an occasion when the early Christians were especially aware of the presence of the risen Christ and were grateful for all the blessings of God.

The phrase "breaking of bread" probably stood for three or four different practices in the early church. It was used as a name for the Lord's Supper. It was used to designate a common meal at which Christians were very much aware of the presence of the risen Christ. It also indicated a common meal which was sometimes a means of providing food for those members of the congregation who were poor and did not have enough to eat. The meal was ordinarily concluded by the Lord's Supper.

6. Finally, we are told that *the early Christians took bread with glad and generous hearts, praising God and having favor with all the people.* There is a joy in the Christian faith. Sadness of heart and sourness of spirit are not Christian virtues. Despair is always a sign of unbelief. There was something winsome about these early Christians. They found favor with people.

It is also true that they did not find favor with some people. Jesus himself was crucified. Peter and John knew prison sentences and death as martyrs. Jesus cautioned us to beware when all men speak well of us. Nevertheless, there are still a winsomeness and a joy about real Christian faith. We have reason to be suspicious of what is happening to our faith whenever we lose heart and become sad and sour in spirit.

CHECK YOUR UNDERSTANDING

1. Tell in your own words what happened on the day of Pentecost. (See Acts 2.)
2. Why is Pentecost important in the life of the church?
3. What things did the early Christians do together?

Explore and Undertake

For Discussion

1. What was God's purpose in creation of human beings? How does it help us understand our freedom as persons?
2. How do we try to hide from God? (See Genesis 3:10.) How do we rebel against God? (See Genesis 11:1-9.) Is it possible to find a place that is outside the range of God's judgment?
3. What difference does God's call of Abraham make in our lives? In what ways does God's call give both blessing and responsibility to those whom he calls? How does your church bless—help—your community?
4. What was God's purpose in giving a king to his people?
5. What does God do when we say No to his call?
6. How does God use voluntary suffering to strengthen the life of his people? What could the suffering servants of God do in your community? What is your congregation doing to meet needs?
7. How did Jesus in his life and work fulfill the expectations of God's people? Why were some people disappointed in Jesus?
8. How does what Christ did affect what you will do tomorrow?
9. What are some of the evidences of the presence of the Holy Spirit in your life? In the life of your congregation?
10. In what ways is your church like the church of the first century? In what ways is it different?

CHAPTER II

The Church,
Particular and Catholic

Having reviewed the movement of the church, the people of God, in biblical history, and having noted biblical teachings about the church, you are now ready for a definition of the church as it exists today. As you study this chapter ask these questions: What is the meaning of the church? What meaning does the church have for me?

The Church, Its Meaning

Begin with the meaning of the word "church." This word is often upon our lips, but not all of us could tell someone else what it means. We can test this for ourselves by asking, What do I understand the word "church" to mean? Your answer probably does not satisfy you. Part of the problem is that we use the word "church" for many things that are connected with the church but which are not really the church.

We call the building the church. The building is an important symbol of the church, and when we see a church building, it reminds us of our faith. We can usually tell by looking at a building whether it is a church or not. Sometimes by looking at the building we know what kind of Christians worship there. But the building is not the church. It is simply the place where the church frequently gathers, worships, and works. The Puritans never called the building in which they worshiped the church. They called it a meeting house, the place where the church meets. The early Methodists insisted on calling the building a chapel, not a church. The building is important and useful and contributes much to the church, but it is not the church.

We also apply the word "church" to other aspects of the life of God's people. For example, we sometimes speak of the organization as the church. Organization is important. Without it we would not be able to have even a small congregation, much less a denomination. Organization is necessary for everything, from church suppers to church school books such as this one. But organization by boards and committees is not the church, even though it is important and useful. The church in some situations could exist with very little organization.

What, then, is the church? The simplest answer is one which has already been made clear from our study of the Bible. The church is the people of God. The word "church" in the New Testament is a Greek word that means an assembly or congregation that has been called out for some purpose. The distinctive thing about the assembly that is the church is that it is God's assembly, called together by him. Probably the best translation of the word would be "congregation," if it were not for the fact that we have for so long used the word "congregation" for one form of the church's life. Martin Luther wanted to change the words of the Apostles' Creed so that it would read, "I believe that there is a Holy Christian people." In the early days of the Reformation, Presbyterians in Scotland frequently referred to themselves as the congregation.

The word "church" came into our language from the Anglo-Saxon language and originally meant "the Lord's." The building where the church meets is the Lord's house. The people are the Lord's people. It is easy to see how "church" became the translation of the New Testament word which means assembly or congregation of people. Certainly no one wants to give up the word "church," with all its meaning. But we must continually remind ourselves that it does not mean a building or institution or an organization. It means the people of God.

Question 54 of the Heidelberg Catechism contains a splendid statement on the meaning of the church:

> What do you believe concerning "the Holy Catholic Church"? I believe that, from the beginning to the end of the world, and from among the whole human race, the Son of God, by his Spirit and his Word, gathers, protects, and preserves for himself, in the unity of the true faith, a congregation chosen for eternal life. Moreover, I believe that I am and forever will remain a living member of it eternally.

How do we recognize the church? What are the distinguishing marks which separate the church from other groups of people? How can we tell if a group of people is the church? This is a difficult question for many Christians today. The difficulty arises out of the fact that Christians are not fully agreed on what makes a church a church. Some would say that in order to have a church you must have a bishop or pope or a particular form of baptism or full agreement as to doctrine. But you have never heard members of your church insist that any of these things is necessary, have you?

The early Protestants taught that the church exists where the Word of God is rightly preached and heard and where the sacraments are rightly administered. According to them, the two distinguishing marks of the church are the preaching of the Word of God and the administration of the sacraments. Some Reformed theologians add discipline as a sign of the church. This does not mean that people have to be perfect to be the church, but that they have to be serious in listening to the Word of God and in seeking to live according to it. Discipline is a way of maintaining the right preaching and hearing of the Word. The sacraments have the same purpose as the Word of God, that of proclaiming the gospel. *So the church exists where the Word of God is heard and in faith and love obeyed.* Nothing else is necessary for the church's existence. Long ago (A.D. 110) Ignatius said that where Christ is, there is the church. Another theologian of the ancient church wrote that where the Spirit of God is, there is the church. These statements point up the fact that the church is where believing people hear the Word of God. The one thing necessary for the church is the Word of God.

The belief that nothing is necessary for the church's existence except the right preaching of the Word and the right administration of the sacraments is one of the broadest and most generous definitions of the church to be found among Christians anywhere. We recognize other churches as Christian even though they are not Presbyterian in order or Reformed in theology, even though they differ with us in many things. We know that the church exists wherever the Word of God is heard and obeyed.

CHECK YOUR UNDERSTANDING

1. What did the word "church" mean to you before you began to study this chapter? What does it mean now?
2. What are the distinguishing marks of the church?
3. According to the early Protestants, what is the church?

The Church Particular

In the New Testament the word "church" is sometimes applied to the Christians who lived in one town (that is, to a local congregation); at other times, to those who lived in one province. At still other times, it is applied to the whole body of Christians in the world. In its most general sense, the church is all the people of God. We are now going to study the meaning of the church (1) as the local congregation and (2) as the whole body of believers.

The New Testament very clearly calls the local or particular congregation the church. Nowhere else is the church so clearly visible to us as in the life and worship of the local congregation. Here we worship. Here we make our public confession of faith. Here we are baptized. Here we are married. Here we make decisions for justice and truth. Here we do deeds of love and mercy. Here in services of praise and thanksgiving we are buried. In these acts of worship and obedience the church exists before our eyes.

Some Christians have been so impressed by this that they insist that the word "church" belongs only to the local congregation. Some Baptists, among others, believe that the church exists in no other form. It is certainly true that except for local congregations there would be no church. Yet it is also true that a local congregation cannot be separated from other congregations. The local congregation can be the church only as it is part of the whole body of believers. So when we say that the church is the local congregation, we must always go on to say that the church is the whole people of God.

The local congregation is always part of a larger community. You know many people who do not worship in your particular congregation. This was not always the case. In Medieval Europe there was one church for each geographical area. This area was called the parish, and the church was the parish church. The parish church was possible because almost everyone was a Christian, at least in name, and there were no denominations as we now know them. The parish church had responsibility for the whole life of the community (political, social, economic) and for every person in the community, whether or not they were active members of the congregation. There was a real advantage in this. Today it is easy for local congregations to feel responsible for their members but not for the community at large.

Many Protestants, including the early followers of Calvin, continued the parish system. Other Protestants rejected it. Some felt that it was a pretense because many people in the community were not in reality members of the church. Many felt that life in the church demanded a more explicit profession of faith than did the parish system.

Sometimes the word "parish" is still used. Your church has probably never officially repudiated the parish system. But the situation in early America made the parish system impracticable. There were no established churches on the frontier. The settlers frequently grew up outside the church and had to be converted and brought into the church by revivals, camp meetings, and the work of traveling preachers. No one church served the whole community. When conditions became settled, there were churches of several different denominations serving the same community. The day when one church served one community (the parish) was gone.

In our day, it has become increasingly evident that all the members of a community are not Christians. Perhaps you have seen in the newspapers reports of controversies about Bible reading and prayer in public schools. Some religious practices are no longer acceptable in many community activities because all members of the community are not Christians.

Still another fact which complicates the life of the church in the community is the high mobility of the American population. One out of every five American families moves each year. Each time church members move their homes they have to reestablish their participation in the life of a local congregation. In a society in which people so frequently change their place of residence, there is always a danger that they will drop out of the life of the church.

In a society in which everyone belongs to the same church and in which the state supports the church, the witness of the church could be very different from the work of the church in our day. Our task is to learn to be a witnessing congregation in a society in which (a) church membership is voluntary (no one is compelled by social pressure to be a church member); (b) church and state (the government) are separate; (c) many different religious groups live in the same community; (d) society is secular, that is, with no official commitments to any faith or style of life; (e) mass media in the form of television, radio, and magazines bring many non-Christian faiths and life commitments into our homes; (f) people are continually on the move, frequently living anonymously in communities in which they have no relatives and few, if any, close friends.

CHECK YOUR UNDERSTANDING

1. What does the phrase "the particular church" mean?
2. What is a parish?

The Church Catholic

When we recite the Apostles' Creed in public worship we declare: "I believe in . . . the holy Catholic Church. . . ." What do you understand these words to mean?

The New Testament uses the word "church" as a designation not only for the local congregation but also for the whole body of believers. There is the one universal church, or, as we say in the ancient words of the Apostles' Creed, the holy catholic church. The word "catholic" means "universal." The universality of the church means there is one church for all nationalities, all classes, all races, all kinds and types of people. Long ago (A.D. 350) Cyril of Jerusalem, in his lectures for those who were preparing for church membership, described the catholicity of the church in these words:

> The Church, then, is called Catholic because it is spread through the whole world, from one end of the earth to the other, and because it never stops teaching in all its fulness every doctrine that men ought to be brought to know: and that regarding things visible and invisible, in heaven and on earth. It is called Catholic also because it brings into religious obedience every sort of men, ruler and ruled, learned and simple, and because it is a universal treatment and cure for every kind of sin whether perpetrated by soul or body, and possesses within it every form of virture that is named, whether it expresses itself in deeds or words or in spiritual graces of every description.[1]

The catholic or universal church is *not* the sum of many local churches added together. Each local congregation, each particular church, is the catholic church in its place. Catholicity is a quality which belongs to every congregation. You can best see the meaning of this as you apply it to your own congregation. How is it a catholic church? Is it catholic as Cyril described "catholic"? A local congregation cannot really be the church if it does not participate in the life of the whole body of believers. How does the local congregation do this? In our denominations we seek to do this through church courts (see Chapter IV). The presbytery or classis is the congregation of Christians in a district. Some presbyteries which are small geographically engage in such activities as a common Sunday evening service during the summer. This practice helps members of the church see that all the Presbyterians in a district are one church. Likewise, there are summer camps and conferences which illustrate this unity of the church.

All the members of a particular denomination in a state or in the several states which that denomination covers cannot worship together, but they can share in a common church life through elected representatives. In addition, the members of any one denomination share together in the support of homes for children and the aged, in the relief of human suffering, in the support of seminaries and colleges. You can think of additional ways in which the congregation of which you are a member shares in the life of the total body of Christians. (See Chapter VIII for further development of this point.)

There is still another question which no doubt has already occurred to you. How can a group of God's people be a denomination and the catholic church at the same time? If people happen to believe that there is one catholic church and that their church is it, then they have no problem. But the Presbyterian Church has never said this. As you are soon to consider the meaning of denominations, it may be enough here to indicate that your church may work with other denominations in local councils of churches, in the National Council of Churches of Christ in the United States of America, and in the World Council of Churches. Just as persons work with other churches of the same denomination in missions, so each denomination works with other denominations in the worldwide missionary program of the church.

The word "church" designates the local congregation and the total body of believers. In a sense, the total body of believers is present only in local congregations. But the local congregation, the particular church, has the right to the name "church" only if it shares in the life and mission of the total body of believers. When the church was largely concentrated in one congregation in and around Jerusalem, it was easy to be both a local congregation *and* the whole body of believers. Now that the church has spread around the world and includes men and women of every nation, race, and class, it is not so easy to be the church in our local congregation and the catholic or universal church at the same time.

The catholic church also includes those who are in heaven as well as those on earth. When we come to the communion table, we gather not only with all God's people on earth but also with all the saints of all ages.

CHECK YOUR UNDERSTANDING

1. What did the word "catholic" mean to you before you began to study this chapter? What does it mean now?
2. How can a particular church be catholic?

The Church in Denominations

Someone may now say that it is all right to talk about the unity of the church, but that the actual fact is that the church is divided into many groups. How can we talk of the church as one or catholic when it is divided into so many denominations?

The division of the one church into many churches is so common a fact that we often take it for granted. Then we discover that we cannot take communion with members of some other churches. Or we find two churches in a community which is not large enough to support one church. We may find two denominations separately engaged in work which could better be done together. Perhaps you have already begun to ask questions about the existence of so many churches, all calling themselves Christian.

One easy solution to the problem is for one church to believe that it is the only true church and that all others are false. Denominations refuse to take this position. Denominations are by definition bodies of Christians who believe they are the church but who do not believe they are the only form of that church. *One* Presbyterian denomination believes that "the unity of the body of Christ, though obscured, is not destroyed by its division into different denominations of professing Christians. All denominations which maintain the Word and Sacraments in their fundamental integrity are to be recognized as true branches of the Church of Jesus Christ."[2]

You frequently hear people speak of "denominations." In fact, you are so familiar with this word that it may come as a surprise to you to know that it has not always been used to describe parts of the one catholic church. It did not come into use until the middle of the eighteenth century, though an occasional writer had used it a century earlier. An earlier way of referring to the division of the church had been to speak of the Baptist way, the Presbyterian way, or the Episcopal way. The word "denomination" means very much the same thing as "way." It is one way in which Christians live, think, and worship. A denomination is admittedly only one of the many manifestations of the true church. The one catholic church manifests itself in many modes of worship, church government, and theological thought. A denomination never believes that it is the only true church and that other churches are false. This is suggested by the meaning of the word "denomination": a denomination does not claim to be the whole church.

The church existed before anyone ever thought of denominations. There may come a time when something will take the place of denominations, for we do not know what forms the church may take in the future. Some have felt that denominations are a scandal and an obstacle to the unity of the church. Others have felt that denominations are a way in which the rich variety of Christian faith and life may come to dramatic expression. Even those who wish to do away with denominations or drastically reduce their number nevertheless want to discover a way to allow varied forms of worship, government, and church life within one church. Some feel that denominations provide this now and that denominations have worked out ways of working together so that their separate existence need not obscure the unity of the church. This is especially the case when denominations recognize one another's members as true members of the church, when their members may share in the same communion service, and when they recognize one another's ministers as true ministers of Christ.

It should be noted that some churches do not refer to themselves as denominations. Yet even they admit that the church apparently exists in various forms and ways. We in denominations following Presbyterian and Reformed traditions do not believe that denominations are the final form of the church. But at present we do not know of any better way of describing the way the church actually is. At the same time we continually strive to find new ways of expressing our unity in Christ.

Let us now review very quickly the various ways in which the church exists. These paragraphs will serve as definitions to help you recognize other forms of the church than your own.

ANCIENT CATHOLIC CHURCH. This is the name which is usually given to the church of the first five centuries. It covered the Mediterranean world, and it spread as far north as Britain, as far east as India, and as far south as Ethiopia. This church did not have the precise organization of our churches today. There were no boards of education and missions. It had no official headquarters, though the bishops of Rome, Constantinople, Alexandria, Antioch, and Jerusalem were the most influential. Yet all the Christians could recognize one another as fellow Christians because they had a common creed, common Scripture, and bishops who were in communion with each other.

MONOPHYSITE CHURCHES OR NON-CHALCEDONIAN CHURCHES. You may have never heard of these churches. They broke away from the Ancient Catholic Churches because of arguments about the doctrine of Jesus Christ. They have existed since the fifth century in Palestine, Syria, Armenia, Egypt (Coptic Church), and Ethiopia (Coptic Church). For many centuries they were isolated from the rest of Christendom by Islam. In recent years they have come again into contact with other Christians through the World Council of Churches. Their membership is estimated at 15,000,000. They have small churches in the United States. (A.G. Pierborn: *Profiles in Belief,* Vol. I.)

EASTERN ORTHODOX CHURCHES. For many reasons the Ancient Catholic Church began to divide between East and West. There were differences of language and culture. The East was Greek, and the West was Latin. The Easterners were meditative and theological. They were especially concerned about the problem of death. The West, on the other hand, was very practical, concerned with doing things, and bothered by the problem of sin and guilt. Other reasons were political. The Roman Empire disintegrated in the West, leaving the Bishop of Rome as the only strong man. The empire continued strong at Constantinople. Gradually Eastern Christians drifted away from the West. The date for the final break is usually given as 1054.

The Eastern Orthodox Churches are located today primarily in

Greece, the Near East, Bulgaria, Rumania, and Russia. They are distinguished by their elaborate worship services and mystical theology. In recent years the rise of Communism has made life difficult for them. Their membership is estimated to be 126,000,000 (1972).

THE ROMAN CATHOLIC CHURCH. The Roman Catholic Church has its roots in the Ancient Catholic Church and medieval Catholicism. Yet modern Roman Catholicism is not the same as medieval Catholicism. The Council of Trent, which met at the time of the Reformation, formulated the doctrine of the church. Many doctrines which had been permissible in the medieval church were no longer permitted. Furthermore, the dogma of the Infallibility of the Pope was proclaimed in 1870. The dogma of the Immaculate Conception of Mary dates from 1854, and the dogma of the Assumption of Mary was given in 1950. Vatican Council II (1962–1965) gave the Church a new openness to contemporary issues and to other Christians and churches. While the Roman Catholic Church is very ancient in many respects, it is also important to note that Roman Catholicism since the Council of Trent is not the same as medieval Catholicism or the Ancient Catholic Church. It is also important to note the new directions in Roman Catholicism since Vatican II.

The Roman Catholic Church differs from Protestantism especially in the authority which it gives to the clergy and in particular to the pope, in the role of Mary in the piety of the church, and in the doctrine of the sacraments. (Other differences between Roman Catholics and Protestants are discussed in the chapter on Protestantism.)

The Roman Catholic Church is world-wide. It has demonstrated remarkable powers to maintain an international character and to survive difficult ordeals. Its membership is estimated to be 581,000,000 (1972).

PROTESTANTISM. Protestantism grew out of the effort to reform the church in the sixteenth century. (The doctrinal emphases of Protestantism are pointed out in Chapter III.) Protestantism is strongest in northern Europe and wherever northern Europeans have settled. Among the Protestant churches are the Lutheran, the Reformed or Presbyterian, the Anglican, the Methodist, the Baptist, and the Mennonite. No one has the authority to make a list of Protestant churches. The boundaries are not clear. Some of the churches listed above originated after the sixteenth century. Some Baptists and Anglicans do not like to be called Protestants. Protestant membership was estimated to be over 218 million in 1972.

THE YOUNGER CHURCHES. The Age of Discovery opened up new continents to European Christians in the sixteenth century. The Roman Catholics immediately began missionary work. The Protestants were not sufficiently established to get fully into the work until the nineteenth century. That century became the really great century of Christian mission. New churches were established all over the world. These churches, especially in Africa, Asia, South America, and the islands of the Pacific, are now reaching maturity. With an entirely different background from American and European Christians, they bring a freshness and a vitality to the church in our time.

PENTECOSTAL CHURCHES. One of the interesting facts in the life of the church today is the rise of Pentecostal churches. These churches get their name from Pentecost because they emphasize the power and work of the Holy Spirit. They also place a great emphasis upon a literal study of the Bible. They are divided into many small groups. While their names vary, they usually include either the words "Pentecostal" or "Church of God." They are growing rapidly in America and especially on the mission fields. It remains to be seen whether they will become a form of Protestantism or a new type of Christian church. The membership of the Pentecostal churches has been estimated at between 8,000,000 and 12,000,000.

THE ECUMENICAL CHURCH. One of the most significant facts in the life of the church today is the Ecumenical Movement. "Ecumenical" means world-wide, and it is a synonym for catholic. It is the movement toward unity in the Christian community. There is no ecumenical church as such, but the name can be given to the Christian churches as they seek to express their unity in Christ. One expression of this unity is the World Council of Churches of Christ, which was established at Amsterdam in 1948 and which includes the majority of non-Roman Catholic Christianity. In recent years the Roman Catholic Church has shown a greater willingness to enter into conversation with other Christians.

It is estimated that there are 983,620,900 Christians in the world today, more than acknowledge any other religion or loyalty. The world population is 4,123,957,000 (1979). The birthrate of the world, however, is such that the Christian population at present is becoming smaller in relation to the total population.

The Church and Social Diversity

The catholicity of the church is also endangered by the social and cultural pluralism of society. Factors of race, class, ethnic origin, education, cultural affinities, and age frequently shape the composition of local congregations and of denominations. Some older congregations such as the downtown churches and the county seat or rural churches may include a significant measure of diversity, but the newer suburban churches are frequently composed of one social and cultural type of people. While Protestantism in America represents the population as a whole, individual denominations are culturally and socially stratified. Presbyterians are, for example, a very middle-class church, probably more so than any other American church, with a relatively high percentage of their membership from the professions and from business. From the earliest times of the Protestant Reformation there has been this affinity between Calvinism and middle-class people. Presbyterianism has undoubtedly been shaped by middle-class characteristics, and the middle class has in part been created by the Presbyterian tradition.

The relationship between the catholicity of the church and a cultural and social diversity is not simple. The less a church is involved in the actual life of people the easier it is for that church to be untouched by cultural and social diversities. The more the life of the church involves the life of the people, the more important these diversities will become for the church. Protestant and Presbyterian churches have always emphasized congregational fellowship, congregational singing, and the sermon. Cultural and social factors significantly determine the capacity as well as the desire of people to participate in these activities. A sermon that is very meaningful for people in one cultural group will have little meaning for those in another. People from different cultural groups like to sing different hymns both as to content and music. On the other hand, all human beings share common human joys, griefs, hopes, and disappointments. All alike pass through the common human experiences of birth, growth, and death. It is critically important that the church should strive to maintain the catholicity of the Christian faith and the catholicity of our common humanity. Many of our differences are good gifts of God which contribute to the richness of our common humanity and to the catholicity of the church. For this reason they must not be denied in the name of some abstract principle of catholicity. The fact is the local congregation participates in the catholicity of the church, but no local congregation ever fully embodies it. Denominations by their very definition claim to participate in the catholic church, but by their being denominations deny that they are the full, much less the only, expression of the one, catholic church.

The Church and the Religions

The Christian community with its tradition exists in a world in which it is surrounded by many other religious communities with their traditions. In recent years Christians have become much more aware of the religious communities which exist alongside them. How does the church relate to other religious communities and traditions?

We must relate to other religious communities in a way that does justice to the Christian's knowledge of God in Jesus Christ and to what we know about other religious communities as matters of fact.

Religious communities and the piety of individuals are a human response to the mystery that encompasses all of life and an expression of the yearning of the human spirit which reaches out for something beyond every human achievement. Some have argued that human beings are not naturally religious, but this does not seem to be the case in the light of the almost universal manifestation of religious practices. As Augustine put it, "Thou hast formed us for thyself, and our hearts are restless till they find rest in thee." In addition, Christians believe that the God who created the world makes himself known in all that he has made. Religious communities, including the Christian community, are a human response to the activity of God. This is to say that all religious communities are (1) in part the product of the revealing activity of God and (2) in part the work of human beings. All religious communities, even those that most truly respond to the claim of God, are flawed and corrupted by the self-interest of the religious. As Christians, we must acknowledge this of the historical Christian communities. Therefore, in our Christian witness to the world we do not proclaim the superiority of Christianity as a religious community, though neither do we unjustly disparage the real evidence of trust and love in Christian communities.

Every reader of the Old Testament knows that religions can be destructive and religious practices a substitute for real trust in God (for example, Amos 5:21–24). The Christian hope is not in religion or in the religious community. Religion and religious communities must be both appreciated and judged as human works in response to what is believed to be the revelation of God. Christians may gladly acknowledge every evidence of truth and goodness in every religion. On the other hand, Christian openness to the presence of God wherever he reveals himself does not mean that all religions are essentially the same or equally valid ways of salvation. As a matter of fact, some religions are very destructive of values Christians cherish.

The Christian witness to the world points to the revelation of God in Jesus Christ, not to the church. Christians believe that the Lord God, creator of heaven and earth, has been embodied in Jesus Christ. In Jesus Christ God's presence is focused. In this sense Jesus Christ is the final revelation, final not in the sense that God has stopped revealing himself, but final in the sense that all other revelations of God are understood in the light of this revelation. For Christians, God is defined by Jesus Christ. (See section on the Nicene Creed.) This means that God in Jesus Christ is the negation and the fulfillment of all religious communities, including the Christian community. Jesus Christ is the judgment against the corruption of all religious communities. On the other hand, Jesus Christ is the fulfillment of every true yearning of the human for God and of every intimation of the presence of the living God.

In an early Christian sermon Peter declared there is salvation in none other name than Jesus Christ (Acts 4:12). Christians believe this. Jesus Christ is the way, the truth, and the life. Therefore, wherever Christians go they tell of what God has done in and through Jesus Christ.

The question is always raised whether those who are not Christians can find salvation. There is no simple answer to this question. Some Christians have wanted to say that only Christians can know the salvation of God, but there has always been a more generous strand of Christian belief which has affirmed that God has many friends who are not of the house of Israel. On the one hand, we are convinced that the only savior is God who comes to us in Jesus Christ. There is no other name whereby we may be saved. So our task is to tell the world what we have known and experienced. On the other hand, no Christian ought to have any desire to limit God's grace or to limit the ways that God who saves us in Jesus Christ may speak beyond our knowing to other people. Our task is to confess to the world what we know has happened, what we have experienced in Jesus Christ, and to invite all people to share with us in the fellowship and worship of the God and Father of our Lord Jesus Christ.

CHECK YOUR UNDERSTANDING

1. What is a denomination?
2. Why do we have denominations?
3. How is the catholicity of the church endangered by social and cultural distinctions?
4. How can you accept many social and cultural differences as good and yet not endanger the catholicity of the church?
5. How is religion the work of human beings? What is the significance of this fact?
6. How is religion the consequence of the work of God?
7. Can you recognize many good things in many religions and at the same time believe that salvation comes only from the God

and Father of our Lord Jesus Christ?

Explore and Undertake

1. Which denominations in your community recognize each others' ministers and members? Which denominations are able to share in a common observance of the Lord's Supper?
2. Study the development of the ecumenical movement. Ask your pastor for help.
3. Study another denomination in addition to your own.
4. Become familiar with one of the religions of the world.

CHAPTER III

The Church, Protestant

We have identified ourselves as the people of the Bible and as the holy catholic church. We also call ourselves Protestants. Members of the churches which developed out of the Reformation of the church in western Europe in the sixteenth century are called Protestants. We are among them. So the question which we must ask now is, What does it mean to be a Protestant?

Protestants: Reformers

Let us begin with the word "protestant." What does it mean? Historically, it is the name that was given to the followers of Martin Luther at the Diet of Speyer in what is now Germany in 1529. (A diet is a legislative assembly.) In 1526 the Diet of Speyer had granted freedom to the followers of Luther by a unanimous vote, but in 1529 the Diet outlawed the Lutherans by a simple majority vote. The Lutherans objected. They drew up a *Protestation,* which maintained that the unanimous decision of one Diet could not be overturned by a simple majority in another. The *Protestation* went on to declare:

> There is, we affirm, no sure preaching or doctrine but that which abides by the Word of God. . . . We are determined by God's

grace and aid to abide by God's Word alone, the Holy Gospel contained in the biblical books of the Old and New Testaments.

Those who were first called Protestants were not simply protesting against something. They were making an affirmation: they were declaring their intention to live by the Word of God. The word "Protestant," in fact, comes from the Latin word *protestari*, which means to make a declaration. The first meaning which the dictionary gives for protest is "to make a solemn declaration or affirmation." Protestants, then, are people who stand for something.

What do they stand for? If you were asked what Protestants stand for, what would you answer? Keep this question in mind as you study this chapter.

Part of the answer to that question is this: Protestants are Christians who insist that the church must be continually reformed by the Word of God. Martin Luther did not set out to establish a new church. In fact, the early Protestants were not content to say that the church began with the New Testament, or even with Abraham. They insisted that it began with Adam, with the first man. God has always had his people in the world. There have been great events in the life of the people of God, such as the call of Abraham, the giving of the Law at Sinai, and especially the coming of Jesus Christ, when the people of God have been renewed and strengthened. But God has always had his people who have heard his voice and in faith and love obeyed. Luther certainly had no idea of starting a new church. When, on October 31, 1517, he posted his historic ninety-five theses on the door of the church at Wittenberg and so challenged others in the church to debate, he wanted to reform, to cleanse an old, old church. There is a story that a follower of Luther was taunted by the question, "Where was your church before Luther?" The Lutheran replied, "Where was your face before you washed it this morning?"

Protestants do not believe that the church is ever perfect on earth. It is frequently tempted, and it sometimes falls into error. For this reason the church must always repent. It must examine its life and practice to see if it is living in obedience to Jesus Christ. The Reformation is not something which happened once in history and need not happen again. It is something which must be happening continually in the church.

Protestants are never satisfied with themselves or the church. They seek always to reform their own lives in obedience to Jesus Christ. They ask if the congregation of which they are members is loyal to Jesus Christ. They ask this same question of their denomination and of the councils to which the denomination belongs.

CHECK YOUR UNDERSTANDING

1. What does the word "Protestant" mean?
2. What are some of the things Protestants stand for?

Protestants: Believers

Protestants have certain beliefs. These beliefs are not just statements to which a person gives mental assent as, for example, the statement that the ocean is three miles deep. Rather, they are ways of understanding life, and they make a great deal of difference in one's personality and in the society in which one lives.

1. Protestants believe in the supreme authority of the Word of God in the life of the church. When Martin Luther stood before the emperor at the Diet of Worms in 1521, he declared:

Since then Your Majesty and your lordships desire a simple reply, I will answer without horns and without teeth. Unless I am convicted by Scripture and plain reason—I do not accept the authority of popes and councils, for they have contradicted each other—my conscience is captive to the Word of God. I cannot and I will not recant anything, for to go against conscience is neither right nor safe. God help me. Amen.

Over against the authority of the pope or church councils Protestants set the authority of the Holy Spirit speaking in Scriptures.

The Westminster Assembly was truly Protestant when it put these questions in the Shorter Catechism:

Q. 2. What rule hath God given to direct us how we may glorify and enjoy him?

A. The word of God, which is contained in the Scriptures of the Old and New Testaments, is the only rule to direct us how we may glorify and enjoy him.

Q. 3. What do the Scriptures principally teach?

A. The Scriptures principally teach, what man is to believe concerning God, and what duty God requires of man.

There are a number of consequences which flow from the belief that the Bible is the supreme authority in matters of faith. The first is the conviction that no pope, no ruler, no institution, no council has final authority. The Bible is the supreme authority and all other authorities must be judged by the Bible. This means that the authority of the church must be limited. It means that the state does not have unlimited authority. All officials and policies of the church and all officials and policies of the state have to be judged by the authority of the Bible. There may come a time when in obedience to the Scripture a Christian must refuse to obey the officials of the church or of the state.

A second consequence of this belief is the Protestants' concern for education. If the Bible is the supreme authority, then Christians need to know how to read it. For this reason Protestants have always built and maintained church schools or have supported public education. They have been concerned that the Bible should be translated into the common language and be made available to everyone.

We take the Bible for granted today. But one of the most thrilling stories in our history is the effort of William Tyndale and other ₃ in sixteenth century England to translate the Bible and to make it available to all the people. In order to do this, they had to go into exile and risk death as martyrs. Tyndale was himself burned at the stake, but not before he produced a translation of the Bible which is conserved in the Bible which we read today.

A third consequence of the Protestant belief in the supreme authority of the Bible has been unfortunate divisions. It is one thing to say that the Bible is the supreme authority. It is another to agree as to what the Bible says. Consequently, Protestants have frequently separated from one another over their differences in the interpretation of Scripture. Sometimes these divisions have been over quite trivial matters. At other times an important question was at stake. Differences in interpretation are not the only reason we have denominations today. Many other factors such as nationality, race, and geography have played their part. But differences in interpretation of the Bible are certainly one of the reasons. One encouraging fact in our time is that Christians, when they study the Bible together, find that their differences are not as real or as important as they once thought.

One way to prevent divisions over the interpretation of Scripture would be to select some individual or council that would make an infallible, or perfect, interpretation of the Bible. But Protestants believe that no person or group of people is either wise enough or good enough to be infallible. Allowing freedom for differences of opinion in the understanding of Scripture is a risk which Protestants believe is worth taking in order to insure that no person or group of persons should claim an authority which belongs only to the Bible. The Bible must remain the supreme authority, not some person's interpretation of it.

Protestants do insist that the interpretation of the Bible which is given to us by devoted and learned scholars, by church councils and assemblies, and by the Christian community through the ages should be taken very seriously. No one ought to reject casually what other Christians have found that the Bible teaches.

2. Protestants believe that salvation is by grace through faith. This means that we are not saved by good works. Martin Luther tried to find salvation by doing many good works. But he could never be sure that he had done enough. He always imagined that he could have done more. Finally, there came the great experience in which Luther realized that he did not have to win or buy God's favor. God's favor was freely given. All he had to do was to accept it.

The meaning of this becomes clear when we imagine what it would be like for children to earn their parents' love. A parent's love cannot be earned. It can only be accepted. Luther discovered that we cannot earn God's forgiveness. We can only accept it. The great joy of salvation is the knowledge that God forgives us even though we do not deserve to be forgiven.

If God forgives us freely, can we do as we please? Do good

works not matter? Luther's answer was that good works matter very much, but that they are not ways of earning God's favor so much as they are ways of thanking him. In our own experience we know that our finest deeds are not those which we do to get something, but those we do to express joy and gratitude. The Christian life is the thankful life. Luther believed that it was impossible to know that God forgives you and loves you without living thankfully. If a person lives without gratitude to God, then this person has never accepted God's forgiveness.

Justification by grace through faith means that salvation is more what we are than what we do. Luther put it like this: Good fruits do not make a good tree. A good tree bears good fruit. Good carpentry does not make a good carpenter, but a good carpenter does good carpentry. Good works are always a consequence of a person's relationship to God.

One practical result of the doctrine of justification by grace through faith has been Protestantism's recognition that all individuals are sinners. All human achievements in the life of the church as well as in society and culture fall short of the glory of God. The saint as well as the scoundrel is a sinner. Both must always be forgiven.

3. Protestants believe in the priesthood of all believers. The medieval church divided the Christian community into two classes, priests and people. The people could confess only to a priest or receive holy communion only from a priest. The priest was necessary for all the seven sacraments of the church except baptism, which could be performed by a layman. A priest was necessary for the Christian life of the ordinary believer.

Protestants declare that all Christians are priests. But what is a priest?

First of all, a priest is one who makes an offering to God. The great high priest is Jesus Christ, who offered himself as a sacrifice. From this sacrifice, offered once and for all, we receive forgiveness. Protestants object to the Roman Catholic doctrine that Christ is offered again in the Mass. Yet in a real sense all Christians are priests who offer themselves as sacrifices to God after the example of Jesus Christ. In Paul's letter to the Romans we are told to offer ourselves to God as a living sacrifice (Rom. 12:1). To be a priest is to offer oneself to God, and every Christian can and should offer his own life as a sacrifice.

A priest is also one who stands for himself before the face of God. Protestants insist that every person must stand for himself or herself before God. This is a responsibility which no one can accept for another. Everyone must answer personally. No one can hand over this responsibility to the church, to the minister, or to the priest. Luther said, "Every man must believe for himself, because sooner or later every man will die by himself."

The priesthood of all believers has sometimes been said to be the right of private judgment. It is truer to say that every person is responsible for the decisions of his or her own life in the presence of God.

This means that Protestantism is not an easy religion. It teaches that you cannot have your religion in someone else's name. *You* are responsible. One consequence of this teaching is seen in what may be called a Protestant personality. Protestants are people who have the ability to think for themselves and to act according to their own judgment. For this reason Protestants, when they have been true to their beliefs, have always been opposed to dictatorships in state and society which deny people the responsibility for living their own lives.

Priests are not only people who stand for themselves in the presence of God. They also stand and pray for their neighbors. Luther declared that every Christian must be a Christ. By this he taught that every Christian must love his or her neighbor as Christ loves each individual. He also taught that we must bear our neighbor's sin as Christ bears our sin. This means that a Christian does not stand apart and gloat over a neighbor's sin. Christians do not self-righteously separate themselves from their neighbor. Christians pray for their neighbors and help them bear their sins.

Priests are responsible for themselves and for their neighbors. This means that a Protestant church is not a collection of individuals who live their independent lives, but a real fellowship in which people who seek to be responsible for their own faith also seek to be responsible for their neighbors' faith and life.

If every Protestant is a priest, is there any need for ordained ministers? Ministers, like all other Christians, are priests. They have the same status as all other Christians before God. Nevertheless, Protestants have always believed that ministers are important. Protestants believe that the New Testament teaches that ministers are God's will for the church. They believe that ministers perform a work which is very important in the life of the church. Every Christian should study the Bible and interpret it. But if this is to be done with real competence and with orderliness, some individuals must be trained and called by the congregation to lead members of the church in doing this work. Protestants believe that good preaching is so important that they insist that those who preach be rigorously trained. Since the sacraments are always to be administered with instruction in their meaning, ministers who have been trained to teach are to administer them. Ministers are like all other Christians in that they are priests. They differ from other Christians only in having a special work in the life of the church, a work which they have been trained and called by the congregation to do.

4. Protestants believe in the sanctity (sacredness) of the common life. The medieval church had divided life into two areas: the religious and the secular, the sacred and the profane. It was possible to be a Christian in the secular world, but those who took Christianity seriously became members of religious orders—priests, monks, and nuns. Protestants reject this division of life into the religious and the secular and declare that *all* of life is sacred. Christians are called by God to express their Christian faith in all of life. Whether Christians are businessmen, teachers, homemakers, farmers, lawyers, or doctors, they are called to be Christians in their daily work.

The work of a minister is not necessarily any more religious than that of a farmer, a teacher, or a doctor. This is God's world, and any good work may be the service of God. This teaching does not mean that the work of the minister is unimportant. It *is* important in the life of the church. The sanctity of the common life does mean that the work of a minister need not be any more the service of God than the work of a farmer or a teacher. Protestantism gives a new dignity to all of life and does not insist that one has to be in church work in order to be a devoted Christian.

5. Protestants have also emphasized the importance of con-

scious, deliberate choice and decision in matters of faith. They have been aware of how close religion always is to magic. In relation to God magic is the attempt to get control of God by fastening God to something or to some technique that is in humanity's control. In relation to human beings magic is the effort to influence human life through the by-passing of consciousness and critical awareness. Protestants therefore rejected any effort to fasten God to the elements in the sacraments or to any formula or technique. God is not at our command and control. Protestants also insist that there can be no sacrament apart from faith, that is apart from conscious choice and decision.

These beliefs in the supreme authority of the Bible, justification by grace through faith, the priesthood of all believers, the sanctity of the common life, the importance of personal decision set Protestantism apart from other forms of Christian faith. They are the special contribution which Protestants bring to the total life of the holy catholic church.

CHECK YOUR UNDERSTANDING

1. What is the final source of authority for Protestants? What are the consequences of the Protestant doctrine of biblical authority?
2. According to Protestants, how is a person saved? What is the place of works in the faith of Protestants?
3. How does the doctrine of the priesthood of believers influence life in the church, the life of the individual believer?
4. What do you understand by the phrase, "the sanctity of the common life"?
5. Consider items 1 and 3–5 under "For Action" on page 48.

Protestants: Doers

The real difference which religious beliefs make is not to be found in books but in life and in society. We cannot really know who a Protestant is until we take a look at the lives of Protestants and the kind of communities which they build.

Of course, not everyone who claims to be a Protestant lives like a Protestant. No one is a perfect Protestant. Nevertheless, we can ask, What are some of the traits which we would expect to find in Protestants and in the communities in which they live?

On the basis of the beliefs which we have been discussing, what kind of person would you expect a Protestant to be? Certainly one trait of the Protestant is the ability to think for oneself and to act for oneself. While Protestants are glad to have all the help that the ministers of their church can give, they know that finally they have to make their own decisions. Protestants would resent their ministers' telling them how they must vote, for example. It is not surprising that Protestants have been great advocates of democracy in government. Many of the creators of our democratic forms of government learned democracy in the church before they learned it in the affairs of government.

Our study of Protestantism would not be complete without some attention being given to some of the ways in which Protestant faith expresses itself.

1. One special expression of Protestantism is hymn singing. Protestants did away with the choirs which had consisted of monks and introduced congregational singing. Luther himself wrote "A Mighty Fortress Is Our God" and other hymns. Calvin emphasized the singing of the Psalms. Among the great Protestant hymn writers are Isaac Watts and Charles Wesley. Congregational singing has always been a characteristic of Protestant worship.

2. A second expression of Protestantism has been an emphasis upon the Christian family. Medieval Catholicism had exalted celibacy (being unmarried) as a higher Christian way of life than marriage. Protestantism insisted that there was no higher way than marriage and the establishment of a Christian home. Many of the Reformers married. The Christian family replaced the life of the monk or nun as the ideal context for Christian living. Luther regarded the home as the school for character. And Protestantism has been strongest when families have taken most seriously their Christian calling.

3. Protestantism has also been embodied in many cultural forms. In literature it has found expression in such works as John Milton's *Paradise Lost* and John Bunyan's *Pilgrim's Progress*. It is rep-

resented in the work of such artists as Rembrandt and in the work of such composers of music as Johann Sebastian Bach. In architecture the Protestant spirit is seen in the churches of Sir Christopher Wren and in the New England Meeting House, as well as in many present-day designs.

Protestantism is something which most of us have inherited. When Protestantism is simply inherited, there is always the danger that it will cease to be Protestantism. A Protestant is always a person who is willing to give up old ways of doing things or to change the course of life in obedience to the will of God. For example, the Protestants of the sixteenth century, with Luther, were willing to "let goods and kindred go, this mortal life also," for the sake of obedience to the Word of God.

Protestants can never be satisfied with themselves as they are or with the church as it is. In order to be a Protestant you have to be reformed continually by the Word of God. There is no end to the reformation to which Protestants are committed.

CHECK YOUR UNDERSTANDING

1. What traits do Protestants generally have?
2. What is the Protestant view of marriage?
3. Protestantism involves a continual reformation. What does this mean?
4. Consider question 1–4 under "For Discussion" and item 7 "For Action" below.

Explore and Undertake

For Discussion

1. What sort of person is a Protestant?
2. What are some of the distinctive ways in which Protestants express their faith?
3. What are the evidences of the presence of Protestantism in the government and culture of our society?
4. In what way do you think God is seeking to reform the church in our day?

For Action

1. Memorize the answers to questions 2 and 3 in the Westminster Shorter Catechism, quoted on pages 39–40.
2. Make a study of the life of Martin Luther or Huldreich Zwingli and dramatize some significant event in the life of each in a meeting of your group. Chapters 14–15 in Roland Bainton's *The Church of Our Fathers,* chapter 12 in Norman Langford's *Fire Upon the Earth,* chapter 12 in Walter R. Bowie's *Men of Fire,* and chapter 14 in the study book *That the World May Know* are resources you may want to use.
3. Make a list of things that you as a "priest without robes" ought to begin to do.
4. Interview friends who are members of other Protestant denominations, such as Methodists, Baptists, and Lutherans, asking them what they believe as Christians. Report what you discover to your group. What beliefs do your friends in other churches share with you?
5. Let a member of the group interview your pastor, asking questions about the training he or she had for the ministry.
6. Study the hymn "A Mighty Fortress Is Our God" as an expression of the faith of Protestants.
7. Let a member of the group read John Bunyan's *Pilgrim's Progress* and report on it to the group. Other members of the group could report on the work of such other Protestants as Rembrandt, Sir Christopher Wren, John Milton, and Johann Sebastian Bach.
8. The Filmstrip "Papacy of Innocent III to Counter-Reformation" in *The Living Church* set includes the work of the Protestant Reformers.

CHAPTER IV

The Church,
Reformed and Presbyterian

We have been asking the question, Who am I? We have been looking seriously at the family tree of our spiritual history. We are people of the Bible. We are members of the one holy catholic church. We are Protestants. Now we shall try to identify ourselves even more exactly. In the total Christian community we are distinguished as Protestants. As Protestants we are still further distinguished as members of Reformed and Presbyterian churches. What do "Reformed" and "Presbyterian" mean?

Rooted in History

A good way to begin to answer this question is with a look at history. The name "Reformed" was given to our forebears on the continent of Europe in the sixteenth century. The name "Presbyterian" originated in Britain in the seventeenth century. Finding out what the names meant originally will yield clues as to what they mean for us today.

Let us begin with the word "Reformed." In a general sense, all Protestants can be called "Reformed." The first Protestants were concerned about the reform of the church in the sixteenth century. Because of this they were called Reformed Christians. Gradually the name came to be applied only to the Christians who followed

Zwingli, Calvin, and other Reformers in Switzerland. These Christians were to be found chiefly in Switzerland, Holland, Scotland, England, France, Hungary, and Germany.

Why were these Protestants called Reformed? The answer is to be found in the fact that they were more thorough in their reformation of the church than were the Lutherans. Queen Elizabeth once referred to the non-Lutheran churches as "The Churches More Reformed." This is the difference: Luther wanted to eliminate only those practices in the life of the church which the Bible condemned. Zwingli and Calvin wanted to reform the church by eliminating everything which the Bible did not require. Zwingli and Calvin were more willing to work out new forms of worship and church organization as well as the reform of theology.

In this way "Reformed" became the official name of many Protestants. In America it is found in the names of the Reformed Church in America and the Hungarian Reformed Church in America. Presbyterian churches which have their origin on the continent of Europe (for example, in France) are called Reformed churches.

In addition to being the name of denominations, "Reformed" is also the name used to describe our theology and doctrine and worship. The use of the word is common to all followers of Zwingli and Calvin. Statements of doctrine and forms of worship which were influenced by these men are called Reformed theology or Reformed worship.

The word "Presbyterian" is much more specific than "Reformed." It refers to a particular type of church government. Presbyterianism is church government by presbyters or elders in church courts (sessions and presbyteries, etc.). In Britain the question of the form of church government was a very live issue. Some wanted episcopacy—church government by bishops; others wanted church government by presbyters. (See "Presbyterian in Government," beginning on page 57, for more information on types of church government.) In the end the form of government in the Church of England was episcopal; in the Church of Scotland, presbyterian. Members of the Church of Scotland began to call themselves

Presbyterians; when they moved to America, they named their churches here Presbyterian.

Most Protestant churches which bear the marks of Calvin and Zwingli are *both* Reformed *and* Presbyterian. If you belong to such a church in Great Britain or to a church established by emigration from Britain, you call yourself "Presbyterian." If you belong to such a church in Europe or to a church established by emigration from Europe, you will call yourself "Reformed."

The influence of the reform in Zurich and Geneva was also great in churches which are called neither Reformed nor Presbyterian. Congregationalists were Reformed in theology but were congregationalist rather than presbyterian in church government. Many Baptists were likewise Reformed in theology but were congregationalist in church government. The Church of England has been called a Reformed church, but it rejects Presbyterian government and tries to preserve more of the life and practice of the ancient Catholic church than did the more radical Reformers.

CHECK YOUR UNDERSTANDING

1. When and where did the word "Reformed" originate?
2. When and where did the word "Presbyterian" originate?
3. What is the reason that some denominations following Calvin and Zwingli are called "Reformed" and others are called "Presbyterian"?
4. When did your particular denomination come into being? What is its relation to other denominations? Can you trace the roots of your denomination back to the sixteenth century?

Reformed in Theology

We have defined "Reformed" as a name given to those ready to reform the church more drastically than those conservative Protestants who were reluctant to part with many of the practices of the medieval church. We have also said that "Reformed" is the name which is given to the theology taught by Calvin and other Reformed theologians.

Let us now ask, What are some of the characteristics of Reformed theology? What distinguishes Reformed doctrines and beliefs from the beliefs of other Christians?

1. *The Lordship and Majesty of God.* Almost everyone who knows anything about John Calvin knows that he believed in the sovereignty of God and in predestination. But not everyone who knows this also knows what Calvin or his followers meant by these doctrines. All Christians believe in the sovereignty of God. Calvinists and Reformed Christians are distinguished simply by the emphasis which they have placed upon it and by the care which they have taken to spell out its meaning for daily life. It is one thing to believe in a doctrine with the top of your mind and another to believe in it with all your heart. You can test this for yourself by asking, What does the sovereignty of God (or any other doctrine) mean to me? The early Calvinists believed in the sovereignty of God passionately, with their hearts as well as their minds.

Reformed Christians have thought of God primarily as energy, activity, intentionality, moral purpose. God is the Lord "who stretches out the heavens like a curtain, and spreads them like a tent to dwell in: who brings princes to nought, and makes the rulers of the earth as nothing" (Isaiah 40:22–23). This conception of God as awesome energy and moral purpose has shaped the distinctive piety of Reformed Christians as the embodiment of the purposes of God in personal life and in history.

Calvin emphasized the sovereignty of God in *nature.* The world, he believed, did not just happen, nor does it run itself. It exists because God wills for it to exist. If God should cease to will its existence, it would no longer exist. The so-called laws of nature are God's laws. The faithfulness of the universe is an expression of the faithfulness of God. (You will study this concept further in Chapter V, "The Church Confesses Its Faith.")

Reformed theology also declares that God is sovereign in history. Let us begin with a look at what God's sovereignty does not mean. It does not mean that human beings are not free. They are free to vote Democratic or Republican, to be capitalists or socialists, to build this kind of community or that. But a person's freedom is limited. It is limited by many facts. Geography, for example, limits human freedom. People living in poor, rocky, mountainous country are not free to build the same kind of community as people living in a fertile river valley. You can think of other limits on human freedom. Yet God has given human beings freedom to make many important decisions in politics, business, and society and in many other affairs which help to make up what we call history.

In the fifth century Augustine wrote that humanity's sin did not take God by surprise. God anticipated that human beings would misuse their freedom, and God had a remedy ready. Believers in Reformed theology have always been convinced that, though a person in freedom may reject God, in the end God's purposes will be fulfilled. Human beings are free to reject God and within limits to live as they please. They are free to fight wars, to live by falsehood, and to deal unjustly with other human beings. But God's sovereignty is such that he uses even evil deeds to accomplish his purpose.

Consider the death of Jesus. Pilate, Caiaphas, and the mob sought in their freedom to put an end to Jesus by crucifying him. But God used their wicked deed for another purpose. The disciples came to see in the death of Jesus a revelation of the love of God. You can probably think of other occasions when an evil deed has in some way been made to serve a good purpose. Reformed theology emphasizes God's control over history. It is a control which allows human freedom but which so overrules wicked deeds that God's purposes are accomplished.

If God is in control of history and if his purposes are going to be fulfilled, then why should I bother to do his will? Many people have asked this question. Perhaps you have. If God is sovereign, it seems that nothing really depends upon human effort. Strangely enough, John Calvin acted as if everything depended upon him! Calvinists have always acted as though God were depending on them, while at the same time believing that God is going to work his purposes out regardless of what they or anyone else might do.

The reason Calvinists have taken their actions so seriously is to be found in another conviction. They are convinced that the sovereign God has chosen them to work out his purposes. Calvin believed that God had elected (chosen) him, not simply to spend eternity in heaven or hell, but to do his work in Geneva. The belief that he was doing God's work gave him enthusiasm for his work. Thus the sovereignty of God does not destroy zeal for doing the will of God; rather it gives new enthusiasm. Calvinists have never retired from history; they have wanted to be part of that history in which God's plan is being fulfilled. They have never been satisfied simply to say their prayers or to be Christians in the privacy of their homes and churches. They have wanted to be God's representatives in the world.

God is also sovereign in the *salvation* of all humans. The theological name for this sovereignty is "predestination" or "election." Calvinists believe that after Adam and Eve sinned, they could no longer turn back to God. Theologians call this the bondage of the will. This may seem strange teaching to you. Most Americans seem to think that, if a person tries hard enough, he or she can do almost anything. It seems strange to say that no matter how hard a person tries, one cannot earn salvation or turn back to God.

Actually, there are a great many things which we cannot do by trying hard. You cannot forget yourself by trying hard. The more you try to forget yourself, the more you think about yourself. It is when something attracts your attention away from yourself that you forget yourself.

You cannot feel grateful by trying hard. You can be polite by disciplining yourself, but *gratitude* is always spontaneous. In a real sense, you cannot help feeling grateful when you are truly grateful.

One of the great sins is pride (self-centeredness, selfishness). This sin is the root of many other sins. A proud person cannot become humble by trying hard. If so,such a person would be proud that he or she was humble. There is no way for self-centered persons to become others-centered by their own efforts. Their own efforts simply concentrate attention upon themselves.

Predestination means that God does for us what we cannot do for ourselves. In Jesus Christ God captures the attention of our lives and turns our hearts toward himself. God chooses us before we choose him.

This does not mean that the Christian does not will to believe in God and to trust him. No one ever believes in God without willing to believe. Predestination does mean that before we ever will to love God, God calls us and moves us to love him. None of the great saints has ever boasted of what he or she has done for God. The great saints are always grateful for what God has done in and through them.

All of this throws light on the meaning of predestination, but mystery still remains. Why is it that some people do not turn to God, at least so far as we know? Some of our Reformed creeds say that God passed over those who do not turn to him and condemned them for their sin. Other Reformed creeds do not say why. They are content to declare that when we do turn to God, we do so because he chooses us.

2. *The Authority of Scripture.* All Christians believe that the Bible is the Word of God. Calvinists are distinguished by the *emphasis* which they place upon this belief. Most Reformed confessions open with a chapter on the Bible and its authority. We have already seen how Calvin went further than Luther in his reformation of the church, wanting to eliminate those things which the Bible did not command as well as those things which the Bible condemned. Reformed theology has always emphasized the necessity for a scriptural foundation for what we do and what we believe.

We have already noted the emphasis which Protestants in general place upon the translation of the Bible into the language of the people. This, too, has been a special emphasis of Reformed Christians. The Bible has been important not only for theologians but also for all Christians. They read it in the home for worship and study.

The authority of God speaking through Scripture means that no other authority has a right to a Christian's total loyalty. The Christian must examine the activities of the State, for example, by the Bible. We must also test our own church life by the Bible, as we saw in our study of Protestantism.

3. *The Life of the Mind as the Service of God.* Christians can serve God in various ways. They serve God by what they do. They serve God by the way they feel. They serve God by how they think. Calvinists have emphasized the life of the mind as the service of God in a way which distinguishes them from most other Christians. Reformed Christians have always thought it especially impor-

tant to know what they believe and why they believe it. This insistence upon knowledge has led to extensive use of the catechism, which summarizes the faith in question-and-answer form. Karl Holl, a church historian, once said that the strength of the Reformed churches was to be found in this emphasis upon knowing what you believe. You have probably found this to be true. The young person who knows what he or she wants or believes has a strength which others lack. And what we think with our mind sooner or later determines how we feel and what we do.

It is increasingly important for Christians to serve God with their minds. One reason for this is the complexity of modern life. For a long time Christians lived in rural communities or in towns. Today more and more people are living in large cities and in an industrial society. How do Christians live in such a society? How do they vote? How do they love their neighbors? The answers to these questions require not only a good heart but a mind which is willing to try to think out what it means to be a Christian. It is important to want to do the right thing, but it is also important to know what the right thing is. Knowing what Christ would have us do about war, about race relations, or about sexual relationships requires the dedication and service of our minds.

Calvinists are thus distinguished by the emphasis which they place on the life of the mind as the service of God. First of all, this means that Christians must know what they believe and why they believe it. Secondly, it means that Christians have learned to think about the problems of life and society as persons whose highest loyalty is to Jesus Christ.

4. *Obedience to God.* Reformed theology is also marked by the emphasis which it has placed upon obedience to God. The Reformers said that the law of God has three purposes: (1) It convicts us of our sins and brings us to confession. (2) It serves to restrain human passions and to maintain public morality. (3) It is a guide to the Christians as they live as Christ's disciples. Calvin was distinguished from other reformers by his emphasis on the third use of the law.

Closely related to this emphasis on obedience to the law is an emphasis upon the moral life. Calvin wrote that the surest test of the genuineness of our faith was the way we treated our neighbors.

Calvin knew that no person is good enough to save self. Every person needs God's forgiveness. But Calvin also believed that we do not have the right to talk about forgiveness until we have done our best to obey the law of God. He knew people who claimed that since God would forgive them, they would not try very much to be obedient. Such people, Calvin insisted, did not know the meaning of forgiveness.

One mark of the Reformed Christian has always been a solid character and moral conduct. Sometimes the Calvinists became legalists; that is, people who wanted to make the Christian life simply obedience to rules. But at its best, Reformed theology has produced men and women who seek to embody the purposes of God in their lives and who also know that they are forgiven sinners.

These four marks have distinguished Reformed theology historically.

CHECK YOUR UNDERSTANDING

1. How have Reformed Christians thought of God?
2. What does "predestination" mean?
3. What do Reformed Christians believe about the Bible?
4. What importance do Reformed Christians place on serving God with one's mind?
5. According to the Reformers, what is the purpose of God's law?
6. What does obedience to God involve?
7. Consider questions 2–6 under "For Discussion" and items 4–7 under "For Action" on pages 61–63.

Presbyterian in Government

Our other name is "Presbyterian." It, too, has a history. It was first used as the name of the church in Scotland in the seventeenth century. As we have said, "Presbyterian" refers to a form of church government, government by presbyters or elders. After the Reformation the Church of Scotland became presbyterian in spite of many efforts to establish an episcopal form of government. For this reason, "Presbyterian" came to be a very appropriate name. In England many Puritans were also presbyterian in their preference in church government. This distinguished them from other Puritans who were Congregationalists and from members of the Church of England who were Episcopalians. Thus the name "Presbyterian" grew out of the struggle as to what was the proper form of church government for the Church of Scotland.

Christian churches are governed in various ways. One form of church government is Congregational. As the name suggests, it is government by the congregation. Important decisions, such as the admission of members, are made by a congregational vote. Each particular congregation governs itself and is associated with other congregations which likewise govern themselves.

Episcopal government is by bishops, who are often regarded as necessary for the existence of the church. The bishops are believed to be in apostolic succession; that is, they are believed to have been consecrated by other bishops in an unbroken line back to the first Apostles. Sometimes this government is exercised through a "college" or group of bishops, as in the Episcopal Church in the United States or in the Church of England. In the case of the Roman Catholic Church, one bishop, the Bishop of Rome, is given supreme power.

What is Presbyterian church government? One very good definition is this: Presbyterianism is church government by presbyters in a series of church courts. In his book *The Presbyterian Churches,* James Moffatt has given an excellent definition. The basic principles of Presbyterianism, he says, are "(a) parity of presbyters; (b) the right of the people, through their representatives or lay elders, to take part in the government of the Church; and (c) the unity of the Church, not simply in faith and order, but in a graduated series of Church courts. . . ."[1]

Let us examine these definitions to see what they mean. The meaning of Presbyterianism can be spelled out in six principles.

1. Presbyterians believe in the unity of the church. This is to say that a particular congregation can be a church only as it shares in the life of other local churches. You can organize a club, and it will be truly a club, even if it stands alone with no relationship with any other clubs. But the church is the church only when it is part of the life of all the people of God.

The church is the whole people of God, not a mere sum of local congregations. At this point you may begin to ask how your local congregation shares in the life of all the people of God. This leads us to the second principle of Presbyterianism.

2. Presbyterians believe that the unity of the church is achieved through a series of church courts. Church courts are composed of elders and ministers. The lowest court, the session or consistory, governs the local congregation. The presbytery or classis is made up of ministers and representative elders in a district. The synod is likewise composed of ministers and elders who represent the church in a larger area composed of three or more presbyteries or classes. The General Assembly or General Synod is the highest court of the church and includes ministers and elders who represent all the presbyteries or classes.

Through these courts Presbyterians share in a common life in the church. (Note: "court" here means not so much a judicial tribune but a council or assembly which exercises executive and legislative as well as judicial functions.) They build new churches, support homes for children and older people, operate colleges, publish church school literature, and plan programs. In some cases presbyteries provide opportunities for all the people from a given area, representing many local congregations, to worship together.

In the New Testament it was not difficult for all Christians to be one church. But today there are millions of Christians living in many different places. It is not easy to be one church. The system of church courts is the way your denomination seeks to realize the unity of the church.

Church courts help members of a denomination to be one church. What shall we say about other Christians who are not members of our own denomination? How are we united with them? This is one of the problems which we face in the life of the church today. At present we achieve a degree of unity through councils which include many denominations. In the United States we have the National Council of Churches. The World Council of Churches includes most Protestant and Orthodox churches. A very important expression of unity is mutual recognition of members, ministers, and sacraments.

Church courts, in addition to helping us achieve unity, also limit the power of any one individual in the church. This is in contrast to the practice in episcopal churches which gives great power to bishops and, in the case of Roman Catholicism, especially to the Bishop of Rome. All power to exercise discipline or govern the church in Presbyterianism is given to the court, not to any individual elder or minister. This leads us to a third principle.

3. A third principle of Presbyterianism is known as the parity of elders. "Parity" means that each elder stands on the same level or has the same authority as any other elder. No elder has any position of authority over any other elder. Ruling elders as well as teaching elders (ministers) may chair committees or serve as moderators of church courts. These positions are necessary and are important to the work of the church, but they do not give the holder any higher rank than any other elder. They are usually held for a limited time, and then someone else is named to them.

4. A fourth principle of Presbyterianism is the right of the people to share in the government of the church by electing their own representatives and officers. The people or their elected representatives have a right to call ministers. Presbyterians have always objected when someone has tried to appoint their minister for them.

Presbyterians have believed that government by elected representatives is the best way to have God's will done in a congregation. If the congregation as a whole tried to govern the church, then important decisions would be made by many people who were not prepared to make these decisions. No single individual is either good enough or wise enough to make decisions for other people. Elected representatives, we believe, will serve better than either the congregation as a whole or any one individual. Electing representatives, we believe, tends to guarantee that the government of the church will be in the hands of persons who have much knowledge and experience in the life of the church. It is intended that the elders be good persons who have a thorough knowledge and appreciation of the Bible, of theology, and of the mission of the church in the world.

5. A fifth principle of Presbyterianism is the authority of the Bible. Presbyterians have always believed that the government of

the church should be formed according to the teachings of the Bible. Some have thought that Presbyterianism is *the* biblical form of church government. Most Presbyterians now believe that no one form of church government is taught in the Bible. They do believe that Presbyterianism is agreeable to what is found in the New Testament. Most Presbyterians say that Presbyterianism is *a* biblical but is not *the* biblical form.

"The authority of the Bible" means that the government of the church must be in agreement with the principles which the Bible teaches, not with any pattern which is to be copied exactly. Many things in the life of the church have to be arranged according to common sense. For example, the early Christians frequently worshiped in the very early hours of the morning. Today most churches have their Sunday service at eleven o'clock.

6. A sixth principle of Presbyterianism is the ministry of compassion given to the office of deacon. Deacons have the special task of visiting and caring for the sick, helping the poor, and ministering to all those who are in need. In recent years deacons have been entrusted with the care of the church building and many other such matters. Their chief work, however, is to help those who are in need.

CHECK YOUR UNDERSTANDING

1. What different forms of church government are there? Which forms are followed by the congregations in your community?
2. What are the marks of Presbyterian government?
3. Name and explain briefly the six principles of Presbyterianism.

Explore and Undertake

For Discussion

1. Trace the ancestry of your denomination back to the Reformers of the sixteenth century.
2. How does belief in the Lordship and majesty of God shape your life? What part may we play in the working out of God's sovereign purpose for the world?

3. What do you believe about predestination?
4. Why do you think it is important to have the Bible in the language of the people? Do you think that present-day versions of the Scriptures will be satisfactory for use a thousand years from now? Why?
5. What does it mean to serve God with your mind? Have there been occasions in your life when you wished you knew more about what you believe?
6. Do you think that there is a clear difference between the typical Reformed Christian and the typical member of another denomination?
7. What is the name of the ruling body in your congregation? What is the name of the presbytery or classis to which your congregation belongs? of the synod? What do congregations do together in the presbytery or classis? in the synod? in the General Assembly or General Synod?
8. Are there any changes that you would like to see made in the government of your denomination? How can the government of the denomination be made to work better?
9. Is there a Board of Deacons in your congregation? What does it do? Who in your church is responsible for its ministry to human need in the community?

For Action

1. Write in your notebook a brief history of your denomination. Indicate the time and occasion for its beginning and show its relation to other Presbyterian and Reformed bodies both at its time of beginning and through the years. Contact your pastor for infomation about resources to use in preparing the history.
2. Prepare an outline presenting the distinctive features of the following three forms of church government: Episcopalian, Presbyterian, and Congregational. Seek the help of your pastor if necessary.
3. Prepare a one-act play based on a dramatic event in the life of John Calvin or Theodore Beza or John Knox. Consult an encyclopedia for information on each man. You may find additional material on Calvin on pages 150–156 in Bainton's *The Church*

of Our Fathers and on pages 133–139 of Langford's *Fire Upon the Earth;* Beza, on page 154 in Bainton; and on Knox on pages 155-159 in Langford's book, on pages 155–156 of Bainton's *The Church of Our Fathers,* and on pages 157–168 in Bowie's *Men of Fire.* See also chapters 16 and 17 of Hageman and See's *That the World May Know.* You may want to present the play at a meeting of the congregation or of the youth of the church.

4. Study the hymn "A Mighty Fortress Is Our God" or "All People That on Earth Do Dwell" and discuss the belief that they express in the sovereignty of God.

5. Read the Ten Commandments (Exod. 20:1–17) carefully. Begin a list of questions about the Commandments to ask during your study of chapter 11.

6. Consider what the standards of your denomination have to say about the sovereignty of God. Chapters III–V of the Westminster Confession of Faith, Sections 5–16 of the Cumberland Presbyterian Confession of Faith, and Questions 2–4 of the Heidelberg Catechism have help for you.

7. Write an essay on the subject "I'm Glad I'm a Presbyterian." Of course, you may substitute "Associate Reformed Presbyterian" or "Cumberland Presbyterian" or "Moravian" or "Member of the Reformed Church in America" for "Presbyterian."

8. Arrange with your pastor for your group to attend a meeting of the session or consistory of your congregation. Inquire through your pastor into the possibility of the group's attending a meeting of the presbytery or classis. After attending each meeting, talk with one another about procedures followed and decisions made in the meeting.

9. Prepare a report on how members of the session or consistory in your congregation are elected. Put it in your notebook.

10. Make a list of the names of the members of the session or consistory and the diaconate in your congregation. Find out if they are elected for life or for a limited number of years.

11. How is your denomination organized? What is the governing body in your congregation called? What is the name of the governing body at the next and other levels? What is the highest court in the denomination?

12. Obtain from your pastor information about the membership of your congregation in a local council of churches; of your synod in a state council of churches; and of your denomination in the National Council of Churches, in the World Council of Churches, and in the World Alliance of Reformed Churches. Invite the help of your pastor in securing information on the inter-church bodies to which your church belongs, and let members of your group draw up a report on the purpose, membership, and activities of one of them.

13. Draw up a list of services that your congregation could perform in the community in a "ministry of compassion." Find out which of these services your congregation (perhaps through the diaconate or some other group) is performing.

14. Invite your pastor to meet with your group and discuss the government of your denomination. If this is not possible, let a member of your group secure a copy of the Constitution or Form of Government of the church, and give a report to the group on what a study of it reveals.

15. Talk about church government with a friend who is a member of a Baptist church or a Christian (Disciples of Christ) church. Find out what is done in official meetings of the congregation. Report to the group on what you learn.

CHAPTER V

The Church Confesses Its Faith

We have identified ourselves as (1) the people of the Bible, (2) members of the holy catholic church, (3) Protestants, and (4) Presbyterian and Reformed Christians. Now we come to the question, What does the church do? What makes up its life?

Our first answer is, "The church *confesses* its faith." Some react with the taunt, "Doesn't the church have something more important to do?" In our society many people do not believe that they are doing anything important unless they are working with their hands or producing something which they can see and handle and use. So we begin with the question, What good does it do to confess one's faith?

Our first answer is that Jesus has invited us to confess our faith. He declared, "So every one who acknowledges me before men, I also will acknowledge before my Father who is in heaven ..." (Matt. 10:32). Paul was probably referring to a practice of the New Testament church when he wrote to the Christians in Rome, "For man believes with his heart and so is justified, and he confesses with his lips and so is saved" (Rom. 10:10). Jesus himself once asked his disciples, "Who do you say that I am?" Peter answered, "You are the Christ, the Son of the living God" (Matt. 16:16). This simple statement by Peter is one of the earliest Christian confessions.

From the very beginning Christians have confessed their faith.

In fact, the practice of confession was begun by the people of God in the Old Testament. As the worshipers brought their offerings of thanksgiving to God, they confessed their faith by proclaiming what God had done for his people in such words as those found in Deuteronomy 26:5-9. The people of the Old Testament also used simple statements as confessions of their faith: "Hear, O Israel: The Lord our God is one Lord; and you shall love the Lord your God with all your heart, and with all your soul, and with all your might" (Deut. 6:4-5).

Christians have also found that confessions of faith serve specific purposes:

1. They have always been a part of worship. The confession is a declaration of loyalty and of trust. Through the words of a confession, individual persons offer themselves, their whole personalities. They declare that they are going to live in this manner and for this purpose. They make known what they intend to do with their lives and how they intend to live. For these reasons the confession of faith is an important part of worship.

2. Confessions of faith are one way in which the church teaches the faith. The confession is usually a brief and exact summary of the faith. The learning of a confession, as well as the offering of a confession of faith, has always been connected with the preparation of young people for full participation in the life of the church.

3. Confessions of faith are declarations of allegiance. Making such declarations stimulates your own faith, just as the pledge of allegiance reminds you of your loyalty to your country. Declaring your faith also tells the world where you stand. Thus, to confess your faith requires courage. It requires courage because many people, perhaps in some cases a majority, in your group or school may not believe as you do. They will try to make you as they are. Sometimes you may be ridiculed or scorned.

4. Confessions of faith enable us to put our deepest convictions into words. This enables us to reflect on our faith, to understand it better and to deepen its meaning for us.

There is another question which arises concerning confessions of faith. What authority does a confession have? We have said that

God speaking through the Bible is the supreme authority. The authority of the confession or creed is under the authority of the Bible. But the creed or confession is a summary of what the church believes the Bible teaches. The creed is what the church has found that the Bible has to say. The church continues to read the Bible, and sometimes the church finds it necessary to change the creed in the light of clearer knowledge of what the Bible teaches. The creed, on the other hand, helps the Christian to read the Bible with understanding and insight.

The Apostles' Creed

One of the ancient creeds of the church is known as the Apostles' Creed. The origin of this creed is to be found in the instruction for baptism in Rome in the second century. This old Roman creed became the mother creed for all the churches in the West which were dependent upon Rome. The wording of the creed varied from city to city. The particular form which we use developed in southwest France, and we find it in a manuscript which is dated about A.D. 710. It gradually replaced all other forms of the creed, partly through the efforts of Charlemagne, who wanted all churches to worship in the same way. Finally it was accepted in Rome. Though the Apostles' Creed gradually grew in the church and did not reach its final form until around A.D. 700, all of the phrases in it were in use in the church before A.D. 100. For this reason we rightly call it the *Apostles'* Creed.

The Apostles' Creed is the best known creed in western Europe and in the United States. It is not so well known among Eastern Orthodox Christians as the Nicene Creed. All of us have confessed our faith by using the Apostles' Creed. For this reason it will serve as a summary of our confession.

I BELIEVE

What do you mean when you say, "I believe"? It has been pointed out that there is an important difference between saying, "I believe *that*" and "I believe *in*." I believe *that* Columbus discovered America in 1492. I believe *in* my friend. This is an important difference, but the New Testament nowhere makes any such distinction. The reason is that faith involves both kinds of belief.

My belief in God may be more like my belief *in* my father than it is like my belief *about* who discovered America. Nevertheless, I do not believe *in* my father without believing *that* my father is a good man, and so forth. Neither do we believe *in* God without believing *that* Jesus Christ is the revelation of God. When we say "I believe," we do not mean merely that we believe the Creed. We mean that we believe in God and believe that he is and does as the Creed declares.

Believing is an act of one's whole being and personality. A person believes with the mind, the heart, and the will. Believing includes knowledge, passion, and commitment. It is an act of the whole person.

Here is a definition of faith which will help you understand what you mean when you say, "I believe":

"What is faith in Jesus Christ? Faith in Jesus Christ is a saving grace, whereby we receive and rest upon him alone for salvation, as he is offered to us in the gospel" (Q. 86, The Westminster Shorter Catechism).

To believe, in the Christian sense, is to be related to God in trust and hope and obedience, through what God has done for us in the life, death, and resurrection of Jesus Christ. To be a Christian is to trust God as we know him in Jesus Christ.

CHECK YOUR UNDERSTANDING

1. In what ways have Christians confessed their faith?
2. What purposes are served by a confession of faith?
3. What is the Apostles' Creed?
4. What is the difference between belief *in* and belief *about?*

"I BELIEVE IN GOD THE FATHER"

What do we mean when we declare, "I believe in God"? This is the most important statement that we can make. In it we declare what we believe to be the most real and most important fact in all the universe. For this reason we cannot casually say, "I believe in God." If we do make this statement without being seriously concerned, then we do not know what we are saying.

Sometimes people say, "I do not believe in God," but they say it with the indifference with which they might say, "It is going to rain tomorrow." When we talk in this way, we are not speaking with understanding or with seriousness.

A great philosopher once said that the denial of God does not necessarily make a person a bad character, but that it does leave him lonely and sad. For a person to deny God is to believe that the things you care for most are at the mercy of the things you care for least. When you deny the existence of God, you have to believe that man with his mind and his personality just happened, that man is just an accident in the history of the universe. One modern philosopher who denied the existence of God concluded that man is the accidental collocations of atoms and that his end will be the debris of a universe in ruins.

One study of the religious life of young people discovered that more young people come to believe in God when they ask if life has meaning than at any other time. Is this true in your case?

You can know more of what we mean when we say "God" by studying the answers to the questions concerning God in the catechisms of the church:

"What is God? God is a Spirit, infinite, eternal, and unchangeable, in his being, wisdom, power, holiness, justice, goodness, and truth" (Q. 4, The Westminster Shorter Catechism).

"Are there more gods than one? There is but one only, the living and true God" (Q. 5, The Westmister Shorter Catechism).

"What do you believe when you say: 'I believe in God the Father Almighty, Maker of Heaven and earth'? That the eternal Father of our Lord Jesus Christ, who out of nothing created heaven and earth with all that is in them, who also upholds and governs them by his eternal counsel and providence, is for the sake of Christ his Son my God and my Father. I trust in him so completely that I have no doubt that he will provide me with all things necessary for body and soul. Moreover, whatever evil he sends upon me in this troubled life he will turn to my good, for he is able to do it, being Almighty God, and is determined to do it, being a faithful Father" (The Heidelberg Catechism, Q. 26).

THE FATHER ALMIGHTY

In the original sense of the creed, the word "father" meant "creator." God is the maker of the universe. Jesus, however, gave the word "father" a much deeper meaning. Christians, in saying the creed, have always had in mind this special emphasis of Jesus. God is the father who loves the world and cares for the world and has authority over the world.

We all have to think of God in words which have meaning in our own experience. When Jesus wanted to tell us who God is, he chose a word from our daily life and called God "Father." He did not mean that God is just like a father. He *did* mean that he could find nothing more like God in daily experience than our knowledge of a good father.

It is clear that the confession does not mean that God is like an *ordinary* father when it adds the word "almighty." No earthly father is almighty. What does "almighty" mean? Some have thought that it means that God can do anything. This false idea has led to many nonsensical questions: "Can God make a stone so heavy he cannot lift it?" "Can God make a square round at the same time it is square?" These questions were asked in the second century by a philosopher named Celsus. A Christian theologian named Origen replied, "He can assuredly, according to us, do anything, that is, anything that can be done without detriment to his divinity, his goodness or his wishes." Another early church theologian, Augustine, gave this answer: "The only thing the Omnipotent One cannot do is that which he does not will to do."

"Almighty" means that God can do whatever he wills to do.

MAKER OF HEAVEN AND EARTH

We do not know exactly what creation is, for none of us has ever created anything. We have always made things out of things which already exist. We sometimes say that we create things, when there is something new in what we have done. But we always use things which exist. The creeds mean creation from nothing. This is beyond our experience.

What, then, does "creation" mean? It means that the world depends upon God for its beginning and its continuing existence. If God should cease to will the world to exist, it would vanish into nothingness or nonbeing. Also, God is in control of the world. While God gives his creation its own reality, its structures, orders, and energy systems, and while God endows human beings with freedom, the final control of the world remains in his hands. God gives human beings the power to do many things, but there is a limit to their power.

A modern theologian has said that there is something humorous about wickedness. Wicked people (a Hitler, for example) think that they are getting away with something, just as small children think they are getting away with something when they are not. Believers who know that God is the creator can laugh at wicked people, because they know that they cannot in the end get away with what they are doing.

The doctrine of creation also means that the world is good. It is good because God made it. In the first chapter of Genesis we read that God looked at the world and found it to be very good. A Christian must likewise believe that the world is good. The sad-faced, unhappy picture which some of us have of a Christian is a false picture. Even though the goodness of God's creation is marred by human sin, there is still something wrong with the Christian who never enjoys living in God's world.

One common idea in the history of human thoughts has been the notion that the world is evil. For people who believe this, salvation is escape from the world. You must not really enjoy living or anything about this world. This idea has continually crept into the thinking of Christians. It has led to the idea that anything you enjoy doing is a sin. Dorothy Sayers, the great detective story writer who was also a theologian, once wrote that for many modern people " 'original sin' means that anything we enjoy doing is wrong."[1]

The doctrine that God created the world also means that we must respect the world as God's creation. Persons who believe that God created the world will not abuse the world. This means that they will not waste natural resources, such as minerals or the fertility of the soil; that they will not abuse living things; that they will respect other men and women who have been made in the image of God. Whenever we abuse the world, we abuse the work of God.

The Westminster Shorter Catechism states the doctrine of creation in these words: "What is the work of creation? The work of creation is, God's making all things of nothing, by the word of his power, in the space of six days, and all very good" (Q. 9). Here the word "day" is not to be understood as a day of twenty-four hours.

CHECK YOUR UNDERSTANDING

1. What do we mean when in the Creed we express faith in God as Father?
2. What is the meaning of our faith in God as "almighty"?
3. What is the meaning of faith in God as creator? What does "creation" mean?

"I BELIEVE IN . . . JESUS CHRIST"

"I believe in . . . Jesus Christ His only Son our Lord." This statement is the beginning of the second and longest paragraph of the Creed. It has to do with Jesus Christ, and for this reason it is the confession which marks us as Christians. As Christians we believe that the God who made the world became "incarnate," that is, "embodied," in Jesus Christ. God made the world, and we may learn much about him from a study of the world. In the same way, we may learn something about anyone from a study of something which he has made. Nevertheless, we never really know another person until this person confronts us and speaks to us. So it is with our knowledge of God. We do know God when we look at what he has made. We see special evidence of his wisdom and his power. But we know God truly only when he becomes embodied in a human life and confronts us personally.

The doctrine of the incarnation is the central Christian confession ("Incarnation" comes from two Latin words *in* and *caro,* which mean "in the flesh"). Paul stated the doctrine this way: ". . . God was in Christ reconciling the world to himself . . ."(2 Cor. 5:19). Actually, the doctrine of the incarnation says three things: (1) We believe that Jesus Christ is truly man; (2) We believe that Jesus Christ is truly God; (3) We believe that in Jesus Christ God and man are united in one personal existence.

This means that when we see Jesus Christ, we know who man truly is. Jesus Christ is a human being as God made human beings to be. When we see Jesus Christ, we also know who God is, for he is God embodied in a human life. Jesus Christ is our answer to the question, Who is God? God is like Jesus Christ. More than this, he is present in Jesus Christ.

We said earlier that the statement "I believe in God" is an important declaration. It is likewise important to know *who* God is. It is especially important to know whether God cares for us, loves us, and forgives us. Is it possible that God does not care, that he does not love? Jesus Christ assures us that he cares, that he loves, that he forgives.

The Apostles' Creed tells us that Jesus Christ is God's "only Son our Lord." The confession that Jesus Christ is the Son of God was a favorite confession in the early church. The title "Son of God" tells us clearly that Jesus Christ is very close to God, so close that we can say that God was in him as he has been in no other.

The word "only" means that God has no other son like Jesus Christ. There is no other revelation like the revelation of God in him. He is so different from other men in his intimacy with the Father that no one else can be called God's Son in the sense in which we in the Creed affirm faith in him as God's only Son.

The second title given to Jesus Christ was likewise popular in the early church. One of the most frequent Christian confessions was the simple statement "Jesus Christ is Lord." This had special meaning for those Christians who lived under the Roman government, which claimed man's absolute loyalty. The Christian said that Jesus Christ, not the emperor, was Lord. This confession also meant a great deal to people who had been told that their lives were controlled by fate, by the stars, by forces over which they had no control. Jesus Christ, not fate, not luck, not the stars, was Lord. When the Christians said that Jesus Christ was Lord, they were declaring that Jesus Christ had authority over the whole world.

This confession, Jesus Christ is Lord, has through the centuries had special meaning for Christians in distress. In an assembly at

Barmen in the time of Adolf Hitler, Christians declared that Jesus Christ, not Hitler, was Lord, and that they would listen only to Jesus Christ.

HE WAS CONCEIVED AND BORN

"... Jesus Christ ... was conceived by the Holy Ghost, born of the Virgin Mary ..." This statement tells us two things about Jesus Christ. The first is that he was born as you and I were born. He was truly man. Many Christians have had difficulty believing that Jesus Christ was a real man. But the Creed here nails down this fact. He was born of a woman named Mary.

Yet this phrase also tells us something else, which seems in contradiction to what has just been said. This birth was unlike all other births. Jesus was conceived by the Holy Spirit. This was a most unusual birth, as the accounts of the shepherds in the fields and the wise men from the East so dramatically tell in the Gospels. Here in the Creed the unusualness, the strangeness, the newness of Jesus' birth is told in theological language. He was conceived by the Holy Spirit.

This statement in the Creed may seem drab when you compare it with the account of the shepherds and the wise men. Nevertheless, when you confess the Creed, you are making the same confession which is made in Matthew 1 and Luke 2.

HE SUFFERED

"[He] suffered under Pontius Pilate ..." Here the Apostles' Creed gives a date to the life of Jesus Christ. Jesus Christ was not just any man, but a particular man who lived in a particular time and place. The church believed that it was important to pin this date down exactly. He lived and died under the Roman governor, Pontius Pilate. The Gospel of Luke has this same concern to tell exactly when Jesus was born. "In those days a decree went out from Caesar Augustus that all the world should be enrolled ..." (Luke 2:1; see also Luke 3:1). Leaders in the early church wanted to make certain that no one would think there was anything vague, indefinte, uncertain about Jesus. Hence, they told exactly when he lived and died.

Christians are concerned about historical dates, because they believe that God most clearly reveals who he is in history. They believe that God reveals himself through the wonders of nature. They believe that he reveals himself through human reason. They believe that he reveals himself in prayer. But he most clearly reveals himself in the great events of history. In the Old Testament the people of God seemed to say, "If you want to know God, see how he delivered Israel from the house of bondage in Egypt." In the New Testament they said, "If you want to know who God is, see what he has done in the life, death, and resurrection of Jesus Christ." They thought the life of Jesus Christ was so important that they gave it an exact date. He suffered under Pontius Pilate.

HE WAS CRUCIFIED AND BURIED

"[He] was crucified, dead, and buried . . ." Again the Creed emphasizes the solid facts of the life of Jesus. There can be no doubt that he was true man, for men suffer and are crucified. Men die and are buried. The burial leaves no doubt that he was dead.

Perhaps you have already asked, Why doesn't the Creed say more about the life of Jesus, about his teaching? As we shall explain later, the Creed does not try to say everything. But here we can ask, Why is this great emphasis put on the death and burial of Jesus Christ?

If you will look at the Gospels, you will find the same emphasis there. About one-third of the material in the four Gospels is devoted to the last week of Jesus' life. Why? The answer must be that their writers thought that this last week was of very great importance.

"The crucifixion of Jesus set men thinking more than anything else that has ever happened in the life of the human race,"[2] declared Scottish theologian Donald Baillie. Can you see why he said it? The remarkable thing is that when people have thought of the death of Jesus, they have thought of the love of God. God loves that much, enough to share in the death of Jesus Christ.

On first thought, you would think the death of Jesus would have made people think the very opposite. They might have thought that the death of Jesus meant that God didn't care what happened to man. But they had seen Jesus loving men, even his enemies, willing to die for them. They had seen that he was willing to bear the guilt of their wrongdoing and forgive them, and that he was ready to forgive from the cross. They had seen Jesus do this. And they knew that they had seen God doing this. ". . . God was in Christ reconciling the world to himself . . ." (2 Cor. 5:19).

HE DESCENDED INTO HELL

"He descended into hell . . ." This phrase represented a common idea in the early church and was added to the Apostles' Creed. Yet it is a difficult phrase. It has a number of meanings:

1. The Westminster Larger Catechism says, "Christ's humiliation after his death consisted in his being buried, and continuing in the state of the dead, and under the power of death till the third day, which hath been otherwise expressed in these words, He descended into hell" (Q.50).

2. John Calvin believed that these words stood for the spiritual suffering of Jesus as he took upon himself the sins of man and knew God's righteous anger upon all sin. The descent into hell points to the inner suffering of Jesus in his spirit, heart, and mind, as the wounds of the nails and spear point to the suffering of his body.

Very much the same meaning is given to these words in The Heidelberg Catechism (Q.44): "Why is there added: 'He descended into hell'? That in my severest tribulations I may be assured that Christ my Lord has redeemed me from hellish anxieties and torment by the unspeakable anguish, pains, and terrors which he suffered in his soul both on the cross and before."

3. Many people in the early church thought that these words referred to a visit by Jesus to the place of the dead. Here he preached to those who had looked forward to his coming in the Old Testament and also to those who did not have a chance to hear him during their lifetime. Some Christians had vivid imaginations of Jesus' visiting hell itself and conquering Satan and rescuing those whom he had enslaved.

Those who have held these views of the early church base them upon such passages as 1 Peter 3:18–20. Read the passage. This is a difficult text, and for this reason Calvin preferred his much simpler and clearer interpretation of the Creed.

HE AROSE

". . . the third day he rose again from the dead . . ." The resurrection of Jesus was the central theme of the preaching of the first Christians. "But God raised him from the dead" was the great glad news. This was the most important event in all of history.

It was important because it overthrew what had been done on Friday. On Friday Pilate, the High Priest Caiaphas, and the senseless mob had crucified Jesus. They thought that they had done away with him. The resurrection was God's answer to those who had so tried to do away with Jesus. The resurrection was also a demonstration of power greater than death. For this reason the disciples called the resurrection the great good news. They even changed their day of worship from Saturday to Sunday, because on this day God raised Jesus Christ from the dead. Every Sunday is an Easter, because every Sunday is a memorial of the resurrection.

Peter, who had gone back to his fishing boats, now became a great preacher of the gospel. Other disciples, ordinary people who had been very sad over the death of Jesus, now became courageous disciples, willing to lay down their lives for the faith. The resurrection brought courage, hope, assurance to the disciples.

What did the resurrection mean for the Pilates, the members of the mob? It could only mean judgment. The resurrection was God's No to Pilate and to all who had raised their voices against Jesus as they cried, "Crucify him!"

Today when we declare our faith that God raised Jesus Christ from the dead, we say something very important about our own lives. The resurrection is both God's Yes and God's No to us. It is God's Yes to those who trust Jesus Christ as Lord and Savior. It is his No to all those who today reject Jesus. For this reason it is strange that Easter is the day when people who never seem to think about God and the serious issues of life choose to come to the church. Easter is judgment as well as hope.

HE ASCENDED INTO HEAVEN

". . . He ascended into heaven . . ." The ascension is the end of the visible and physical presence of Jesus with his disciples. It is the end of one way of his being with them, and the beginning of a new way.

The people of God live within the limitations of history. We are limited by space: we cannot be everywhere at once. We are limited by time: time runs out before we finish our work, for example. These same limitations affected the work of Jesus during his earthly ministry. His ascension means that he is no longer limited in this way. Because this is true, the people of God are not altogether limited by space and time and death. The meaning of the ascension is well stated in John 14—16.

HE IS ON THE RIGHT HAND OF GOD

". . . and [He] sitteth on the right hand of God the Father Almighty . . ." This phrase tells where Jesus Christ is now and helps us to understand his ascension. When the early Christians said that Jesus went up into heaven, they did not mean necessarily that heaven is a place just above us. That is an impossible idea, as our modern knowledge of the universe makes clear. They did mean that Jesus Christ in his humanity as well as his divinity is with God. In Acts 1:9 we are told that a cloud took him out of the sight of his disciples. The cloud here, as elsewhere in the Bible, is a symbol of the divine presence.

The right hand of God is not one literal, particular place. Martin Luther once said that the right hand of God is everywhere. Sitting "at the right hand of God" simply means that Christ is the active, reigning Lord of the world. John Calvin wrote: "When Christ is said to be in heaven, we must not view him as dwelling among the spheres and numbering stars. . . . Not that it is a literal place beyond the world, but we cannot speak of the Kingdom of God without using our ordinary language" (Commentary on Ephesians 4:10).

The first Russian astronaut reported that he scanned the heavens and did not find God anywhere. He should not have expected to find God in outer space any more than in the space of the earth. For God has his space which is different from ours; we do not know and understand it. Our problem is that we do not even know what our space is. When we begin to think about it, we are left in mystery. Try to think of space going on forever. You can't, can you? Try to imagine space coming to an end. You can't do that, either. There are many things which we do not know about space, our space as well as God's. When we say that Jesus Christ is at the right hand of God, we are saying that he is everywhere, unlimited by space and time.

Consider the following quotations from the Heidelberg Catechism:

"How do we understand the words: 'He ascended into heaven?' That Christ was taken up from the earth into heaven before the eyes of his disciples and remains there on our behalf until he comes again to judge the living and the dead" (Q.46).

"Then, is not Christ with us unto the end of the world, as he has promised us? Christ is true man and true God. As a man he is no longer on earth, but in his divinity, majesty, grace, and Spirit, he is never absent from us" (Q.47).

"What benefit do we receive from Christ's ascension into heaven? First, that he is our Advocate in the presence of his Father in heaven. Second, that we have our flesh in heaven as a sure pledge that he, as the Head, will also take us, his members, up to himself. Third, that he sends us his Spirit as a counterpledge by whose power we seek what is above, where Christ is, sitting at the right hand of God, and not things that are on earth" (Q. 49).

"Why is there added: 'And sits at the right hand of God'? Because Christ ascended into heaven so that he might manifest himself there as the Head of his Church, through whom the father governs all things" (Q. 50).

HE SHALL COME

". . . from thence He shall come to judge the quick and the dead." Those who knew that Jesus Christ had been raised from the dead and had ascended to the heavens also knew that he would come again to judge the living and the dead. Human life and human history do not just end. They end face to face with God. Just as the death of Jesus was not the end of him but the occasion for the resurrection, so our human history will not just end in death.

At the end there will be God—God as we have known him in Jesus Christ. Just as Easter overthrew the work of Pilate and those who crucified Jesus, so will Jesus Christ overthrow much of the work which we do in human history. But just as the resurrection gave new hope and courage to those who trusted in Jesus and wiped away the tears of those who were in sorrow, so Jesus Christ will save every life of faith and hope and love.

Thus, this confession of a Christ who will judge the living and the dead is not a vague statement about something which will only happen a long time from now. It is a confession about what also happens in our lives here and now.

CHECK YOUR UNDERSTANDING

1. What does "incarnation" mean?
2. What do we mean when we declare faith in Jesus Christ as "God's only Son"?
3. In what respect was the birth of Jesus Christ like any other birth? In what respect was it different?
4. Jesus Christ suffered, "was crucified, dead, and buried." What meaning does that statement have?
5. What is the significance of Christ's resurrection from the dead? Of his descent into hell? Of his ascension? Of his being at the right hand of God? Of his coming again?

"I BELIEVE IN THE HOLY GHOST"

Now we come to the doctrine of the Trinity. We have spoken of God as the Father Almighty, creator of heaven and earth, and of God in Christ. Now we consider the Holy Spirit. ("Ghost" means "spirit.")

Does this mean that we believe in three gods? If God were just another man, then we would not have great difficulty knowing who he is. But since God is God and not man, we do have a great deal of difficulty. Our best answer to who God is is in the doctrine of the Trinity. In this doctrine we say that God has revealed himself to us in three different ways. He has revealed himself as our creator who is beyond our comprehending and on whom we utterly depend. He has confronted us in Jesus Christ. He is known to us in worship, in prayer, in the deep experiences of life as a Holy Spirit. Yet the God whom we know as our creator and as our redeemer in Jesus Christ and as the Holy Spirit is one God.

God is *one*. He is not one in the sense that there is one God when there might be two or three. In the Christian sense of "God," there cannot be more gods than one. If one can think of God and then can imagine a number of gods, he has not thought what the Christian means by God.

This one God is *triune;* that is, he is three in one. The Westminster Shorter Catechism speaks of three persons in the Godhead (Q.6), but it does not mean by "person" a separate individual, as the word commonly means to us. When the word "person" was first used in the doctrine of the Trinity, it meant the mask which an actor used in a drama or the role which he played in the drama. In the doctrine of the Trinity, "person" simply means a way or mode in which God is God. The doctrine of the Trinity means that God is continually and personally related to us in three different ways.

"I believe in the Holy Ghost . . ." In these words we affirm that God is everywhere present and that he is at work in the church and in the lives of his people. God is never far away. Whenever we call upon his name, he is there.

The word "spirit" is a vague word in our language. It frequently means something unreal, ghostlike. But we also use the word in a very real sense. We talk about the spirit of a person. When we use the word in this sense, we mean something very much like basic selfhood. This is near to the meaning in the Creed. The Holy Spirit is the presence and power of God in the world which he has made. This presence and power are especially known in the church.

What, now, is the nature of the power and presence of God which we call the Holy Spirit? The answer which the New Testament always gives is that the Spirit is Christ's Spirit. It doesn't mean much to say that a person has a great spirit unless we know the person. It would not mean much to say that God's power and presence were in our midst, if we did not know God. We do know God in Jesus Christ, and so we know that the Holy Spirit is the Spirit of Christ.

Likewise, we say that the Holy Spirit is bound by the Word of God. The Holy Spirit is the same God who inspired the writing of the Bible. The Holy Spirit speaks to us the same word which was spoken in Christ and in the Bible. Lhis gives us some basis for judging whether a person is moved by the Spirit by asking if he or she seems to be moved by the Spirit of Christ whom we know in the Gospels.

The importance of this affirmation of the Creed is clear. When we say, "I believe in the Holy Ghost," we declare that God is present and powerful in our midst, in our own lives. We declare that we can *know God,* not just something *about* him.

Finally, how may each of us know the Holy Spirit personally? There is no magic formula which we can repeat. There is no way to compel the Holy Spirit to make himself known to us. But there are some things which we can do. We can read our Bibles. We can think about Jesus Christ and his will for our lives each day. We can have as our companions those who do trust God and seek to do his will. No one can guarantee the presence of the Holy Spirit. But if we do these things it is likely that we shall know him.

CHECK YOUR UNDERSTANDING

1. In what sense is God one?
2. What is the meaning of the doctrine of the Trinity?
3. Who is the Holy Spirit? How can we test the claim that a person is moved by the Spirit?
4. How can a person come to know the Holy Spirit?

"I BELIEVE IN . . . THE . . . CHURCH"

"I believe in . . . the holy Catholic Church . . ." We do not believe in the church in the sense that we believe in the Holy Spirit. We believe there is a holy catholic church, but our faith rests in God, not in the church. But we do have faith in the church as the people of God.

We have already looked at the meaning of the words "catholic" and "church" in Chapter II. What, now, does the word "holy" mean? It originally meant "separate". It came to mean that which has to do with the divine and which is separated from all worldly uses. As the righteous and ethical nature of God was emphasized, holiness came also to mean "the righteous and the moral." Christians are holy because they have been set apart for God's purpose and because they live in obedience to him.

In what sense is the church holy? There were some in the early church who wanted to say that the church was holy because its members were holy. But this was not a firm foundation for the church, because you could never be sure that all the members were holy. Others said the church is holy because its ministers are holy, but this too was a feeble foundation. Of course, both members and ministers *ought* to be holy. But is there not some more certain basis for saying that the church is holy?

The church is holy because God has chosen the church and set it apart, because the Holy Spirit is present in the church, and because the means of God's favor and grace are there: the Bible, the sacraments, and prayer. The church does not depend upon what its members do so much as upon what the Holy Spirit does. Even a sinful minister who fails miserably as a Christian may be the means by which a person hears the Word of God and in faith obeys.

THE COMMUNION OF SAINTS

This phrase has had a number of interpretations. The most common interpretation is that the communion of saints is the fellowship of all the people of God.

When we confess belief in the communion of saints, we declare that the church is a fellowship of all the people of God in heaven and on earth. The communion of saints also means that Christians share their gifts with one another. John Calvin emphasized this point. The gifts which we share are not simply gifts of food and material things, but gifts of the spirit. A person who has one spiritual strength helps another person who is struggling against some temptation or spiritual weakness. (Read 1 Corinthians 12:14—13:13; Galatians 6:1–5.) Consider this word from The Heidelberg Catechism (Q.55):

What do you understand by "the communion of saints"? First, that believers one and all, as partakers of the Lord Christ, and all his treasures and gifts, shall share in one fellowship. Second, that each one ought to know that he is obliged to use his gifts freely and with joy for the benefit and welfare of other members.

THE FORGIVENESS OF SINS

"I believe in . . . the forgiveness of sins . . ." This is the central theme of the Gospels. Jesus proclaimed the forgiveness of sins. (Read Mark 2:1–2; Matthew 9:2–8; and Luke 5:18–26.) Nevertheless, it was easy for the church to forget this. Some sins, such as murder and adultery, seemed unforgivable. Many Christians came to feel that there was no forgiveness for these sins. We can understand why they felt this way. They were concerned that Christians should live as Christians. Nevertheless, the church must never forget that at the heart of the gospel is the forgiveness of sins.

We sometimes say we forgive a person when what they did does not really matter to us. But this is not real forgiveness. It is indifference. Whenever you forgive someone for what he has done to you, you have to be willing to bear the pain of his wrongdoing. Someone has well said that wherever there is forgiveness, there is suffering on both sides—the suffering of repentance on the side of the forgiven and the greater suffering of atonement on the part of the forgiver. Forgiveness cannot be easily given. The price has to be paid by the forgiver. Neither can forgiveness be easily accepted. We would all much rather "pay our way" than accept forgiveness from someone else.

Here again our own human experience helps us to understand the Creed. If someone has done you a wrong which has hurt you deeply, and you have genuinely forgiven him, then you have had a glimpse of what is meant when you say in the Creed, "I believe in . . . the forgiveness of sins."

Why is it that some people continue to commit the same deed for which they have been forgiven? Is it because they have never really known what it is to be forgiven? Do they mistake "I forgive you" for "I don't care"? The Heidelberg Catechism (Q.56) speaks this word to the point we are considering:

What do you believe concerning "the forgiveness of sins"? That, for the sake of Christ's reconciling work, God will no more remember my sins nor the sinfulness with which I have to struggle all my life long; but that he graciously imparts to me the righteousness of Christ so that I may never come into condemnation.

THE RESURRECTION AND THE LIFE

"I believe in ... the resurrection of the body; and the life everlasting." Death is the universal fact: every person dies. Over against this fact the Creed asserts the Christian hope in the resurrection of the body. The resurrection of the body does not so much mean the resurrection of the particular chemical elements which make up the body as the resurrection of the person. The word "body" here means much the same thing that we mean when we speak of somebody. We do not know in detail what the form of the resurrected body will be. The particular point which the Creed makes is that the risen life will not be some vague immortality of the spirit, only remotely connected with the life which we now live in the body.

Someone has said that we know very little about the furniture of heaven or the temperature of hell. We do know that life after death will be life with Christ. What is important for us now is to live our lives for those things which will be important then.

The last phrase of the Creed, "and the life everlasting," was added to affirm the permanence of the resurrection of the body. It is possible to be raised from the dead only to die again, as in the case of Lazarus. The resurrection is to the life everlasting.

You began your study of the Creed by noting that the confession of faith is no dull routine performance. It is always an act of *courage*. It is a declaration of *allegiance*. It is public affirmation of your *intentions* in life. Now that you have reviewed the Creed, it is important to think about the meaning of the Creed for your own life. What do *you* mean when you stand and confess the Apostles' Creed?

CHECK YOUR UNDERSTANDING

1. In what sense is the church holy?

2. What does the phrase "the communion of saints" mean?
3. What is the forgiveness of sins?
4. What is the meaning of belief in the resurrection of the body and the life everlasting?

Explore and Undertake

For Discussion

1. Does the recital of the Apostles' Creed in worship ordinarily have meaning for you?
2. How does putting your feelings or faith into words help?
3. How important to a person is his or her faith?
4. What would life be like to be without God? What are some things that lead you to believe in God?
5. Do you agree with the theologian who declared that there is something humorous about the lives of wicked people? Have you seen something humorous in the lives of wicked individuals whom you have known or heard about?
6. Is there anything wrong with enjoying life?
7. How does Jesus Christ as God's Son help us to know God?
8. What does belief in Jesus Christ as Lord have to say about the sort of decisions you make when you are at home? at school? with "the gang"?
9. Was Jesus Christ a real man?
10. What meaning does the death of Jesus have for you?
11. Which interpretation of the phrase "He descended into hell" satisfies you most?
12. To what in your life does the resurrection of Christ say Yes? To what does it say No?
13. Where is Jesus Christ now? What meaning does where he is have for you?
14. How does it help to know that at the end there will be God?
15. Why is it impossible for the Christian to believe in more than one God?
16. Why should we speak of the Holy Spirit as personal?

17. In what sense is *your* congregation a part of the holy catholic church?
18. In what sense is your congregation a communion of saints? How do you share in this communion?
19. Do you sometimes find it hard to forgive someone who has wronged you? What does God's willingness to forgive us tell us about God?
20. How does faith in the resurrection of the body and the life everlasting help a person to face life with courage?
21. Go over the articles in the Apostles' Creed. In what sense does each one express both belief *about* and belief *in?*

The Nicene Creed

The Nicene Creed is not as familiar to us as the Apostles' Creed. Yet it is a more universal creed for it is used by Eastern Orthodox churches as well as Roman Catholic and Protestant churches. In one sense the Nicene Creed is the most important Christian creed, for it emphasizes the most important claim. It declares that God, Creator of heaven and earth, was truly and personally present in Jesus Christ. Christians are people for whom God is defined by Jesus Christ.

The origin of the Nicene Creed is both alike and different from the origin of the Apostles' Creed. It is different in that it grew out of a theological debate in the church. It is alike in that it is a revision of a local church's creed.

The theological controversy that lies behind the Nicene Creed had to do with the question Who is Jesus Christ. The Christian community had always spoken of Jesus Christ as if he were God. They had spoken of him as the Lord, the Savior, Word of God, Son of God, Son of Man, prophet, priest. All of these titles refer to his activity, to his relation with his disciples, and to his value or meaning for them. For a long time this was sufficient.

Many persons outside the church as well as within wanted to know more about how Jesus can have this meaning for us. These questions came to a focus in the preaching and teaching of an Alexandrian presbyter named Arius. Arius did not ask what does Jesus

Christ mean to me, but who is Jesus Christ. This is a more basic question, for what Jesus Christ means to me depends upon who Jesus Christ is.

Is Jesus Christ God or is he a creature? Arius' answer to this question was clear. Jesus Christ is a creature. Arius was willing to give Jesus many wonderful titles such as the firstborn among all creatures or the noblest of all creation. He thought of him as a most wonderful human being or demigod. Arius believed in the utter separation of God from his creation, and he wanted to protect the divinity of God at all costs. Hence he could not believe God shared his being with a human being.

All the theological resources of the church were concentrated in this debate, for it was clear that it had to do with the most important Christian doctrine. Moreover, the Emperor Constantine had recently become a Christian, and he wanted the Christian community to unify the empire, not divide it. Hence Constantine gave his support to the calling of a church council at Nicea in 325 to settle this theological debate. This was the first universal church council since the Jerusalem Council in Acts 15.

The Council decided after much debate that Arius was wrong, and the Council was determined to say that in Jesus Christ God is truly present. In Jesus Christ we are not dealing with another creature, another human being, however wonderful, but with God, the Creator himself. The Council faced the problem of making this conviction very clear. The Arians had the ability of twisting words to suit their own meaning. Hence the Council had to find words that Arius could not twist to his own meaning. So they took a creed that was being used in a church in the eastern Mediterranean world, probably in Palestine, and inserted in it four phrases that Arius could not say. These four phrases were (1) "from the essence (being, reality, substance) of the Father"; (2) "true God from true God"; (3) "begotten not created (made)" (begotten here means a going from or an extending forth of a being); (4) "of the same essence (being, reality, substance) as the Father." The crucial phrase is "of the same essence as the Father." The Council was saying that in Jesus Christ we are confronted not simply with a great human being, not with someone like God but by God himself. If Jesus is only like God, then we have to determine how much he is like God. If Jesus is only like God, someone more like God may now come. In other words if Jesus is only like God, he cannot be the final revelation. But if in Jesus Christ we are truly confronted by God himself then there is no further word. As John's Gospel puts it, we have seen the Father. Read and study John 1:1–18, Colossians 1:15–20, Hebrews 1:1–4.

The action of no council is truly authoritative until it is confirmed by the wisdom of the Christian community itself. Hence the creed of the Council of Nicea was vigorously debated for the next fifty years. The church tried many substitutes for the crucial phrase "of the same essence as the Father." Among these substitutes were "like the Father," "like the Father in all things," "exact image of the godhead," "of like essence with the Father," "like the Father according to the Scriptures." None of these phrases proved satisfactory. They were too imprecise and subject to too many interpretations. Increasingly, church people decided that the Council of Nicea had said better than any other what Christians had found Jesus Christ meant to them and what the Scriptures taught. The Council of Constantinople in 381 reaffirmed the work of the Council of Nicea in 325. What we call the Nicene Creed today was related to this Council, and has three of the decisive phrases that the Council of Nicea in 325 inserted into its creed.

The great theologian of the Nicene Creed was Athanasius. Athanasius understood that if the Son or the Word (logos) is a creature, then his knowledge of God is of the same order as our knowledge. As the firstborn among all creatures he may know more of God than other creatures but his knowledge is still that of a creature. Furthermore, if the Son is a creature, then he cannot have the value of God for us and he cannot unite us to God.

For these reasons the Nicene Creed became the most universal of Christian creeds and the most important. It dealt with the most serious heresy or false doctrine, and it made the most important Christian affirmation.

The Nicene Creed made it necessary for the Ancient Catholic Church to harness all of its theological abilities in formulating other Christian doctrines.

Christians had always said that Jesus Christ was truly man, truly human, as well as God. Now they had to work all of this out in clearly stated doctrine. At the Council of Chalcedon in 451 the Church declared that Jesus Christ was truly God and truly man in one acting, personal subject. We have some clue how the Divine Self and the human self can be united in one acting, personal subject in the way two human persons penetrate each other's life. Some times one person "lives in" another person so much that we say there goes so and so in another person. This is a faint analogy, but it is a clue to what the church attempted to say.

The church also had to work out the doctrine of the Trinity. Christians had always said that God is one and that God shares his being with no other. Christians also said that God is present in Jesus Christ and that the Holy Spirit is God. The doctrine of the Trinity was the effort of the Church to say how one God is personally and always related to us as the Creator on whom we utterly depend and whose thoughts are beyond our thoughts, and as the Redeemer who confronts us in Jesus Christ, and as the Life Giver and Sanctifier whom we know in Christian experience.

REFORMED CONFESSIONS

We have limited our exposition of the faith in this chapter to the universal catholic confessions of the Ancient Church which we share with all Christians. This is proper for an introductory text. As we develop in our church life we shall need to study the more comprehensive and the more distinctive Reformed confessions. In this book we have become familiar with Reformed catechisms.

CHECK YOUR UNDERSTANDING

1. Why is the Nicene Creed the most important Christian Creed?
2. What is the central teaching of the Nicene Creed?
3. What phrases in the creed make this teaching clear?
4. Why did the Nicene Creed make it necessary for the Ancient Catholic Church to formulate carefully other doctrines?

For Action

1. Look up what an encyclopedia has to say about the following

creeds of the church: the definition of Chalcedon, the Athanasian Creed, the confessions of the Protestant Reformation. Put in your notebook the following information about each creed: the date and place it was drawn up, the purpose it served, the distinctive beliefs it affirms. Do the same thing for the catechism and/or the Confession of Faith which your church accepts. John Leith's *Creeds of the Churches* contains the texts of many creeds.

2. Write a biography of Augustine, a leader whose work has significantly affected the creeds of the church down through the centuries. Sources to turn to for help are encyclopedias, pages 60–63 in Langford's *Fire Upon the Earth,* pages 56–60 in Bainton's *The Church of Our Fathers,* chapter 9 in Bowie's *Men of Fire,* chapter 5 of the CLC study book *That the World May Know,* and *Augustine: His Life and Thought* by W. T. Smith (John Knox, 1980). Put the biography in your notebook.

3. Write your own statement of Christian faith. Add to it as you study this chapter. Perhaps you would want to begin each statement with the words "I believe."

4. As you study this chapter, consider what the standards of your church affirm about the several articles of faith given attention in the Apostles' Creed. Consider especially chapters 2, 4–5, 8–9, and 27–29 in The Westminster Confession of Faith; articles 5–7, 10–16, 27–33, and 99–103 of the Cumberland Presbyterian Confession of Faith; questions 26–58 in The Heidelberg Catechism; and the sections 3, 4, 5, and 9 of the Catechism of the Moravian Church in America.

5. Memorize Philippians 2:5–11.

6. Learn the Apostles' Creed if you do not already know it.

7. Study what Jesus said about the Holy Spirit in the following passages: John 14:18 and 26; 15:26; and 16:7–15.

8. Study the hymn "Holy, Holy, Holy! Lord God Almighty!" in the light of what the church believes about God.

9. Study 1 Corinthians 12:12–27. What do you learn about the church and the communion of saints?

CHAPTER VI

The Church Obeys

The church confesses its faith. The church obeys. Chapter V and this chapter belong together. Confession of faith is *obedience* to the commands of Jesus. Obedience is likewise confession of faith. We know much about what people believe by what they say and by what they do. To understand what it means to obey, we need to begin by asking two questions: What is the will of God? And why should we obey God?

First, what is the will of God? What is the law of God? Some *have* believed that they obeyed the will of God when they killed their children in sacrifice to God. Some have believed that they did the will of God when they put to death people whom they thought to be witches. Others have believed that they were doing the will of God when they went on long pilgrimages or kissed the bones of a dead saint. How may we learn what the will of God is?

The answer which your church gives to this question is clear. The will of God has been made known to us in Jesus Christ and in the words of Scripture. We have believed that the will of God in its moral demands is clearly expressed in two places. The first is in the Ten Commandments, which are a brief summary of the will of God, and the second is in the words and deeds of Jesus Christ.

The Christian life as obedience to the commands of God has been the dominant way in which Calvinists and Presbyterians have understood the Christian life. It is important, however, to note two qualifications. First, the will of God is more than moral demands, more than laws to be obeyed. It is also grace and mercy. Secondly, the Christian life as obedience to the commands of God is not the only way of thinking about the meaning of the Christian life. The Christian life can be understood as the responsible life, the answering life. It can be conceived as the imitation of Christ. It can be thought of as the spontaneity and the freedom of a life made free by Christ. It can be conceived as the embodiment of purposes of God, as Calvin himself and many other Reformed Christians have also thought of it. Hence, in this chapter it is important to remember that the Christian life as obedience to God's commands is a very important and characteristic Presbyterian way of understanding the Christian; but it is not the only way, and it does not exclude other ways of understanding the Christian life.

Thirdly, obedience has connotations for us today that are different from the meaning it had at the time of the Reformation. Hence, we must beware of thinking of obedience to the laws of God according to the model of obedience to commands in the army or to laws and regulations of the government. In this chapter we have kept the old term but we need to remember that no one word is adequate and that the meanings of words change. The obligated life is another way of saying the obedient life without giving the impression that the Christian life is simply obedience to rules according to the model of the army or government regulatory agencies. Other ways, as just indicated, of saying what Reformed theologians of the sixteenth and seventeenth centuries meant by obedience is to conceive of the Christian life as the responsible life or as the fulfillment of the purposes of God.

Protestants have always been careful to insist that the commandments of *men* are not the commandments of God. It has been easy for people to think that what they desire and will, what they find pleasant and attractive, is also the will of God. It has also been easy for people to label what they do not like, what they find repulsive, as sin. Many human activities, many styles of life that are objectionable to us, are not sin. Many human activities and styles of life that we may find attractive do not necessarily fulfill the purposes of God. Before the time of the Reformation, the medieval church required the people to do many things which were not commanded in

Scripture. The church also threatened those who did not obey these commands with damnation. Can you think of any illustrations of this temptation to make a human command into a command of God? Can you imagine situations where this might be true? For example, if our church were to say that in order to be a member of the Presbyterian Church you must be a middle class person, an advocate of a particular cause or style of life, a United States citizen, this would be adding to the commands of God.

Theologians call this imposing of human commands upon people *binding the conscience*. *The Confession of Faith* declares, "God alone is Lord of the conscience, and hath left it free from the doctrines and commandments of men which are in anything contrary to his word, or beside it in matters of faith or worship." The church can make a regulation that worship will be at 11:00 A.M. on Sunday. The congregation has to abide by this. Only in this way can there be orderly worship. Without this regulation there would be confusion. This is not binding the conscience. But if the church should say you must worship at 11 o'clock *in order* to be *saved,* this would bind the conscience. God has not specified any time of worship. We may choose any time which is convenient. If the church were to say that only those who do not smoke cigarettes or marijuana or drink alcoholic beverages can be church members, would this be binding the conscience?

The following catechism questions are helpful in determining what is the will of God:

> But what are good works? Only those which are done out of true faith, in accordance with the Law of God, and for his glory, and not those based on our own opinion or on the traditions of men (The Heidelberg Catechism, Q. 91).
>
> What is the duty which God requireth of man? The duty which God requireth of man, is, obedience to his revealed will (The Westminster Shorter Catechism, Q. 39).
>
> What did God at first reveal to man for the rule of his obedience? The rule which God at first revealed to man for his obedience, was the moral law (The Westminster Shorter Catechism, Q. 40).

Wherein is the moral law summarily comprehended? The moral law is summarily comprehended in the ten commandments (The Westminster Shorter Catechism, Q. 41).

What is the sum of the ten commandments? The sum of the ten commandments is, to love the Lord our God, with all our heart, with all our soul, with all our strength, and with all our mind; and our neighbor as ourselves (The Westminster Shorter Catechism, Q. 42).

Why should we obey God? This is a *second* question. We have already seen that we cannot earn God's favor. We cannot buy our salvation by being good. We have noted that God forgives us our sins. A modern play says that every crook will argue, "I like committing crimes. God likes forgiving them. Really the world is admirably arranged."[1] Well, why should we be good? Why should we obey, if God will forgive us anyway?

There are three answers to this question. The first is that God made us. He made us for fellowship with himself. He made us so that our lives are complete only when they are lived in obedience to him. To refuse to live according to God's will is to violate our nature as his children.

Automobiles are made to run on gasoline. If you put kerosene in them they may chug along, but they will not run very well. If we try to run life otherwise than as God intended, we too will end up in trouble.

Calvinists have frequently said that we obey God in order to give glory to him. "Glory" is not a word which we use very much. We are likely to think of glory as something which a king or sultan demands. This is not what Calvinists mean. Calvinists mean that we glorify God when we recognize that God is the creator, the maker of man and of this wonderful and mysterious universe. Human beings must always feel a certain awe in his presence. Calvinists would say that those who speak of God as "the man upstairs," or "a living doll" (as one movie actress is reported to have said), simply do not know what they are talking about. To know God as the creator is to know that one must obey him.

The second reason or motive for obedience is gratitude. Whenever a person is forgiven, he or she is always thankful. In fact no one can truly accept forgiveness without being thankful. The forgiven person obeys God, not in order to earn God's favor, but to give thanks for the goodness which God has shown.

Likewise, when we know God as our creator, we are thankful. We celebrate our thanksgiving for all the good things of this life during the Thanksgiving festival in November. This festival serves as a special reminder of God's goodness. But the Christian's life is a life of giving thanks every day in the year. Consider this word in The Heidelberg Catechism (Q. 86):

> Since we are redeemed from our sin and its wretched consequences by grace through Christ without any merit of our own, why must we do good works? Because just as Christ has redeemed us with his blood he also renews us through his Holy Spirit according to his own image, so that with our whole life we may show ourselves grateful to God for his goodness and that he may be glorified through us; and further, so that we ourselves may be assured of our faith by its fruits and by our reverent behavior may win our neighbors to Christ.

A third reason or motive for obedience is that through our obedience God works out his purposes in our families, in our schools, in our communities, in our nation, and in our world. God uses good works, even when they are not perfect, to help other people, to relieve suffering, to overcome injustice.

CHECK YOUR UNDERSTANDING

1. How has God made known his will?
2. What is the place given good works in The Heidelberg Catechism?
3. Why should we obey God?
4. Consider question 1 under "For Discussion" and items 1–3 under "For Action" on pages 128–129.

The First Four Commandments

The Ten Commandments occupied a central place in the worship and life of the people of God in the Old Testament. They are given a central position in the description of the life of the Covenant People in Exodus 19–23. (The Ten Commandments are in chapter 20.) And they stand at the beginning of Moses' speech concerning the covenant in Deuteronomy 5:1—11:32.

The Commandments are the direct speech of God to his people. They were almost certainly used in the worship of the people. They can be translated, "You do not have any other God before me," as well as "You shall have no other God before me." Both of these statements are accurate translations of the original language. But the variation makes it clear that the commandments are a description of the people of God. The people of God do not kill, do not commit adultery, do not steal.

The Commandments are divided into two tables. The first table deals with man's relation to God and with the worship of God. The second table deals with human relationships. But the two tables cannot be separated. The proper worship of God in obedience to the First or Second Commandment means also that a person does not kill or steal.

Jesus emphasized the importance of the Ten Commandments. When a rich young man asked him what he should do to inherit eternal life, Jesus asked him about obedience to the Commandments. Never did Jesus reject the law of Moses. He did reject many of the additions and interpretations which had grown up around it. But Jesus himself pointed to the law as the way of life of the people of God, and he deepened its meaning.

Jesus fulfilled the law and deepened its meaning first of all by embodying it in his own person, as it could never be expressed in propositions. He also fulfilled the law by amplifying it and interpreting its meaning. He related the outward deed to the motive of the heart. He faced squarely the dilemma created when obedience to one law conflicted with obedience to another, as when obedience to the law of the Sabbath did violence to value of neighborly love. Jesus also fulfilled the law by always keeping the law in the context of the gospel. He never canceled the demands of the law, yet he was open and helpful to those who failed to keep the law. The only persons whom he could not help were the righteous who thought they kept the law and did not know they too needed forgiveness. Jesus said, "For truly, I say to you, till heaven and earth pass away, not an iota, not a dot, will pass from the law till all is accomplished" (Matt. 5:18). Yet, when the Pharisees asked his disciples, "Why does your teacher eat with tax collectors and sinners?" he said, "Those who are well have no need of a physician, but those who are sick. Go and learn what this means, I desire mercy not sacrifice. For I came not to call the righteous but sinners to repentance" (Matt. 9:11–13).

(Roman Catholics and Lutherans combine the First and Second Commandments and divide the Tenth. Hence, their numbering of the Commandments differs from ours. The Hebrew numbering is the same as that used by Reformed and Presbyterian churches.)

THE FIRST COMMANDMENT

"You shall have no other gods before me" (Exod. 20:3)—this is the first commandment. Study this:

> What is required in the first commandment? The first commandment requireth us to know and acknowledge God to be the only true God, and our God, and to worship and glorify him accordingly (The Westminster Shorter Catechism, Q. 46).
>
> What is forbidden in the first commandment? The first commandment forbiddeth the denying, or not worshipping and glorifying, the true God, as God, and our God; and the giving the worship and glory to any other, which is due to him alone (The Westminster Shorter Catechism, Q. 47).

Almost everyone who reads this book believes in God, in the one God. In this age, only ignorant people would believe in more gods than one. In fact, someone may protest that the trouble is that many people do not believe in even one god. But let us not go too fast in this direction. Is this the true situation? Do we not have many gods? Do we not worship, heed, and obey the gods of money, of popularity, of pleasure, of convenience, of success, of nation, of church? You can make your own list. In any case, it is clear that modern people *do* have the problem of too many gods, or rather, of false gods.

In answer to the question, What means it to have a God?, Martin

Luther replied, "Whatever thy heart clings to and relies upon, that is properly thy God." In this sense, most of us have many gods.

On the top of our minds, of course, we do believe in the one God. But in the actual living of life, do we? Obedience to the First Commandment must be lived as well as spoken. In actual life we need to hear this commandment.

Does loyalty to God leave any place for lesser loyalties to home, to nation, to one's work? We sometimes hear of people who refuse to obey their country's laws, or who give up their daily work, or who have even left their families in order to obey God. Does obedience to God destroy family, nation, and daily work? Not necessarily. If God is truly God, then he is great enough to include every honorable and wholesome loyalty. Loyalty to God includes even demands, every true loyalty to family or nation or daily work. There do come moments when a person in loyalty to God must reject loyalty to nation or to family, but this is always a solemn and serious decision.

THE SECOND COMMANDMENT

"You shall not make for yourself a graven image, or any likeness of anything that is in heaven above, or that is in the earth beneath, or that is in the water under the earth; you shall not bow down to them or serve them; for I the Lord your God am a jealous God, visiting the iniquity of the fathers upon the children to the third and fourth generation of those who hate me, but showing steadfast love to thousands of those who love me and keep my commandments" (Exod. 20:4-6).

Note the following catechism answers:

What is required in the second commandment? The second commandment requireth the receiving, observing, and keeping pure and entire, all such religious worship and ordinances as God hath appointed in his word (The Westminster Shorter Catechism, Q. 50).

What is forbidden in the second commandment? The second commandment forbiddeth the worshipping of God by images, or any other way not appointed in his word (The Westminster Shorter Catechism, Q. 51).

No knowledgeable person worships a graven image, a piece of sculpture. The only people who do this live in remote places where they have no schools. Why should we stop to consider this commandment?

Again, we must not go too fast in this direction. We may not worship a piece of sculpture, but many modern people do worship a false idea of God. We imagine the image of the God we would like to have rule over us, and then we worship him. A few years ago a British minister wrote a book entitled *Your God Is Too Small*. In it he pointed out that many people think of God as a big man, a policeman, or an indulgent Santa Claus. We may no longer have images in stone and wood, but we still have mental pictures of God. Many of these pictures of God are false and harmful.

We have to have some image of God. Where can we find the true image? The New Testament tells us that the true image of God is Jesus Christ. (Study Colossians 1:15–20 and Hebrews 1:1–4.) Our images of God must be continually transformed and corrected by the revelation of God in Jesus Christ.

Our Protestant forefathers always applied this commandment to worship. In worship men and women learn more about God than in any other way. Many people learn much of their theology from the hymns that they sing or from the architecture of the church. If the hymns or the architecture or the prayers give a false image of God, this is a serious matter. Obedience to this command means that we must be careful in worship to obey God and not our own ideas of God.

This commandment has also been applied to works of art, sculpture, paintings. Calvinists used to insist that it was wrong to try to represent God in a painting or sculpture. First of all, we have never seen God. Secondly, God is so much more than can be represented in any work of art, that all representations of him would misrepresent him. Art itself is a gift of God. Calvinists took art seriously, and for this reason they insisted that *any* use of art must be theologically correct.

THE THIRD COMMANDMENT

"You shall not take the name of the LORD your God in vain; for the LORD will not hold him guiltless who takes his name in vain" (Exod 20:7).

What is required in the third commandment? The third commandment requireth the holy and reverent use of God's names, titles, attributes, ordinances, word, and works (The Westminster Shorter Catechism, Q. 54).

What is forbidden in the third commandment? The third commandment forbiddeth all profaning or abusing of anything whereby God maketh himself known (The Westminster Shorter Catechism, Q. 55).

In the Bible, a name is not just a label. It is the living person. To abuse the name is to abuse the person. If someone hits a stop sign with a rock, we think of this as a thoughtless and damaging deed. But if someone throws a rock at the American flag, we feel outraged. In a sense, the abuse of the flag is the abuse of the name of our country.

How do we abuse the name of God? We abuse God's name when we use his name carelessly and thoughtlessly in speech. It may seem to be a small matter, just words. Yet a careless use of God's name in speech robs the name of its meaning and makes it useless for serious conversation. Careless use of God's name and of holy things also does something to a person's life. It robs one of a sense of awe, of wonder, of the capacity for deep feeling. When people lose the capacity for awe and for a sense of the holy, they have lost something which is very precious.

People abuse God's name when they use it for the sake of falsehood. Courts require oaths to guarantee that truth shall be told. It would be much better, Jesus said, if every person's Yes could simply be Yes. To have to bolster a person's Yes or No with an oath means only that you cannot ordinarily expect this person to tell the truth. The great tragedy is that, even when people take oaths, they sometimes do not tell the truth.

People abuse God's name when they lightly take some obligation assumed in the presence of God's name. God's name is invoked, and persons pledge that some responsibility will be met. When they fail to do so, they abuse God's name.

God's name is taken in vain when it is used as a magic formula. Many people still use God's name as though it were some secret formula from the Arabian Nights. This commandment forbids the confusion of magic and faith. Magic wants something for nothing, blessing without obligation. But faith always involves loyalty, trust, commitment. Magic is the attempt of human beings to use God, and to accomplish something in a way not bound by our creatureliness, by space and time.

The positive duty which this commandment imposes upon us is the obligation to take God seriously in every area of life.

This commandment will become more meaningful to you if you will pause and think of the *specific* things which it means for you.

THE FOURTH COMMANDMENT

"Remember the sabbath day, to keep it holy. Six days you shall labor, and do all your work; but the seventh day is a sabbath to the LORD your God; in it you shall not do any work, you, or your son, or your daughter, your manservant, or your maidservant, or your cattle, or the sojourner who is within your gates; for in six days the LORD made heaven and earth, the sea, and all that is in them, and rested the seventh day; therefore the LORD blessed the sabbath day and hallowed it" (Exod. 20:8–11).

What is required in the fourth commandment? The fourth commandment requireth the keeping holy to God such set times as he hath appointed in his word; expressly one whole day in seven, to be a holy Sabbath to himself (The Westminster Shorter Catechism, Q. 58).

Which day of the seven hath God appointed to be the weekly Sabbath? From the beginning of the world to the resurrection of Christ, God appointed the seventh day of the week to be the weekly Sabbath; and the first day of the week, ever since, to continue to the end of the world, which is the Christian Sabbath (The Westminster Shorter Catechism, Q. 59).

How is the Sabbath to be sanctified? The Sabbath is to be sanctified by a holy resting all that day, even from such worldly employments and recreations as are lawful on other days; and spending the whole time in the public and private exercises of God's worship, except so much as is to be taken up in the works of necessity and mercy (The Westminster Shorter Catechism, Q. 60).

Someone has said that this commandment really puts to us the question, Who owns time? The Bible has a great deal to say to us about time. It condemns the abuse of time in no uncertain words.

Time is one of God's gifts to us. It is a gift we cannot hoard and put away. We can only use it. The way we use it determines whether it shall bless us or curse us. There are few more important questions which a person faces than this: How shall I use the time which has been entrusted to me?

This commandment teaches important truths about the use of time. First, time must be used for the worship of God. In a general sense all of life must be the worship of God. Yet it is important that a portion of life be set aside for the *special* worship of God. Our daily work often demands full attention. We cannot work and think about God at the same time. We need certain periods which we devote entirely to listening to the Word of God and heeding it.

From the very beginning the people of God have set aside a certain time when they have worshiped God as his people. The Christians of the New Testament changed the day of worship from the last day of the week to the first, because it was on this day that Jesus rose from the dead. Every Sunday is an Easter. Christians have called it "the Lord's Day." It is especially appropriate that we should worship on the day which celebrates the resurrection. But there is nothing especially holy about a particular day. The important principle is that human beings should worship God, that they should worship regularly, and that they should worship in the company of his people.

There was a time when on Sunday people were subject to many laws which limited what they could do. Called "Blue Laws," they forbade certain amusements and business operations. In some cases, these laws have not yet been repealed. Many persons still rightly insist that all businesses be closed on Sunday, not as a religious duty, but as a way of organizing community life so that most people may be free of business responsibilities on the same day. But many people in our society do not worship God. This makes it increasingly difficult for Christians to maintain regular worship. We are tempted to do what non-Christians do on Sunday. But we should beware of imposing Christian obligations upon non-Christians.

Time must be used not only for worship but also for *rest*. The commandment speaks of cessation from work for servants and even for animals. One purpose of the commandment was to provide relief from work. Today we have laws against child labor and laws limiting the work week to forty hours or less. Nevertheless, many still work too hard; for example, some work forty hours a week at one job and additional hours at a second job. Others are overwhelmed by work on their houses or yards. Even though we have laws to protect those who labor, some wear out spirit and body by too much work.

Sometimes people get so used to work they cannot rest. Most of us know people who want to work all the time. Work becomes their god, their master. In Genesis we read that God rested. Man should learn to rest.

Time must also be used to *work*. The commandment says, "Six days you shall . . . do all your work." Some people are mastered by their work, but others do not take it seriously enough. People who are lazy waste valuable time. A person who works hard for something which is not worth working for also wastes time. Some spend their lives working for something which is positively evil.

Protestants, influenced by the doctrine of vocation, have always emphasized constructive work as a way of fulfilling God's purposes. There is a moral obligation to produce what one consumes, to contribute more to society than one takes out. In our society some now feel this old Protestant work ethic is being forgotten. Is this true?

The really serious questions which a person has to answer in life are few. Two of these are, What shall I do with my time? and How shall I invest my life?

CHECK YOUR UNDERSTANDING

1. In what two places are the Ten Commandments found in the Bible?
2. What is the meaning of the division of the commandments into two tables?
3. What was Jesus' view of the Ten Commandments?
4. What does each of the first four commandments require? What does each one forbid?
5. Consider questions 2–8 under "For Discussion" and items 2 and 4 under "For Action" on pages 128–129.

The Last Six Commandments

THE FIFTH COMMANDMENT

"Honor your father and your mother, that your days may be long in the land which the LORD your God gives you" (Exod. 20:12).

What is required in the fifth commandment? The fifth commandment requireth the preserving the honor, and performing the duties, belonging to everyone in their several places and relations, as superiors, inferiors, or equals (The Westminster Shorter Catechism, Q. 64).

With this commandment we pass to the commandments which deal with personal relationships. In it we are told how God's people are to live within the family. Life in the family is important, since the welfare of society and of the church in large measure depends upon the home.

The family faces new problems in every age. This commandment originally was concerned with the treatment given to older people. This is a duty which rests upon adults rather than children. The care of older people is still a serious concern. Medicine and better living conditions enable many people to live to a very old age. Various agencies help them. But the family still has responsibility for them.

But the duties which the fifth commandment imposes upon us

are much broader than specific concern with the care of older people. They include respect for parents and attention to duties in the home. God placed children in families, so that in the life of the family they might be trained and prepared for adult life.

The fifth commandment also calls for respect for the faith of parents. Christian faith is handed down from parent to child. Some of us were born in homes where Christian faith was confessed. One of the great obligations which is placed upon parents is the teaching of the faith to their children.

Of course faith cannot be simply handed down. It must become your own. You cannot inherit faith, courage, hope, as you inherit money or land. Faith cannot be simply taken from your parents. It must become part of your own life. Making the faith of the family your own is sometimes quite difficult. It may involve protest against your parents' faith, and sometimes protest is justified. But this commandment obligates us to take our parents' faith seriously. Their faith has behind it the wisdom of many who went before them.

THE SIXTH COMMANDMENT

"You shall not kill" (Exod. 20:13).

What is required in the sixth commandment? The sixth commandment requireth all lawful endeavors to preserve our own life, and the life of others (The Westminster Shorter Catechism, Q. 68).

What is forbidden in the sixth commandment? The sixth commandment forbiddeth the taking of our own life, or the life of our neighbor unjustly, or whatsoever tendeth thereunto (The Westminster Shorter Catechism, Q. 69).

Why is human life precious? Why is it wrong to abuse another human being? Nicolas Berdiaev, Russian philosopher who died in exile in Paris in 1948, once said, "Where there is no God, there is no man." He meant that when we forget God, we come to think that man has no dignity in himself. He has value only if he belongs to "my" nation, to "my" race, to "my" group. In Arthur Koestler's novel, *Darkness at Noon,* a Communist defines an individual as "the quotient of one million divided by one million. . . ."² In other words, an individual is just a number. If he is no more than this, he can be put to death when he no longer serves the needs of the State or of some other individual.

But Christians believe that every human being is a child of God. God made each person in the divine image. God loves everyone. For this reason no person has the right to abuse another. Each person has a dignity given by God, even when that person is in rebellion against God. John Calvin once said that God represents himself to us in our fellow men, and in their persons demands what is due himself.

None of us is ever likely to kill another person. But this does not mean that this commandment does not concern us. There are *many* ways of harming other persons. Furthermore, the commandment carries the positive obligation to respect human life.

THE SEVENTH COMMANDMENT

"You shall not commit adultery" (Exod. 20:14).

What is required in the seventh commandment? The seventh commandment requireth the preservation of our own and our neighbor's chastity, in heart, speech, and behavior (The Westminster Shorter Catechism, Q. 71).

What is forbidden in the seventh commandment? The seventh commandment forbiddeth all unchaste thoughts, words, and actions (The Westminster Shorter Catechism, Q. 72).

The first concern of this commandment is with the sacredness of marriage. It was God's intention that marriage should be between one man and one woman, for life. When two people are married, God's name is invoked; and they pledge their faithfulness to each other as long as they live. This commandment tells us that faithfulness in marriage is a mark of the people of God.

But this commandment has to do with duties broader than faithfulness in marriage. This commandment has to do with our attitudes toward persons of the opposite sex. Sex is part of God's creation and is good and wholesome. It belongs to the fullness and joy of life. But wrong attitudes toward sex sometimes are expressed in evil thoughts and words and deeds. Such attitudes can destroy the goodness of sex and make it a source of great evil.

This commandment also requires us to respect the dignity of other people. Sometimes one person abuses another person by deceiving that person as to his or her real intentions. Sometimes a person abuses another by using the body of another person for his or her own enjoyment. That is to treat the other person as a thing, and that is wrong.

THE EIGHTH COMMANDMENT

"You shall not steal" (Exod. 20:15).

What is required in the eighth commandment? The eighth commandment requireth the lawful procuring and furthering the wealth and outward estate of ourselves and others (The Westminster Shorter Catechism, Q. 74).

What is forbidden in the eighth commandment? The eighth commandment forbiddeth whatsoever doth, or may, unjustly hinder our own or our neighbor's wealth or outward estate (The Westminster Shorter Catechism, Q. 75).

The order of the commandments is suggestive. Life, family, and now property are declared to be sacred. The Bible teaches that all things belong to God and that possessions are a trust from God. Thus no person owns anything absolutely, to do with it as he pleases. We can rightly use our possessions only for purposes which are worthy, and we must always be ready to help our neighbor in need.

This commandment protects possessions and forbids taking what does not belong to one. Society likewise makes this same prohibition and punishes those who abuse or steal the possessions of another person.

Nevertheless, stealing goes on. Newspapers report the big robberies and also the petty thefts. Customers steal millions of dollars' worth of merchandise in supermarkets. Stealing also takes other forms. Sometimes it is poor workmanship or false advertising. Sometimes it is cheating on examinations or homework. We could add to the list.

The importance of the commandment is obvious. The prohibition of stealing is necessary for the sake of society. Community life could not exist without respect for property, at least in some form. But the basic prohibition against stealing the property of others must not keep us from looking further. The commandment raises the whole question of our relation to things, to possessions. This again is one of those few but basic questions which every person must answer.

Why do people steal? Some steal because they want something for nothing. Some steal because of greed. Some steal because they want things so badly and are so mastered by things that they are willing to take that which does not belong to them. Others are so mastered by the desire for things that they treat other persons unfairly in order to make money.

Let us come at the commandment from another point of view. What does it mean for the rich in relation to the poor? Almost everyone who reads this book is richer than most of the people who have ever lived and most of the people who live in the world today. What does this commandment mean to those of us who have at least enough in a world where most of the people go to bed hungry each night?

Read the story of Jesus and the rich man (Mark 10:17–22). What meaning does this story have for our interpretation of the eighth commandment?

THE NINTH COMMANDMENT

"You shall not bear false witness against your neighbor" (Exod. 20:16).

What is required in the ninth commandment? The ninth commandment requireth the maintaining and promoting of truth between man and man, and of our own and our neighbor's good name, especially in witness-bearing (The Westminster Shorter Catechism, Q. 77).

What is forbidden in the ninth commandment? The ninth commandment forbiddeth whatsoever is prejudicial to truth, or injurious to our own or our neighbor's good name (The Westminster Shorter Catechism, Q. 78).

This commandment is specifically concerned with the sacredness of the witness which is given in court. The people of God will tell the truth when they witness about their neighbors in court. In court sometimes one's life, always his or her future well being, depends upon the truthfulness of witnesses. Without truthfulness in courts there can be no justice.

The meaning of the commandment is much broader, however, than this one concern. Along with the other commandments, especially the sixth and seventh, this commandment demands respect for persons. The people of God so respect and honor the other person that they speak the truth about that person.

This commandment certainly involves the obligation to tell the truth. (Study Matthew 5:33–37.) Human society depends upon people's speaking the truth. But there is something more important: our desire to tell the truth. The strength of this desire reveals who we are and what our real attitude toward other people is. Persons who do not desire to tell the truth do not respect themselves or their neighbors.

This commandment demands that we speak only the truth concerning other people. A person's reputation is a priceless possession. To destroy a person's good name is in a sense to kill the person. It is better to steal a man's purse than his good name. What does this commandment mean when we are tempted to engage in gossip?

This commandment carries with it the obligation to speak the truth about the issues of the day. Falsehoods have contributed to wars, to race riots, to bad government. Falsehoods make life with other people difficult in every way.

Can one be too eager to speak the truth? The answer is Yes, when someone wants to speak the truth for the wrong reason. There are people who like to speak the truth in order to hurt other people. For this reason Paul warns us to speak the truth in love (Eph. 4:15).

THE TENTH COMMANDMENT

"You shall not covet your neighbor's house; you shall not covet your neighbor's wife, or his manservant, or his maidservant, or his ox, or his ass, or anything that is your neighbor's" (Exod. 20:17).

What is required in the tenth commandment? The tenth commandment requireth full contentment with our own condition, with a right and charitable frame of spirit toward our neighbor, and all that is his (The Westminster Shorter Catechism, Q. 80).

What is forbidden in the tenth commandment? The tenth commandment forbiddeth all discontentment with our own estate, envying or grieving at the good of our neighbor, and all inordinate motions and affections to anything that is his (The Westminster Shorter Catechism, Q. 81).

With this commandment we pass from the outer deed—murder, adultery, theft, falsehood—to the inner thoughts and motives of the heart. The Bible does not teach that all our desires and wishes are good. It takes very seriously the fact that many of our desires and wishes are bad. Out of the thoughts of the heart and mind flow our misdeeds. Someone has declared, "The word translated *covet* seems to mean 'indulge in thoughts which tend to lead to the actions named in the previous commandments.' "[3]

It is easy to see how covetousness plays havoc with a person's attitude toward things. Setting one's heart upon things—upon cars, boats, vacations at the beach, clothing—can lead to a materialism which judges a person's life by the things he possesses. Shallowness is the judgment on this covetousness.

Covetousness also plays havoc with human relations. The commandment speaks of coveting another's household; that is, another's family, or another's wife; but it includes covetousness in all human relationships. We may covet someone else's friends and seek to destroy their friendship. We may be selfish with our friends and refuse to let anyone else share in our friendship and play.

Covetousness also plays havoc in a person's own life. Coveting fame, position, honor, and the approval of one's fellows leads people to do things which otherwise they would be ashamed to do.

Someone may protest, "Isn't it a worthy thing to covet a good name, to covet good friends, to covet a comfortable home? The answer is Yes, and No. The answer is Yes insofar as our desires for these things are expressions of our loyalty to God. The answer is

No insofar as these things can be had only by compromising our honor and our honesty or by hurting our fellowman.

The people of God are folk who have learned that the one really indispensable thing in life is God himself. A very fine paragraph in Paul's letter to the Christians in Philippi (4:10–13) will help us to understand this commandment, if we study it and apply it to our own lives.

Why are some people never satisfied with what they have? Why are some people who have very little more content than some who have very much? Is the trouble to be found not so much in what one has as in what one is?

CHECK YOUR UNDERSTANDING

1. What does each of the last six commandments require? What does each one forbid?

The Law of Christ

Jesus thought of his work as fulfilling and completing the work of Moses. He did not come to destroy the law but to fulfill it. The confidence with which he used the law astonished his hearers. It is not surprising that his disciples came to think of him as the new lawgiver, the new Moses.

The Gospel of Matthew emphasizes this work of Jesus. He is the teacher and the lawgiver. His disciples hear and obey his words. Through the centuries the imitation of Christ has been a constant theme of Christian discipleship. Whatever else Christians are, they are people who seek to fulfill the purposes of God in their lives.

As we have already noted, Jesus is more than a new lawgiver. Christian life is more than obedience. At the heart of the Christian gospel is the forgiveness of sins, the mercy and grace of God. We must never forget this. Nevertheless, we must also remember that only persons who have tried their best to obey the law have any right to talk about the forgiveness of sin. The command to be perfect as our Father in heaven is perfect must never be separated from the promise of forgiveness and mercy, for none of us is perfect.

The most familiar summary of the teachings of Jesus is the Sermon on the Mount, found in Matthew 5—7. On the first reading, this appears to be a single sermon which Jesus gave to his disciples. Closer study shows that it is a summary of many sermons and teachings of Jesus.

It is sometimes said that the Christian life is following the Sermon on the Mount. It is this. But you have reason to wonder whether the person who makes this statement has read the Sermon carefully. Surely no person can read the Sermon and finish it, believing that he is able completely to live the life described in the Sermon. If Christian faith is obedience according to the Sermon, then none of us can be a Christian.

Most Christians have known that after they do their best to follow the teachings of the Sermon, they will still be *far* short of its commands. But if we cannot obey the Sermon, then is it of any use? The answer is Yes. The Sermon serves several good purposes for us. It keeps before us God's intention for our lives, reminds us of our failures, and calls us to new obedience.

We must see in the Sermon more than laws. Laws are important. In most situations they do tell what we should do. When a person loses his pocketbook and we find it, it is enough for us to know, "You shall not steal." When we are asked to speak the truth in ordinary situations, it is enough to know, "You shall not bear false witness."

But many decisions are more difficult to make. Then law does not tell us what we must do, but rather serves as one guide in making a decision. Then we have to figure out what we must do in obedience to Jesus Christ. For example, we are told in the Sermon to turn the other cheek (Matt. 5:39). What does this mean when a robber breaks into your home, endangering the lives of some who are sleeping? No law can tell us in advance what we must do in such extraordinary situations.

Furthermore, in some situations obedience to one commandment or value may seem to involve disobedience to another. Perhaps you can think of some such situations. Reinhold Neibuhr tells about a boy he encountered in his first pastorate who supported his widowed mother by selling newspapers on a busy street corner. The only way he could sell newspapers on this corner was to keep other newsboys away by force. So he asked his minister what he should do. Should he keep other boys away by force, sell his papers, and support his mother? Should he give up the corner, fail to sell his papers, and fail to support his mother? The situation becomes more difficult if some of the boys he kept away from the corner had to support *their* mothers also.

For this reason we must not think of the Sermon on the Mount simply as a code of laws. It is a guide to show how we are to obey Jesus Christ in each situation. Sometimes the simple commands tell us what to do. Sometimes we have to think, study, and figure to decide what we must do to obey Jesus Christ. Many times we shall not live up to the demands of the Sermon on the Mount. But always it tells us how God commands us to live, and it continually challenges us to live that way.

CHECK YOUR UNDERSTANDING

1. What is the place of the law in the Christian life?
2. Where is the most familiar summary of the teachings of Jesus?

God's Design for Life: A Study of Matthew 5—7

You have probably studied the Sermon on the Mount several times in your years in the church school. Perhaps you have studied it on your own, at home. But to see the meaning of the law of Christ clearly, a fresh look at the Sermon at this time should be helpful. The outline below is based on Archibald M. Hunter's *Design for Life*. We shall follow his exposition of the Sermon as it is simple and clear. As you study the Sermon according to the outline, you may want to obtain a copy of that book to guide your study.

I. The Life Described
   A. Its Characteristics (the Beatitudes: Matt. 5:3–12)
   B. Its Influence: Salt and Light (Matt. 5:13–16)
   C. Its Relation to the Old Order (Matt. 5:17–20)
   D. Its Outworking (Matt. 5:21—7:12)
      1. In Thought, Word, and Deed (Matt. 5:21–48)
         a. No Murder, No Anger (Matt. 5:21–26)

    b. No Adultery, No Lust (Matt. 5:27–30)
    c. No Divorce (Matt. 5:31–32)
    d. Oaths (Matt. 5:33–37)
    e. Retaliation (Matt. 5:38–42)
    f. Love (Matt. 5:43–48)
2. In Worship (Matt. 6:1–18)
    a. Almsgiving (Matt. 6:1–4)
    b. Prayer (Matt. 6:5–15)
    c. Fasting (Matt. 6:16–18)
3. In Trust and Devotion (Matt. 6:19–34)
    a. True Treasures (Matt. 6:19–21)
    b. The Single Eye and the Single Service (Matt. 6:22–24)
    c. Trust and Tranquility (Matt. 6:25–34)
4. In the Treatment of Others (Matt. 7:1–12)
    a. Judge Not (Matt. 7:1–5)
    b. Discrimination (Matt. 7:6)
    c. In Prayer (Matt. 7:7–11)
    d. The Golden Rule (Matt. 7:12)

II. The Way of Life: Profession and Practice (Matt. 7:13–27)

Professor Hunter has written:

As we call ourselves followers of Christ, we must acknowledge that Christ does set before us a real design for living which challenges every thoughful disciple. He does tell us: (1) the kind of people we ought to be; (2) the influence we ought to exert in the world; (3) the way in which, as Christians, we ought to behave socially; (4) the kind of worship we ought to render; (5) the attitude we ought to have towards earthly and heavenly treasures; and (6) the manner in which we should treat our fellow-men. And most of us know, as Dr. Joad says, that "Christ's prescription for good living . . . is the right prescription." (A. M. Hunter, *Design for Life* (London; SCM Press, Ltd. 1952), pp. 113–114)

It is also important to note before one begins to study the Sermon on the Mount that the sermon is far more than a system of morals. It is first of all a "summons to faith, an invitation to a total trust that takes the 'Father' as the absolute center, and that experiences all of life as a gift" (Eduard Schweizer, *The Good News According to Matthew*, p. 197). The Lord's Prayer and great passages on the Christian life as a life of trust and joy are at the heart of the sermon.

Design for Life in the Kingdom of God, Matthew 5—7

I. The Life Described (Matthew 5:3—7:12)

  A. Its Characteristics (the Beatitudes) (Matthew 5:3–12)

The word "blessed" has an otherworldly sound to most people today. We are not certain that we want to be called blessed. For this reason we have to ask further as to what Jesus meant by the word. One synonym for blessed is happy. But this word may be too shallow. We too often use it when we mean nothing more than that a person is having a good time. One translator says that the word could be translated "congratulations." Jesus is saying, Congratulations to the poor in spirit for yours is the Kingdom of heaven. "The man who lives like this is getting the best out of life, living the kind of life that is really worthwhile."

The Poor in Spirit. Who are they? Certainly they are not the poor-spirited. There is nothing Christian about a sad face and a pessimistic outlook. Neither are they simply the poor who do not have enough of this world's goods. The poor in spirit are those who are aware of their need of God. They are those who are oppressed by the evil in their own lives and in the world about them.

They That Mourn. Who are the mourners? All of us someday will mourn the death of loved ones. The New Testament promises comfort, strength, to those who trust God in such losses. But the word mourner reaches further. Surely it includes those who mourn with others, who share and bear the burdens of others. Surely it also includes those who mourn their sins.

The Meek. Who are the meek? The meek are not the weak, the fearful, the cowed. The meek are strong of heart and mind. Yet they are not always asserting their egos, demanding their rights, grabbing for more at the expense of those who are weaker. Neither are the meek those who do not become angry. They have the capacity for great anger in the presence of wrong. Note how Jesus looked with anger upon brutality. They do not become angry simply because they do not get their way or because their egos are hurt.

Those Who Hunger and Thirst for Righteousness. Hunger and thirst mean intense desire. But what is the meaning of righteousness? Righteousness means uprightness, justice. Surely it means that here. But it means more. The righteousness of God is also what God does for our salvation. Thus righteousness for us is not simply conformity to a law. Those who hunger and thirst do not depend upon their own power to achieve righteousness, but upon God. They eagerly desire the triumph of every good cause. In sum, they long for salvation.

The Merciful. The merciful are the sympathetic, the kind, and the forgiving. There is nothing strange in the promised reward. Only those who are merciful can receive mercy.

The Pure in Heart. The heart is the window through which we seek God. If it is dirty from evil thoughts and desires then our vision of God is obscured.

The Peacemakers. Peace is a great word in the Bible. It means more than absence of war or strife. It means that persons are in right relations with one another. Those who seek to build good, helpful relations between human beings do God's work in the world. They are rightly called his children.

The Persecuted for Righteousness' Sake. Note that it is not the persecuted, but the persecuted for *righteousness' sake.* The Bible does not promise that the good will be popular. In the Bible good people continually make people angry, and they do not win popularity contests. But again, we must note that the cause of persecution is righteousness.

Each Beatitude promises a reward. Do people get rewards for being good? Isn't this paying a person for being good? The answer depends upon the meaning of rewards. The following sentences from C. S. Lewis are worth careful study:

There is the reward which has no natural connection with the things you do to earn it, and is quite foreign to the desires that ought to accompany these things. Money is not the natural reward of love; that is why we call a man mercenary if he marries a woman for the sake of her money. But marriage is the proper reward for a real lover, and he is not mercenary for desiring it. A general who fights well in order to get a peerage is mercenary; a general who fights for victory is not, victory being the proper reward of battles as marriage is the proper reward of love. The proper rewards are not simply tacked on to the activity for which they are given, but are the activity itself in consummation. (*Transposition and Other Addresses* [London: Geoffrey Bles, 1949], pp. 21–22.)

After reading this paragraph, what do you think of the appropriateness of rewards?

B. Its Influence: Salt and Light (Matthew 5:13–16)

We do not have in the Bible exact instructions as to how we are to live in our time and place. Obedience to God varies from time to place. The obedience that a slave could give to God in the Roman Empire is different from the obedience which a free person in America can give today. The slave was limited in what he could do. The American can vote, can write letters to the newspapers, can raise his voice in protest against wrong doing. You can think of the freedom which you have in obeying God which a person in East Germany today does not have.

The Bible does tell us something of our responsibility. We are to be salt and light. Salt gives taste to food and saves it from corruption. Light chases darkness away. Now try to answer for yourself, What does it mean for me to be the salt of the earth and the light of the world in the time and space where I live?

C. Its Relation to the Old Order (Matthew 5:17–20)

As we have already said, Jesus Christ did not come to end the work of Moses but to fulfill and complete it. He stripped away all the additions to the law of God, and he taught the deeper meaning of the law.

D. Its Outworking
1. In Thought, Word, and Deed (Matthew 5:21–48)
   a. No Murder—No Anger (Matthew 5:21–26)

   What does verse 24 mean for our worship today?

   Does this prohibition mean that we shall never become angry? When does it mean that we shall never become angry? When does a Christian become angry? Anger that is induced by oversensitivity of our own egos is usually destructive, but there is a legitimate place for anger when human values are at stake.
   b. No Adultery—No Lust (Matthew 5:27–30)

   We must remember that sex is part of God's creation and is therefore good. This means that it must be honored, respected, and disciplined.

   What do these verses mean for those who engage in dirty talk and jokes about sex, for those who trivialize life, for those who lose the sense of dignity in being a human being?

   What do they mean for the boy or girl who betrays the confidences of other boys and girls? What does it mean for the person who wants to use and abuse the body of and personality of another person for his or her own enjoyment?
   c. No Divorce (Matthew 5:31–32)

   The very important teaching to remember is that God's intention is that marriage should be between one man and one woman for life. Divorce is always the denial of this intention. Our church teaches that divorce in some instances is the lesser of two evils. But it is always the denial of God's intention for marriage.

d. Oaths (Matthew 5:33–37)

Persons use oaths because they do not tell the truth. A Christian's Yes or No should be enough. When we tell the truth, we do not have to take oaths. Oaths are a sign of the falsehood among us.

e. Retaliation (Matthew 5:38–42)

If we continue to answer hate with hate, we simply increase the amount of hate in the world. The only possible way to end hate is by answering it with love. Love may not (and frequently does not) end hate, but it is the only possibility of ending hate.

Is it possible to live without retaliating in our world? If it isn't, how can we obey this commandment?

f. Love (Matthew 5:43–48)

Love is more than simply liking another person. It is an attitude of positive good will toward the other person. In this sense we may love people who are not necessarily our friends or close associates.

What many people call love is selfishness. They love those who love them and give them gifts. Everybody loves like that. Christians are distinguished by the fact that they have good will toward those who do not love them.

What are you doing more than others in loving your neighbors?

2. Its Outworking in Worship (Matthew 6:1–18)

a. Almsgiving (Matthew 6:1–4)

True worship is never public display. Almsgiving had a much more public role in the Palestine of Jesus' day than in ours. Nevertheless, those words still have meaning for us. The generosity which God approves is the quiet helping of a person without any expectation of public acclaim.

Now that so much help of those in need is done by the government, how can Christians fulfill this command of Jesus?

b. Prayer (Matthew 6:5–15)

As we shall study prayer, and the Lord's Prayer in particular, in the next chapter, we shall not do so now. It is important for us to note here that Jesus emphasized sincerity in prayer. Are many of the public prayers in the worship of the church repetitions for us? If so, why?

c. Fasting (Matthew 6:16–18)

Not many Christians today fast. Yet fasting is a very ancient Christian practice. It was a form of discipline. Such discipline enabled Christians to control their own desires and served to remind them of the conditions of others. Certainly Jesus did not condemn fasting, though he did condemn a false sort of fasting.

Should we revive the practice of fasting? Should we fast on certain days in order to give what we would have eaten to those who do not have enough to eat?

3. Its Outworking in Trust and Devotion (Matthew 6:19–34)

a. True Treasures (Matthew 6:19–21). Many people spend the time and energy of life seeking those things which won't amount to much when they come to die. A true treasure is one which abides. What are some of the things which will be important for us at the end of our days?

These words also remind us that we must begin to prepare ourselves to enjoy those things which will be in heaven. Hell might very well be being in heaven and not liking it.

b. The Single Eye and the Single Service (Matthew 6:22–24). One of the perils of life is that we shall waste our energies and time doing a variety of things which are good in themselves but relatively unimportant. We may even try to divide life between God and the devil. This does not work. A person can have only one master.

Have you ever noticed that persons with average ability can accomplish very much if they devote all of their energies to one purpose? Is not the same thing true of the Christian life?

c. Trust and Tranquility (Matthew 6:25–34). This is one of the very great passages of the Bible, and it should be committed to memory.

Christians believe that this world is our Father's home and that we are never beyond his love and care. For this reason poise, dignity, trust, and confidence characterize the life of Christians. They do not become frantic in fear or distress. They do not become over-anxious about tomorrow.

4. Its Outworking in the Treatment of Others (Matthew 7:1–27).

a. Judge Not (Matthew 7:1–5). It is necessary to make judgments. On another occasion, Jesus himself said, "By their fruits you shall know them." There is a difference which is important between a kind person and a brutal person, between a truth-telling person and a liar. What then does Jesus mean here?

Jesus here points to those who enjoy gossip which runs down other people. He speaks against those who emphasize the weakness of other people in order to bolster their own egos.

b. Discrimination (Matthew 7:6). Holy things are not to be abused. Do we sometimes bring abuse upon the faith of the Church, the Bible, and the sacraments by trying to impose them on people who do not and will not appreciate them? We do not invite persons to church with the same casualness that we invite people to go to a ballgame.

c. In Prayer (Matthew 7:7–11). A psychologist has said that the most important thing you can know about people is where they want to be five years from now and how hard they intend to work to get there. This is also true in prayer and in the Christian life. Here Jesus assures us that what we shall be in the Christian life is limited by what we want to be.

d. The Golden Rule (Matthew 7:12). Here Jesus sums up our obligations to others. We are to treat all people as we wish to be treated. What does this mean for us? In our relations with people of other races? In our relations with people who are weaker than we are?

II. The Way of Life: Profession and Practice (Matthew 7:13–27)
All of our days we have heard the words of Jesus. Most of us have known the Sermon on the Mount for a long time. Now only one question remains. Have I built my life upon these words of Jesus? Or have I built my life upon shifting sands which will certainly give way when the going is rough?

The Summary of the Law

Consider Jesus' summary of the law in Mark 12:28–31. Here it is clear that Christian obedience demands the love of the entire person—heart, soul, mind, and strength. Christians offer God the deeds of life. They offer God the devotion and feeling of their hearts. They offer God the service of their minds. They offer God the whole of life.

Christians sometimes live one-sided lives. Some seek to *do* things for God, but they do not want to offer to God their hearts or their minds. Others feel their religion very deeply, but they do not do anything in the service of God. Still other persons worship God with their minds, but they never feel their faith very deeply. The great commandment calls on us to offer God the whole of life.

It is important for us to remember that there is no *one* type of Christian person. In the New Testament a great variety of people became disciples of Jesus. There was impulsive, robust Peter, who frequently talked before he stopped to think. It is hard for us to imagine Peter as a university professor. On the other hand, there was Paul. We *can* imagine him as a university professor. Then there was Barnabas, who was a warm-hearted, generous man. We can imagine that people liked to be with him and that they always felt better when they talked with him. Mary enjoyed the presence of Jesus but Martha expressed her love for Jesus by doing the practical chores. The church would lose much if all of us were alike. There is no one way to be a Christian. We need persons like Peter, Paul, Barnabas, John, Mary of Bethany, Mary Magdalene, and Priscilla in every congregation.

Christian obedience does not demand that we all be alike. It does demand that we offer to God the *whole* of life.

Love for God is confidence and trust in God. It is this trust in God that gives the Christian serenity, dignity, and poise amid the challenges of individual life, the vicissitudes of history, and before the final test of death.

The second commandment calls for us to love our neighbors as ourselves. A person must love himself. If a person doesn't love himself, he is not likely to love anyone else. But how do we love ourselves as Christians? Here are some of the ways we properly love ourselves: We respect ourselves as children of God. We give ourselves a certain dignity. We love ourselves even when we do wrong and don't deserve being loved. We love ourselves as individuals, not simply because we belong to a certain group.

We are commanded to give to our neighbors this love that we direct to ourselves and that we want for ourselves. Someone may raise the question, "Who is my neighbor?" A man once asked Jesus this question. In his reply Jesus did not give him directions as to how to determine who was his neighbor, but he did tell the story of the Good Samaritan (Luke 10:29–37). He ended his story by asking another question, "Which of these three, do you think, proved neighbor to the man who fell among robbers?" The important question to ask ourselves is not, Who is my neighbor? but, Am I a neighbor?

Here, then, is Jesus Christ's summary of the Christian life—love for God and love for neighbor. This is the life of the people of God—trust in God and openness to one's neighbor. Each of us must ask, Is this my life? Is this the life of the congregation to which I belong?

CHECK YOUR UNDERSTANDING

1. How did Jesus summarize the law?
2. How are you tempted to live a one-sided life?

3. What opportunities do you have to be a neighbor to other persons?
4. Consider items 2 and 8–9 under "For Action" at the end of this chapter.

Moral Inquiry

The divine command to love God with all of our minds has special application to the moral life. The Commandments and even the Sermon on the Mount can be studied in such a way that the Christian life appears to be obedience to clear and simple rules. But when we begin to reflect upon the Commandments and the Sermon, upon our human situation, upon our convictions about God, we see that the Christian life is deeper and more complex than simple conformity to rules. Moral inquiry and reflection is a Christian necessity and duty. We have to *think* about the way we must live as Christians.

The attempt to define the moral life simply in terms of external rules leads to *legalism.* The Christian life cannot be defined by rules alone. Rules may be superficial, dealing only with surface behavior. Rules can never fully anticipate the possibilities that are open to human freedom. Rules can never deal adequately with all the factors that are involved in many human situations. Those who live simply by rules, the legalists, frequently become self-righteous and brutal toward those who fail by their rules. And they sometimes become excessively concerned with their own purity. Finally, rules do not move the hearts of human beings, and they are not able in themselves to sustain human relations. They are most effective in coercive situations, as when supported by the power of the state with its police force or its tax collecting machinery.

The attempt to define the Christian life in terms of rules also leads to *moralism,* which is closely related to legalism. Moralism is defined in different ways, but here it means the insistence upon a particular rule, value, or principle at the expense of other rules or values and with no regard for the complex facts in the human situation. Moralism always has a simple answer to very complex problems. Thus, the attempt to define the moral life in terms of rules or laws leads to irrelevance, a loss of contact with what is actually happening. Whenever a pattern of life is imposed on people without an understanding of their situation, this pattern is sooner or later rejected as arbitrary and out of touch with the real world.

Living morally requires the use of the mind as well as the support of a good heart. We have to think about how we shall live as Christians. We are not given ready-made answers to how we should live from Bible reading alone, from prayer alone, or from good intentions alone. In many situations we do not have the choice between the simple good and the simple evil. The most notable instance of such a situation historically has been war. No Christian would ever believe that war is a simple good, but many times Christians have participated in war. In some situations the choice of one value or good means the denial of another value or good. We can think of instances when the refusal to take life means the loss of life, or when feeding hungry children means taking food from hungry older people. You will be able to think of situations in your own life in which no rule can tell you in advance what you as a Christian should do or of situations in which you have to choose one value at the expense of another. Furthermore, rules or values are helpful not when they are arbitrarily imposed but when they are internalized, assimilated into one's own person. This happens when a rule or value is meaningfully related to a person's actual situation and to other rules or values. Hence, moral inquiry, the task of thinking responsibly about conduct, is a basic Christian obligation.

How do we determine how we shall live as Christians? We have at least four guides or aids to help us decide how we shall live.

(1) Rules which prescribe conduct as well as values and principles which give more general guidance for conduct are a very significant indication of how Christians should live. The fact that rules and principles when taken alone are inadequate guides, for reasons that have just been indicated, does not mean they are unimportant. They are an indispensable element in understanding Christian conduct. Note the importance of commandments in the Bible.

(2) Theology is also important in determining moral behavior, especially our doctrine of God and our understanding of God's pur-

poses in the world. Our theological convictions about who God is, about who a human being is, and about the meaning of human history influence how we act in the world.

(3) Our analysis and interpretation of the actual human situation and our interpretation of the moral significance of particular circumstances is also an important factor in moral inquiry. We need to know what is actually happening, what is possible, and how our different values such as respect for human life and truth telling relate to the situation and to each other in that situation.

(4) A fourth factor that helps determine how we live as Christians is our basic understanding of the nature of the Christian life. Thomas á Kempis conceived the Christian life as the imitation of Christ, Martin Luther as the life of the person made free by Christ, John Calvin as obedience or as the fulfillment of the divine purposes, H. R. Niebuhr as the answering, responsible life. Each of these visions of the Christian life has its own strengths and weaknesses and each gives a particular style to the Christian life. All four of these factors are important in our thinking as Christians about the moral life. When any of the four is neglected, we weaken our ability to think constructively about how we should live.

The moral life for Christians presupposes trust in God and a good heart. It also requires the use of the mind to discover how the purposes of God can be fulfilled in our lives, in our community, and in the world. Hence, as we grow in trust and devotion to God we need also to grow in our ability to think responsibly about how we should live as Christians.

Finally, it must also be said that just as it is possible to overemphasize the simplicity of the Christian life and to restrict it to rules, so likewise it is possible to overemphasize its complexity. In most situations it is enough to know that we as Christians must tell the truth and respect other human beings as children of God.

CHECK YOUR UNDERSTANDING

1. Why are rules alone an inadequate guide for determining how we shall live?
2. What factors are important guides to our reasoning when we think about how we ought to live as Christians?

3. What are some of the most important ways of understanding the Christian life? Which image of the Christian life appeals to you?

Explore and Undertake

For Discussion

1. Have you felt that God has used your obedience to work out his purposes?
2. How are you tempted to serve more than one god?
3. When must a person reject his friends or family in order to be loyal to God?
4. What is your conception of God? What do you have in mind when you think about him?
5. How may we abuse the name of God?
6. Have you expected God to work magic in answer to prayer?
7. How are we to use the gift of time?
8. How can you keep the Lord's Day holy when you need to prepare for a test over the weekend? When you are away from home on vacation?
9. Why should you take seriously the faith of your parents? What are some problems you have as you seek a faith of your own?
10. Why do we place high value on human life?
11. How are we tempted to harm persons who are different from us?
12. A state puts a person to death for a crime. Discuss this practice in the light of the Sixth Commandment.
13. What would you do if someone in a group with you began telling dirty jokes?
14. How do you avoid getting into situations in which you will be tempted to do something wrong?
15. Why do people steal? What is wrong with stealing?
16. How can you destroy a classmate's good name?
17. When do you find it difficult to tell the truth?
18. When have you felt that you shouldn't tell the truth?
19. What is the right attitude to take toward possessions?
20. What is the secret of being content with what you have?

21. Is it possible for a person to obey perfectly the teachings of the Sermon on the Mount?
22. Have you been in situations in which there has seemed to be no law to tell you what to do?

For Action

1. Study the questions and answers related to the Ten Commandments in The Westminster Shorter Catechism (questions 39–82) or the Catechism in the Cumberland Presbyterian Confession of Faith (42–84) or The Heidelberg Catechism (questions 92–115).
2. Memorize the following passages: the Ten Commandments (Exod. 20:3–17); the Great Commandment (in Mark 12:29–31); the Beatitudes (Matt. 5:3–12), Micah 6:6–8, and Matthew 6:25–33.
3. Read and report to the group on J. B. Phillips' *Your God Is Too Small.*
4. What is the purpose of laws?
5. Write an essay on the subject "What My Parents Have Done for Me." Place it in your notebook.
6. Write a story about what might happen when a young person carelessly tells a falsehood about a classmate at school.
7. Write out the Beatitudes, putting them in words that have special meaning for you. Put what you do in your notebook.
8. Write a brief description of several Christians whom you know who seem to be quite different from one another. Then write a paragraph on the subject "Why I Am Glad Everyone Isn't Alike."
9. Study the hymn "O Master Workman of the Race." What clues does it give as to how to obey God?

CHAPTER VII

The Church Worships

The church obeys and confesses. And the church worships. Worship must not be separated from obedience and confession, for in worship the church both confesses and obeys. Yet worship is a distinct activity of the church. It merits our special attention.

What does worship mean? The dictionary tells us that worship comes from an Anglo-Saxon word, "weorthscipe," which meant "ascribe worth." In the New Testament one word for worship means "work." Worship, then, is the service of God. Another New Testament word for worship means "to prostrate oneself, to adore."

We cannot find the full meaning of worship in these dictionary meanings. For Christian worship is a *specific* way of ascribing worth to God, or of serving God, or of giving oneself in adoration. The directory for worship and work in one denomination states, "Christian worship depends upon and is a response to the presence of God, the Father, Son, and Holy Spirit, and to what God has done for us and for our salvation, which we acknowledge by acts of adoration, confession, thanksgiving, petition, and obedience."[1]

Christian worship is the acknowledgment of God as he makes himself known to us in Jesus Christ through the work of the Holy Spirit. We do not worship just any god, but the God and Father of our Lord Jesus Christ.

In worship we offer the sacrifice of praise, thanksgiving, and obedience. The most important fact in our worship, however, is not what we do, but what God does. We worship not so much to do something for God as to receive what God gives and to hear what God says. If worship were primarily what we do, it would not be so important.

Consider the following definition of worship:

... worship, to be Christian, must embody and set forth before the eyes of the worshipper the great historic facts of the Christian revelation so that the worshipping Church may respond in penitence and thanksgiving, dedication and praise.[2]

Worship is public: we worship publicly when the Christian community is gathered for worship. Worship is also private: we worship as individuals and as families. But even when we worship privately, we worship not as solitary individuals concerned only with ourselves, but as members of the church.

Some may protest, "Why is worship important? It is much more important to be doing something." This is what many so-called practical people think. Yet worship does shape and mold a person's life. If you know how and what a person worships, you know a great deal about the person. The hymns we sing, the prayers we hear and make our own, the reading and the preaching of the Word of God—these have more influence upon the kind of person we shall become than most of us suppose. This is the reason that the church has been so concerned that worship be true and pure, for false worship harms a person just as true worship makes a person strong.

How does worship influence what happens in your home, your city?

CHECK YOUR UNDERSTANDING

1. What does "worship" mean? What is the meaning of Christian worship?
2. What differences does worship make in our lives?
3. Consider questions 1–4 under "For Discussion" and items 1–2 under "For Action" on pages 153–154.

Our Heritage in Worship

One of the ways in which Christians differ from one another is in their manner of worship. There are differences among congregations in a denomination and differences among denominations. Our worship has been influenced by the history of the Reformed and Presbyterian churches. At least four important influences have shaped our worship today:

1. ZWINGLI—FAREL

The first great Protestant Reformer in Switzerland was Huldreich Zwingli (1484–1531). Zwingli was the leading preacher in Zurich, and the Reformation really began there with his fresh and vigorous preaching of the Word of God. When he began to revise the worship of the church, he transformed it into a preaching service. Even though he was an able musician, he eliminated music. For Zwingli, the sermon was the center of worship. When we say we are going to preaching or to hear a sermon, we are, in a sense, disciples of Zwingli.

William Farel, a French reformer, was responsible for the beginning of the Reformation in Geneva. Following Zwingli's example, he entitled his liturgy "The Manner Observed in Preaching." His order of service was as follows:

Prayer and the Lord's Prayer
Proclamation of the Word
The Law of God
The Confession of Sin
The Apostles' Creed
Prayers of Intercession

Neither Zwingli nor Farel planned to celebrate the Lord's Supper very frequently. For them, worship was primarily the proclamation of the Word of God.

2. JOHN CALVIN

John Calvin assisted Farel in Geneva. Later he was himself the chief reformer there. While a pastor in Strasbourg, he worked out a liturgy which went beyond the simple preaching service of Farel. His service of worship was as follows:

Scripture Sentence
Prayer of Confession
Assurance of Pardon
The Commandments
Psalm
Prayer for Illumination
Scripture and Sermon
General Prayer
The Apostles' Creed
The Lord's Supper
The Benediction

More important than Calvin's order of worship are the principles which he believed should govern worship. These principles were set forth in the preface which he wrote to his liturgy.

Biblical Basis. Worship, Calvin insisted, must be in accordance with the Word of God. While the Bible does not tell us whether or not to sing at a particular point in the service, it does contain teaching in the light of which we can make such a decision.

Simplicity. A second principle which Calvin insisted upon was simplicity. He objected to all the extra ceremonies which the medieval church had added to the services of worship. He opposed the pompous and the theatrical.

Intelligibility. Worship must be intelligible. This means, first of all, that it must be in the common language. We take this fact for granted today, but it was one of the great reforms of the Protestants. It means also that we must know the meaning of what we do in worship and why we do it.

Calvinists were able to worship with plain church buildings and plain liturgies, without props, because they were prepared to worship. They knew the Bible and theology. They were disciplined to prayer. They did not need aids and props for worship.

Edification. True worship helps us to grow into the fullness of the maturity of Jesus Christ. The real test of worship is whether we leave trusting God and loving our fellow man. A service in the church may give us the most wonderful feeling, and it may keep us entertained; but if it does not send us forth more Christlike, it is not worship.

The Singing of Psalms. Calvin believed that the congregation should participate in worship through singing. Music is powerful in moving the thoughts and emotions of people. For this reason he wanted singing to be a part of worship. But for the same reason he removed the organ from worship and insisted that the music should be simple. The music must not attract attention from the words, which are the prayers of the people.

Calvin believed that the words of a song, sung in worship, should be very carefully chosen. He knew that he could not go wrong if the Psalms, inspired words of Scripture, were used. Calvin had the Psalms set to verse and music. The Calvinists became known as Psalm singers. Some sang only Psalms.

The Sacraments. Unlike Zwingli and Farel, Calvin emphasized the role of the sacraments in worship. He moved the baptismal font from the rear of the church to the front, beside the pulpit, so that the congregation could see what was taking place. He believed that baptism should be a part of the public worship of the people of God. (See the section on sacraments beginning on page 143.)

Calvin also wanted the Lord's Supper celebrated each Sunday. The authorities in Geneva would not permit this, and Calvin had to be content with a frequency of once each quarter in each church. This became the general Presbyterian and Reformed practice.

3. THE PURITANS

Another influential movement in the history of our worship was Puritanism. The Puritans believed that the first reformers had not sufficiently reformed worship according to the Word of God.

Puritans were first of all great preachers, and they made the sermon the central part of worship. Thus they gave additional support to the worship of Zwingli and Farel.

Second, the Puritans were opposed to service books, that is, books containing prescribed services of worship including the prayers. They especially objected to the *Book of Common Prayer* of the Church of England. They saw that many ministers simply read the services from this book, and they felt that the book produced an idle and unedifying ministry. They substituted a directory of worship for the service book. The directory gave the rules governing worship rather than the forms of worship themselves. For example, it told how to pray, but it did not provide a prayer which could be read.

Calvin had prepared a service book which did give the minister freedom to vary at least one prayer and other parts of the service. John Knox had used the *Book of Common Order* in Scotland, a service book which contained set forms and prayers. After the Westminster Assembly, the *Directory of Publick Worship* became part of the constitution of English-speaking Presbyterian churches. Thus service books dropped out of the life of the church. Only recently have they been brought back in.

On the continent of Europe, leaders in Pietism, a movement which emphasized personal religion, likewise objected to set forms. Many of them objected to use of the Gloria, the Lord's Prayer, and the Apostles' Creed. They wanted worship to be free and spontaneous. This, in part, is the reason that many Presbyterian churches in America did not use the Apostles' Creed or Lord's Prayer very frequently in worship.

A third emphasis of the Puritans was in opposition to read prayers. Some believed that prayer had to be extemporaneous in order to be genuine. Some allowed a studied prayer, one that had been prepared by the minister. They were united in objection to prayers that were read.

4. THE AMERICAN FRONTIER

The settlers who came to America found themselves in a new situation. There were no churches on the frontier. There was no community pressure to attend worship. The vast majority of the settlers dropped out of the regular patterns of church life. It is estimated that in 1790 only five or six persons out of every hundred were members of the organized church.

The stately worship which was suitable for Europe was out of place on the frontiers. Unlike European congregations, a majority of those who attended church services in America were not members of the church. For this reason every service had a missionary thrust in which those who were present were urged to become members of the church.

Our situation today is different. Most of those who attend services of worship now are members of the church. Special revival services, common even forty years ago, are not so frequent now. Nevertheless, the influence of the frontier situation lingers in the worship of the church in America.

Another contribution of the American experience to worship is the integration of the offering for the support of the church into the worship service. Offerings have always been a part of worship. The peculiar American situation of a newly settled land and the separation of church and state contributed to the conviction that the church should be maintained by all the people. The church in the United States is unique in that it is maintained neither by the state, nor the land owners, nor the nobility, nor the rich, but by members generally. The offering is the expression of this conviction in the worship of the church.

There were and are other influences that shape our worship. But these four are the major ones. They suffice to teach us that there is no *one* form of Christian worship. There is not even one form of Presbyterian and Reformed worship. A form of worship that is suitable in one situation may not enable people to worship God in another.

Yet even in the varieties of worship certain elements remain the same. Every service includes adoration, confession, and thanksgiving, and the reading and preaching and hearing of the Word of God. Even when the forms of worship are not ones which we find congenial to our practices, we still can recognize and appreciate what the worshiper is doing. Worship must grow out of the life and the faith of the people of God in a particular situation.

The principles which govern worship remain the same. For this reason Reformed and Presbyterian worship will always have certain characteristics, though the form may vary.

CHECK YOUR UNDERSTANDING

1. What was the center of worship for Zwingli?
2. What principles for worship did Calvin advocate?
3. What do we in our worship owe to the Puritans? What was their emphasis in worship?
4. Consider items 3 and 4 under "For Action" on page 154.

The Public Worship of God

Is a book of common worship used by congregations in your denomination? Such a book contains forms for the worship of the congregation and for the sacraments, marriages, funerals, and various other services of the church. If copies of such a book are available in your church, get a copy and keep it in hand as you study this chapter.

Below is a listing of the parts in the First Order of Morning Worship in *The Book of Common Worship,* used in many Presbyterian and Reformed congregations. Study this service, comparing it, part by part, with the service of worship in your own congregation. To do this, it would be advisable for each member of the group to have a copy of *The Book of Common Worship* and of the worship bulletin used in your congregation on a particular Sunday. If copies of the former are not available in sufficient number, try to locate at least one copy for use in connection with your study. The service follows:

First Order of Morning Worship
Call to Worship (verses of Scripture, read by the minister)
Adoration (a prayer by the minister)
Confession (a prayer said by the minister and people)
Assurance of Pardon (to be said by the minister)
Psalter (a Psalm, chanted or read responsively by the minister and people)
First Scripture Lesson
Hymn or Anthem
Second Scripture Lesson
The Creed
Hymn or Anthem
Prayers of Thanksgiving, Supplication, Intercession, and Communion of Saints, Followed by the Lord's Prayer (by the minister and people)
Offering
Doxology and Response or Prayer of Dedication
Hymn or Anthem
Sermon
Hymn
Benediction

The Worshipbook which was published by three Presbyterian churches in 1970 gives the following basic structure for the service of the Lord's Day including the Sacrament of the Lord's Supper.

The Basic Structure	Additions and Variant Forms
Call to Worship	
	Versicle
Hymn of Praise	
Confession of Sin	
Declaration of Pardon	
Response	(Gloria, Hymn, or Psalm)
Prayer for Illumination	(Or, the Collect for the Day)
Old Testament Lesson	
	Anthem, Canticle, or Psalm
New Testament Lesson(s)	
Sermon	
	Ascription of Praise
	An Invitation
Creed	
	Hymn
	Concerns of the Church
The Prayers of the People	
The Peace	
Offering	
	Anthem or Special Music
	Hymn or Doxology
Invitation to the Lord's Table	
The Thanksgiving	
The Lord's Prayer	
The Communion	
Response	
Hymn	
Charge	
Benediction	

The theological background for this order of worship is found in the *Directory of Worship* of the United Presbyterian Church.

As you compare the service of morning worship in your congregation with the above services, ask such questions of it as these: Is the order in both services generally the same? Where is it different? What may be the reason for the difference?

PRAYER IN WORSHIP

Prayer is a universal fact. Even those who do not attend churches pray on occasion. "There are no atheists in foxholes," someone has said. But what is prayer? Is it simply an emergency request to whatever gods there be to get you out of a jam? It can be that, when offered in sincerity. But in Christian worship it is more.

There is a splendid definition of prayer in The Westminster Shorter Catechism:

> Prayer is an offering up of our desires unto God, for things agreeable to his will, in the name of Christ, with confession of our sins, and thankful acknowledgment of his mercies (answer to question 98).

The model prayer is the Lord's Prayer. It came in answer to a request from disciples of Jesus, "Lord, teach us to pray." We can learn how to pray as we study this prayer which our Lord taught his disciples. Let us study it. (See Matthew 6:9–13, King James Version.)

"Our Father which art in heaven"—with these words the prayer begins.

> The preface of the Lord's prayer, which is, *"Our Father which art in heaven,"* teacheth us to draw near to God, with all holy reverence and confidence, as children to a father, able and ready to help us; and that we should pray with and for others (The Westminster Shorter Catechism, answer to question 100).

Others have called God "Father," but Jesus made it our best name for God. No other earthly name says so clearly who God is. "Father" stands for authority and for love. "Which art in heaven" sets God apart from any earthly father, lest we should think of God as just a very big father. Note the pronoun "our." God is not just *my* father, or yours. He is *our* father.

There is much theology in these opening words. Some of this you can work out for yourself if you will answer these questions:

What does it mean for me to call God "Father"? What does it mean to say "our Father"?

Every prayer, including the Lord's Prayer, begins with an acknowledgment of God and of who he is.

"Hallowed be thy name."

> In the first petition, which is, *"Hallowed be thy name,"* we pray that God would enable us, and others, to glorify him in all that whereby he maketh himself known, and that he would dispose all things to his own glory (The Westminster Shorter Catechism, answer to question 101).

A name in the Bible, as we have already seen, is more than a sign; it stands for the whole person. The name of God has been made known to us in Jesus Christ. When we say "hallowed be thy name," we are asking that the God whom we know in Jesus Christ be exalted, that his name not be profaned. What are some of the ways in which we profane God's name? We profane the name of God when we use it carelessly in speech. We also profane God's name when our lives are inconsistent with the faith we profess.

"Thy kingdom come."

> In the second petition, which is, *"Thy kingdom come,"* we pray that Satan's kingdom may be destroyed, and that the kingdom of grace may be advanced, ourselves and others brought into it, and kept in it, and that the kingdom of glory may be hastened (The Westminster Shorter Catechism, answer to question 102).

The kingdom of God is the reign of God. Here we pray that it will now be clearly seen in our lives, in our communities, in our world. Of course, God reigns even when we rebel against him. We only destroy ourselves by rebellion. So our prayer is primarily that God's reign will come in our own lives and in our world, that we and our world may not destroy ourselves in mad rebellion against his will.

It is said that Augustine prayed, "Thy kingdom come, but not now." Do we sometimes pray in this same sense?

"Thy will be done in earth, as it is in heaven."

In the third petition, which is, *"Thy will be done in earth, as it is in heaven,"* we pray that God, by his grace, would make us able and willing to know, obey, and submit to his will in all things as the angels do in heaven (The Westminster Shorter Catechism, answer to question 103).

This petition is parallel to the one just before it. God's will and God's kingdom are the same. Most people want their own will to be done. Here we pray that not *our* will but *God's* will shall be done.

"Give us this day our daily bread."

In the fourth petition, which is, *"Give us this day our daily bread,"* we pray that, of God's free gift, we may receive a competent portion of the good things of this life, and enjoy his blessing with them (The Westminster Shorter Catechism, answer to question 104).

Here we have an answer to the question, Is it all right to pray for material things? One commentator has said that the prayer calls for bread, not cake. Another has noted that it asks for daily bread, not for stored-up riches. It recognizes that material needs are important and that God is concerned about them.

When we pray this prayer, we acknowledge that we depend upon God for daily bread. God has given rain, sunshine, and fertility to the earth. Our very lives depend upon God's faithfulness.

Our prayer also obligates us. Again note the pronoun "our." Can we pray this prayer without sharing our abundance with those who do not have daily bread?

"And forgive us our debts, as we forgive our debtors"

In the fifth petition, which is, *"And forgive us our debts, as we forgive our debtors,"* we pray that God, for Christ's sake, would freely pardon all our sins; which we are the rather encouraged to ask, because by his grace we are enabled from the heart to forgive others (The Westminster Shorter Catechism, answer to question 105).

"Debts" here is a synonym for "sin." It is a good one. When we sin, we put ourselves in debt. We are obligated to make amends. But in our own strength we cannot make amends. We have to ask forgiveness. Forgiveness means that God pays our debt. If you have ever forgiven someone a real wrong which was done to you, a wrong for which amends could not be made, you have some understanding of what this means. George Bernard Shaw once said that forgiveness is impossible. A person has to pay his debts. He was right. The debt has to be paid. But in the forgiveness of sins, God pays it.

Yet we dare not ask for forgiveness if we are not willing to forgive. The people who know that they have been forgiven find it possible to forgive their neighbors. On the other hand, those who are unwilling to forgive their neighbors can hardly accept forgiveness.

"And lead us not into temptation, but deliver us from evil . . ."

In the sixth petition, which is, *"And lead us not into temptation, but deliver us from evil,"* we pray that God would either keep us from being tempted to sin, or support and deliver us when we are tempted (The Westminster Shorter Catechism, answer to question 106).

What does "temptation" mean? If it means something evil, God would not lead us there. If it means a trial or test of our faith, we ought not to shrink from it. Faith grows strong by testing.

Nevertheless, none of us can risk temptation carelessly. No matter how many times we overcome, the next time we may slip. Only fools place themselves in situations in which they may be tempted beyond their ability to resist. When such temptations come to us, we must meet them.

But we dare not carelessly and casually subject ourselves to them.

"For thine is the kingdom, and the power, and the glory, for ever. Amen."

The conclusion of the Lord's prayer, which is, *"For thine is the kingdom, and the power, and the glory, for ever, Amen,"* teacheth us to take our encouragement in prayer from God only, and in our prayers to praise him, ascribing kingdom, power, and glory to him, and in testimony of our desire and assurance to be heard, we say, *Amen* (The Westminster Shorter Catechism, answer to question 107).

This conclusion was probably not in the original prayer, and some churches omit it. However, such tributes to God were used in the Bible and in the early church. Certainly this part is appropriate here, as it is to the conclusion of any prayer. All prayer includes the acknowledgment of God's power and majesty, the power and majesty which created the world and which raised Jesus Christ from the dead.

CHECK YOUR UNDERSTANDING

1. What are the elements that seem to be a part of each complete service of worship?
2. What is the place of prayer in worship?
3. For what do we pray in each petition of the Lord's Prayer?
4. Consider question 6 under "For Discussion" and items 5-13 under "For Action" on pages 153–155.

The Sacraments

A sacrament is holy ordinance instituted by Christ, wherein, by sensible signs, Christ and the benefits of the new covenant are represented, sealed, and applied to believers (The Westminster Shorter Catechism, answer to question 92).

Sacraments are the gospel acted out. They are an outward sign of God's gracious presence. In this sense there are many sacraments. Even the universe itself is a sacrament, a sign of the presence of God. But in the worship of the church we limit the sacraments to those which we believe Jesus Christ established. They are Baptism and the Lord's Supper.

You may raise the question, Why do we need sacraments? Are not words sufficient? Our common experience tells us that words are not. A deep feeling which cannot be put into words can be communicated by the expression on one's face. A wedding ring confirms vows which are spoken. A handshake is a part of a true greeting of a friend. In many areas of life we resort to acts to say what words cannot say or to confirm what words have said.

BAPTISM

Baptism is the sign of membership in the Christian community. It is an initiation sacrament. As such it is applied to those who confess their faith in Jesus Christ and to those who are born in the fellowship of a Christian home and in the fellowship of the church.

Baptism is a sign and a seal (1) of the forgiveness of sins, (2) of our communion with Jesus Christ, and (3) of our welcome into the household of faith.

There are two questions about baptism which lead to different answers among Christian people: How shall we baptize? and Whom shall we baptize?

Let us look at the first question, How shall we baptize? Reformed and Presbyterian churches, among others, baptize by pouring or sprinkling water on the head. Baptist churches, among others, baptize by immersion. There does not seem to be any way to settle this question in a final way. The New Testament does not specify any particular mode. Both forms of baptism were practiced in the early church. The word "baptize" means "to bathe" as well as "to dip or to immerse."

Does pouring or immersion better symbolize the meaning of baptism? Here again we do not find a clear-cut answer. As a sign of the gift of the Holy Spirit, of cleansing, and of forgiveness, baptism is well symbolized by pouring. Paul, however, speaks of baptism as death and resurrection, and here the symbolism of immersion is more suggestive.

Reformed and Presbyterian churches have never considered the question of the mode of baptism as of the greatest importance. Persons who have been baptized by immersion are not rebaptized when they become members of Reformed and Presbyterian churches. Their baptism by immersion is accepted as valid.

The second question is more important: Whom shall we baptize? Baptists have insisted that only adult believers who make their own confession of faith shall be baptized. Reformed and Presbyterian churches baptize children of Christian parents as well as adult believers.

Baptists point to those who have been baptized in infancy who in adult life show no sign of Christian confession. Karl Barth, a Reformed theologian, has been so disturbed by this fact that he once exclaimed, "Both Hitler and Stalin, both Mussolini and the Pope stand under the sign [of baptism]".[3]

If both Hitler and the Pope as well as many devout Protestants have been baptized in infancy, can the baptism of infants have any real significance?

Here are some of the answers which Reformed and Presbyterian churches have given to these questions:

First, baptism is a sign and seal of what God does. God forgives. God calls people to be members of his church. God gives his Holy Spirit. The baptism of infants underscores what God has done. The really important thing in baptism is not the believer's act but God's act.

Secondly, in the providence of God, the birth of children into the fellowship of the Christian home and of the church is significant. Such children grow up in the church. There is never a time when they are out of the church. Seldom is there a particular moment when they become consciously aware that that they are members of the church. There is no question that such children have a heritage in the faith which does not belong to those born outside the church.

The baptism of children who are born in the church places a serious responsibility upon the church. First of all, the church must be reasonably certain that such children are born to Christian parents in the fellowship of the church. The church has sometimes baptized children of parents who had the very loosest connection with its life.

Furthermore, the church and the parents must take with utter seriousness their obligation to rear their children in the nurture of the Lord and in the fellowship of the church. At baptism the church as well as the parents confess its faith, and the church as well as the parents pledge themselves to rear this child in the Christian community.

Moreover, the baptism of infants means that we have to take seriously the admission of persons to the Lord's table. John Calvin emphasized the necessity of examining all those who come to the table of the Lord as to their knowledge and their Christian life. As persons are admitted to the Lord's table, they confirm for themselves the vows which were taken for them by their parents and by the church when they were children. Recent actions of some church courts have opened the Lord's Supper to baptized persons prior to communicant or confirmation classes.

Someone may protest that we cannot know that a child who is born in a Christian home and in the fellowship of the church will grow up as a member of the church. This is true. But neither can we know that adults who are baptized after they make their confession of faith will continue in this confession. In both cases we baptize only when there is evidence which makes it reasonably certain that this person is in the church. There are no statistics, but it is probable that the promises of infant baptism, at least in America, are fulfilled in as great proportion as the promises of adult baptism.

A service for baptism is found in *The Book of Common Worship* and also in *The Worshipbook*. Get a copy of either book and study the baptismal service. Also watch carefully when there is a baptism in your congregation. Then you will be ready to ask yourself, What did my baptism mean? Martin Luther, in dark moments of discouragement, always took heart when he remembered that he had been baptized. Can you see why he did?

THE LORD'S SUPPER

What is the Lord's supper? The Lord's supper is a sacrament, wherein, by giving and receiving bread and wine, according to Christ's appointment, his death is showed forth; and the worthy receivers are, not after a corporal and carnal manner, but by faith, made partakers of his body and blood, with all his benefits, to their spiritual nourishment and growth in grace (The Westminster Shorter Catechism, Q.96).

The Lord's Supper is one of the most characteristic acts of the church. From the beginning one of the high points in the life of the church has been the gathering of the people of God at the table of the Lord. It is a thrilling fact to remember that for almost two thousand years not a Sunday has passed that Christians somewhere on this planet have not gathered at the table of their Lord.

The earliest written account of the Lord's Supper is found in Paul's Letter to the Christians at Corinth (A.D. 50-52). Read this account in 1 Corinthians 11:23-26.

Here we find all the acts which are familiar to us in the celebration of the Lord's Supper. The prayer of thanksgiving, the taking and breaking of the bread, the taking of the cup, the anticipation of the coming of the Lord—all of these acts call to mind the life and death of Jesus Christ.

The bread and the wine are appropriate symbols. Bread and wine have always been symbols of the truth that man is dependent upon something not himself. Common eating has been a clear symbol of our common need. In addition, the bread and the wine have been symbols of God's blessing and human toil. In the ancient celebrations of the Lord's Supper, the people brought the bread and wine from their own gardens. This was the origin of the offertory. Here, the offering of the people, the fruit of creation and of human toil, became a means of the gracious presence of Jesus Christ among his people. When we make our offering in money today, it is more difficult to imagine that the bread and wine are our gifts. Yet this is what they are.

But the elements are not simply bread and wine. They are *broken* bread and *poured* wine. The breaking of the bread and pouring of the wine, symbols of the broken body and the shed blood, are as important as the elements themselves. There is additional symbolism which we frequently miss today. Ideally, in the Lord's Supper there are one loaf and one cup. We all eat from one loaf and drink from one cup and we become one body. The celebration of the Lord's Supper in large gatherings does not make it practical to use literally one loaf or one cup. An ancient prayer, which goes back to the days of the New Testament, declared, "As this broken bread was scattered (as corn) over mountains, and being gathered together became one, so may thy church be gathered together from the ends of the earth into thy kingdom. For thine is the glory and the power through Jesus forever."

What is the meaning of the Lord's Supper? Let us see.

1. *The Gospel.* First of all, the Lord's Supper is a proclamation of the gospel, as is baptism. It is the gospel acted out. It has no other purpose than the purpose of the Word—to present Jesus Christ as Lord and Savior.

2. *The Presence of Jesus Christ.* Christians have always believed that Jesus Christ is truly present in the celebration of the sacrament. The broken bread and the poured wine have been occasions of his presence. Christians have differed over *how* he is present. Sometimes the popular view of the sacrament has been nothing more than crude magic, according to which the bread and wine are literally changed into the body and blood of Christ. In the late medieval period people even argued about what would happen if and when a mouse ate some of the consecrated bread. Ignorant people even tried to get a piece of the host (the consecrated bread) to use as a charm. No official church pronouncement approved these practices. However, the doctrine of transubstantiation (look up that word in the dictionary) as it developed in the medieval period did lead to such problems.

Reformed and Presbyterian churches have always emphasized the *real* but *spiritual* presence of Jesus Christ in the Lord's Supper. Spiritual means personal presence. The following paragraphs from a book by Professor Donald Baillie of Scotland will help to make this clearer to you:

> But what do we mean by Real Presence? Is it different in the sacrament from the kind of divine presence we can have at any time when we draw near to God?
>
> It is important to note that even apart from the sacrament we are bound to distinguish several degrees or modes of the divine presence. To begin with the most general, we believe in the *omnipresence* of God. He is everywhere present. And yet we also say that God is with those who trust and obey Him in a way in

which He is not with others. We say, God is with them. And we say that God's presence is with us *more* at some times than at others. We speak of entering into His presence in worship, and we ask Him to come and be with us and grant us His presence. We say that wherever two or three are gathered together in His name, He is there in the midst of them. And then in apparently a still further sense, we speak of the Real Presence in the sacrament. What does all that mean?

Surely the first thing we have to remember is that God's presence is not strictly speaking a *local* or *spatial* presence at all, but a spiritual personal relationship which we have to symbolize by spatial metaphors.

. . . There may even be two persons together in a room without their being in more than a minimal way *with* each other, because they are not encountering each other in a genuine relationship. So "We can . . . have a very strong feeling that somebody who is sitting in the same room as ourselves, sitting quite near us, someone whom we can look at and listen to and whom we can touch if we wanted to make a final test of his reality, is nevertheless more distant from us than some loved one who is perhaps thousands of miles away or perhaps, even, no longer among the living. We could say that the man sitting beside us was in the same room as ourselves, but that he was not really *present* there, that his *presence* did not make itself felt" (Donald M. Baillie, *The Theology of the Sacraments* [New York: Charles Scribner's Sons, 1957], pp. 97, 98, 99).

3. *Remembrance.* The Lord's Supper is a memorial which refreshes our memory. It focuses our attention upon the actual, historical life, death, and resurrection of Jesus Christ. It helps us to remember.

4. *Thanksgiving.* The Orthodox churches of the East call the Lord's Supper the Eucharist. "Eucharist" is the Greek word for "thanksgiving." From the beginning the celebration of the Lord's Supper has been a time for thanksgiving for creation; for the good things of this life; and, above all, for the love God has shown in the

redemption of the world in Jesus Christ and for the means of grace and the hope of glory.

5. *Communion.* The Lord's Supper is a communion. It is a communion first of all with Jesus Christ. It is also a communion of Christians with one another in the body of Christ.

6. *Supper.* We are fed at the Lord's Supper spiritually, by faith. Those who come to the supper with understanding, expectancy, commitment, and faith are nourished by all that Jesus said and did, by his resurrection from the dead, and by his intercession at the right hand of God.

7. *Declaration of Faith.* The most important thing which happens at the Lord's Supper is what God does for us. Yet when believers come to the Lord's table, they do something too: they declare their faith to the world. They make their declaration of allegiance: The Lord's Supper is a pledge of allegiance.

This leads us to the indispensable condition for participation in the sacrament of the Lord's Supper, which is faith. There is nothing automatic in the benefits to be received in the Lord's Supper. There is no magic. The Lord's Supper becomes a means of God's grace only when it is received in faith. Faith includes knowledge and understanding, personal commitment and dedication. John Calvin and many of his followers used to emphasize the fencing of the table; that is, the barring from the table of all those who lacked knowledge and who did not give evidence of repentance and faith. The table should not be profaned by carelessness or pretense.

There is no better way to conclude our study of the Lord's Supper than to call to mind the denunciation the Hebrew prophets heaped upon those who used sacraments as magic. There is nothing automatic or magical about any sacrament or ceremony. Note the word of the Lord in Amos 5:21-24.

CHECK YOUR UNDERSTANDING
1. What is a sacrament?
2. Of what is baptism a sign? How is baptism to be administered? to whom?
3. Of what is the Lord's Supper a symbol? What is its meaning?
4. Consider questions 6-9 under "For Discussion" and items 14–18 under "For Action" on pages 153–155.

Weddings and Funerals

WEDDINGS

Among other occasions for worship are weddings. The wedding of Christian people is never a private matter. The church has a stake in the marriage of those who are the church. Hence, there has been for many years the custom of having weddings in the church. Here the name of God is invoked as a home is established—a home through which a part of God's purpose for all mankind will be worked out.

The church building is not a mere auditorium or the parlor of a justice of the peace; it is a sanctuary, a place for worship. For this reason, weddings in the church ought to be different from weddings held elsewhere. The music may include hymns. The ceremony will speak of God's purposes for marriage. The necessary furniture of the church—pulpit, table, baptismal font, open Bible—will not be obscured or hidden by flowers. The conduct of those present at rehearsal and wedding will be that of Christian folk.

FUNERALS

There were so many abuses connected with funeral services in late medieval times that many early Protestants objected to any service for the dead. Yet most Reformed and Presbyterian people have agreed that the death of a Christian is an occasion for worship. Death is a great threat to community, to life, to faith. In worship the congregation hears the Word of God and replies to the challenge of death.

When the Christian congregation is gathered for a funeral, it does at least four things: (1) It affirms that the Christian community cannot be broken by death. The church is composed of the living and those who have departed from us. In Christ, the head of the church, we still have communion with one another. Moreover, the reality of the Christian community is demonstrated. Members of the church gather to support members who have suffered loss.

(2) The Christian community declares that death is not the destruction of a life of faith and love. The conviction that God raises the dead is openly declared.

(3) The Christian community, perhaps using the Apostles' Creed, declares its faith in the face of death. Apart from faith, death seems to suggest that everything ends without meaning and without hope.

(4) The funeral is an occasion for the Christian community to give thanks for a life which has been lived in faith and love.

A funeral can be an occasion for pagan display of wealth. It can be expensive. It can be wholly lacking in faith. But it *can* be the occasion when God's Word is read and heard, when Christian faith is declared with passion and devotion, when God's grace in a human life is acknowledged.

Personal and Private Worship

Christians worship publicly in the assembled congregation. They also worship privately. Private worship must not be understood in contrast to public, congregational worship, for in private worship the Christian still worships God not simply as an individual but as a member of the Christian community. John Calvin declared that because of our sluggishness we need to set aside certain times for prayer. "Those hours should not pass without prayer, and during them all the devotion of the heart should be completely engaged in it. These are: when we arise in the morning, before we begin daily work, when we sit down to a meal, when by God's blessing we have eaten, when we are getting ready to retire" (*Institutes of the Christian Religion,* III, XX, 50). Not everyone can manage so many periods for prayer, meditation, devotional Bible reading. Yet the very secular, pluralistic, chaotic character of American life makes it all the more necessary that we find time for such concentrated moments of prayer, meditation, and devotion. The importance of having at one's command a store of biblical passages that are especially suited for devotion and personal faith and some of the great prayers of the church is clear. In the practice of private devotions we discover one of the greatest values in committing some of the treasures of the Christian life to memory. Most denominations including such organizations as the American Bible Society also provide aids to daily devotion.

CHECK YOUR UNDERSTANDING
1. In what way is the church an appropriate place for weddings?
2. What does a funeral in the church accomplish?

Explore and Undertake

For Discussion

1. Look at this definition of worship: ". . . to worship is to quicken the conscience by the holiness of God, to feed the mind with the truth of God, to purge the imagination by the beauty of God, to open the heart to the love of God, (and) to devote the will to the purpose of God." Discuss this definition in the light of your usual experience in worship as an individual and as a member of a congregation.
2. What difference would it make in your private devotions if you were not a member of the church?
3. What would be the effect on the Christian faith in your community if services of public worship were outlawed?
4. Is there a connection between the sort of songs we sing and the sermons we hear, and the sort of persons we become?
5. Discuss the meaning of the Lord's Prayer, phrase by phrase. As you do, keep such questions as the following in mind: Why is it good to begin prayer with an acknowledgement of God and of who he is? How may we hallow God's name at home, at school, in the community, in the church? What might happen if all the members of your study group were to submit themselves completely to the reign of God? If, as someone has said, God's will is done perfectly, constantly, and willingly in heaven, what do we ask for when we pray, "Thy will be done in earth, as it is in heaven?" Does the petition "Lead us not into temptation" say something about places we should not go?
6. What values do you see in the use of material things like water and bread and wine and in physical acts like shaking hands with a friend?
7. What are the benefits of infant baptism? What risks does the church run in baptizing infants?

8. How does observance of the Lord's Supper stengthen the individual? the church?
9. Are there any automatic benefits to be derived from participation in the sacraments of the church?
10. Ask an adult, perhaps a parent, about the differences between a civil marriage and a church wedding. Discuss what you learn in your study group.
11. Look at the marriage vows in such a book as *The Book of Common Worship*. Most couples repeat the vows after the minister, but some memorize the vows. What value is there in learning the vows?

For Action

1. Ask several members of your congregation what worship means to them. Report what you learn to the group, and record it in your notebook.
2. Write out your own definition of worship.
3. Write an essay on the worship of your congregation.
4. Apply the principles of John Calvin to the worship of your congregation.
5. Plan together a service of worship for use some Sunday in your group, following some definite theme.
6. As suggested on pages 136–138, study the morning worship in your congregation, comparing it with that given in *The Book of Common Worship* or *The Worshipbook*.
7. Study Psalms 51, 142, and 146. What mood of worship does each psalm express?
8. If you do not already have a time for private devotions daily, begin the practice of daily worship.
9. Study the questions and answers in the catechism related to the Lord's Prayer (The Westminster Shorter Catechism, questions 99-107; Cumberland Presbyterian Catechism, questions 98-105; The Heidelberg Catechism, questions 118-129).
10. Look up the following words in a dictionary, and put their definitions in your notebook: adoration, confession, petition, supplication, and intercession.
11. Write out six brief prayers. Write prayers of adoration, confession, thanksgiving, petition related to your own need, in-

tercession for others, and dedication. Put them in your notebook.

12. Study the hymn "All People That on Earth Do Dwell" as a hymn that expresses the mood that should be dominant in our worship.

13. Look at the topical index in the hymnbook used in your congregation. Choose several hymns that might be used in each of the several parts of a service of worship.

14. Study and memorize the definitions of the sacraments in the catechism (The Westminster Shorter Catechism, questions 92, 94, 96; Cumberland Presbyterian Catechism, questions 91, 93, 95; and The Heidelberg Catechism, question 66).

15. Memorize 1 Corinthians 11:23–26.

16. Ask friends who are members of churches in other denominations "How are people baptized in your congregation? Why?" and "Are infants baptized in your congregation?" Report to the group on what you learn.

17. Write an essay on the subject "I'm Glad I Was Baptized in Infancy" (if you were).

18. Let the group study the booklet on symbolism, *Symbols of the Faith,* perhaps in Sunday evening meetings. Invite parents to share in the study.

19. Write an essay on the subject "A Christian Funeral."

20. Have an adult who has read *The American Way of Death,* by Jessica Mitford, report on the book to the group. Discuss funeral practices in your community.

Prayers of the Church

GENERAL PRAYER OF CONFESSION

Almighty and most merciful Father; We have erred and strayed from Thy ways like lost sheep. We have followed too much the devices and desires of our own hearts. We have offended against Thy holy laws. We have left undone those things which we ought to have done; And we have done those things which we ought not to have done; And there is no health in us. But Thou, O Lord, have mercy upon us, miserable offenders. Spare Thou those, O God, who confess their faults. Restore Thou those who are penitent; According to Thy promises declared unto mankind in Christ Jesus our Lord. And grant, O most merciful Father, for His sake; That we may hereafter live a godly, righteous; and sober life; To the glory of Thy holy name. Amen.

GENERAL PRAYER OF THANKSGIVING

Almighty God, Father of all mercies; We Thine unworthy servants; Do give Thee most humble and hearty thanks; For all Thy goodness and loving kindness to us and to all men. We bless Thee for our creation, preservation, and all the blessings of this life; But above all for Thine inestimable love in the redemption of the world by our Lord Jesus Christ; For the means of grace, and for the hope of glory. And, we beseech Thee, give us that due sense of all Thy mercies; That our hearts may be unfeignedly thankful; And that we show forth Thy praise, not only with our lips, but in our lives; By giving up ourselves to Thy service, And by walking before Thee in holiness and righteousness all our days; Through Jesus Christ our Lord; To whom, with Thee and the Holy Spirit, be all honor and glory; World without end. Amen.

GENERAL PETITIONS

O Lord, support us all the day long, until the shadows lengthen and the evening comes, and the busy world is hushed, and the fever of life is over, and our work is done. Then in Thy mercy grant us a safe lodging, and a holy rest, and peace at last; through Jesus Christ our Lord. Amen.

GRACE BEFORE MEALS

The Lord bless this food to our use, and us to His service. Amen.

Lord, help us to receive all good things from Thy hand and use them to Thy praise. Amen.

Heavenly Father, make us thankful to Thee, and mindful of others, as we receive these blessings; in Jesus's name. Amen.

Father in heaven, sustain our bodies with this food, our hearts with true friendship, and our souls with Thy truth; for Christ's sake. Amen.

Refresh us, O Lord, with Thy gifts, and sustain us with the bounty of Thy riches; through Jesus Christ our Lord. Amen.

Blessed be Thou, O God, who givest us day by day our daily bread; in the name of Jesus Christ our Lord. Amen.

Lord Jesus, be our holy Guest,
Our morning Joy, our evening Rest;
And with our daily bread impart
Thy love and peace to every heart. Amen.

These prayers are found along with many more in *The Book of Common Worship*. See also the *Book of Common Order* and *Contemporary Prayers* from the Church of Scotland.

CHAPTER VIII

The Church Serves

The church confesses its faith, obeys, and worships God. The church also serves God. Confession, obedience, and worship, of course, are ways of serving God. In this chapter we shall look closely at other ways the church serves God.

When the Bible wishes to describe the Christian or the church, it frequently makes use of the image of a servant. The Christian is the servant of the Lord. The church is God's servant. In the Old Testament, Israel is frequently called "God's servant" (1 Kings 8:23; Ps. 69:36; Isa. 41:8–9). Isaiah 53 is a moving description of the Servant of God. Many Christians believe that this remarkable statement is fulfilled only in Jesus Christ.

Jesus Christ himself was called by the early Christians "the servant of God." (See Acts 3:13) Jesus described himself as a servant: "For the Son of man also came not to be served but to serve ..." (Mark 10:45). He said, "... I am among you as one who serves" (Luke 22:27).

Jesus taught his disciples that they were to be servants. When he washed his disciples' feet (read John 13:1–11), he vividly illustrated the fact that he was a servant, and he said to his disciples, "... you also should do as I have done to you." It is not surprising that the Apostle Paul called himself a servant of Jesus Christ (Romans 1:1) or that the New Testament church should think of its life as a ministry.

There is no question that one of the most important pictures which we have of the church is that of a servant. The Christian and the church are not called to be God's favorites, idly to enjoy his favors. They are called to be servants, doing his will and suffering with and working with him in the world. The church is to be the servant of God, and this means also the servant of man and the servant of the world. (In this connection, see Matthew 25:34–40.) We are in the world as those who are called to serve.

What is the service of God? What does it mean to be the servants of God today? Perhaps the best way to answer this question is to note specific ways in which the church serves God.

The Church Presents God's Call

Jesus came preaching the gospel of the Kingdom of God and calling people to repentance. In this way he served God, and by serving God he served the world and man. There is nothing more important that we can do than to tell people about God and his love. There is nothing more important that we can do than to call people to repent of their sins and to believe the gospel, the good news about God. We call this telling people of God and of his love "evangelism." "Evangelism" comes from a Greek word meaning "good news." Evangelism is the proclaiming of the good news about God which was revealed in Jesus Christ.

How do we do the work of evangelism?

1. We proclaim the gospel through the lives which we live. Paul thought of Christians as living epistles (2 Cor. 3:2–3). The message of their faith was written in their lives. The only proclamation of the gospel which many people will ever hear is the one which we tell by the way we live.

Many people became members of the early church because they were attracted by the love which the Christians expressed. Tertullian, a church historian who lived in the second century, reported that the enemies of Christians, noting their care for the helpless, declared, "Look how they love one another."

2. We also proclaim the gospel through the services of worship in the church. While our services of worship are for the Christian congregation, they are also for all others who wish to worship. In all

of these services, the good news is proclaimed. Christian people, as well as those outside the church, need continually to hear the gospel.

3. The church devises other ways in which to proclaim the gospel to the world. One way is the establishment of new congregations in areas where there are no churches and in new centers of population. Another way is a ministry through radio and television. Still another means is proclamation through printed books, magazines, and pamphlets. One of the best ways is personal witness.

4. One form of evangelism is so far-reaching that it deserves special attention. This is the world mission of the church, the work of taking to the people everywhere the good news about God. This is the same work which we do in our communities, but telling the good news to people in all parts of the world is a tremendous task. Thousands of persons especially equipped for it take part in this world-wide ministry.

In the book of Acts we are told that Jesus charged his disciples with these words: ". . . you shall receive power when the Holy Spirit has come upon you; and you shall be my witnesses in Jerusalem and in all Judea and Samaria and to the end of the earth" (Acts 1:8). One of the most thrilling stories in all of history has been the fulfilling of this commission of Jesus to his disciples. In obedience to this command, young men and women have left homeland, parents, and friends. They have gone to the far corners of the earth. The result is that today there is hardly a place on this planet where there is no Christian church. The long march which Paul began as he crossed from Asia to Europe has covered the known world. Of course, the church is weak in many places. The miracle is that the church is in such places at all. Never in all of history has any other movement been so widespread and commanded the loyalty of so many people.

One of the interesting things about the missionary movement is that young people have frequently led it. In 1806 a group of college students at Williams College in Massachusetts had the vision of telling people across the seas the good news about God. The great missionary work of the nineteenth century in the United States can be traced to a prayer meeting held in that year at a haystack near the college campus by Samuel J. Mills and other students. At the end of that century, other students formed the Student Volunteer Movement and with great enthusiasm went out to try to evangelize the world in one generation.

One of the great new facts in the life of the church today is the existence of strong churches in many areas of the world where there were no churches 200 years ago. In fact, many of these churches now send missionaries to other lands. Some of their great preachers, like D. T. Niles of Sri Lanka (Ceylon) have preached in America. New churches thus are sending missionaries back to the countries from which missionaries first came to them.

Rapid changes in transportation and in communication have brought about great changes in the ways Christians proclaim the gospel. Airplanes and radios have made old methods out of date. The intense nationalism in many new nations has brought about changes in missionary methods. Today missionaries urge people to take responsibility for the support and management of their own congregations as soon as possible. Thus the missionary helps the new church assume responsibility for the work.

CHECK YOUR UNDERSTANDING

1. What passages in the Bible tell us that the church is to serve?
2. What does "evangelism" mean? How do we do the work of evangelism?
3. How widespread is the Christian faith in the world? What part have young people had in the missionary movement in America?
4. What new facts have brought about changes in the way the church carries out its mission?
5. Consider questions 1–3 under "For Discussion" and items 1–8 under "For Action" on pages 168–170.

The Church Teaches

In addition to telling people the good news about God, the church also teaches people about God and his will for their lives. This is another way in which the church serves God, and by serving God serves people and the world. Presbyterian and Reformed Christians have always emphasized the importance of teaching.

They have believed that it is important for believers to know what they believe and why they believe it.

It is important that we know the facts about our faith and the church. We need to know the Bible; that is, we need to know what is in it and how to use it. We need to know something about the history of the church. The secularization of our society which has no commitment to Christian faith means the church must do more in the way of teaching than was true a few decades ago. Much of the Bible and many facts about Christian faith were learned in the public schools and in society generally. This is no longer true. It is almost impossible to be a Christian, much less to grow in the faith, without some knowledge of the Bible, of church history, and of theology.

It is important also that the church should teach us more than facts, as necessary as they are. It must also teach us to think as Christians.

What does it mean to think as Christians? Christians do not use a different logic from that used by other people. Their minds do not work any differently from the minds of others. But they do find that the revelation of God in Jesus Christ gives them a clue, an insight for interpreting, understanding, and making sense out of what is happening in their lives and in the world.

Suppose you are confronted with a decision about how to treat another person. In making this decision you will need the facts which are available to all. But there is something else that you as a Christian will need to take into account: this other person is a child of God. (The non-Christian may believe that a person is little more than an animal, a unit of production, or an accident in the history of the universe.) In making your decision about how to treat your neighbor, the fact that you are a Christian makes a great deal of difference.

The great purpose of Christian teaching is to help people make their decisions and form their opinions in the light of what Jesus Christ has revealed about God. It is important that you learn to think as Christians as you decide whether you will join a club, how you are going to behave on a date, what you are going to do as your lifework. It is important that you learn to think as a Christian as you form opinions about the great issues of the day—in energy problems, in environmental issues, in war and peace, in everything.

CHECK YOUR UNDERSTANDING

1. What is the great purpose of Christian teaching?

The Church Relieves Suffering

Christians have always been convinced that the relief of human suffering is a service of God. One of the notable things that Jesus did was to relieve human suffering and pain. The concern to relieve suffering has always been a characteristic of Christian people when they have been true to their faith.

In the ancient church, the congregation had congregational suppers to which the poor could come to get food. As the church grew, this was no longer possible. The church had to devise other ways. Today Christians in America send every year through Church World Service millions of dollars' worth of food to people who do not have enough to eat.

The church has also been concerned with sickness and pain as well as with hunger. The churches have established hospitals. They have sent out doctors and nurses as well as preachers to minister to those in need around the world. Among the great missionary doctors have been Wilfred Grenfell of Labrador and Albert Schweitzer of Africa.

There are other ways in which the church has sought to relieve human suffering. The church has built homes for children who have no home and for the aging who can no longer manage their own homes. You can probably think of additional ways in which the church has helped people in need.

Today the government and other organized groups have taken over many of the tasks which used to belong to the church. The government provides for the needs of those who are out of work and for those who cannot afford the medical care they need. The government builds great hospitals. New forms of insurance give many people protection against sickness and unemployment and old age. Some regret that this work of the church has now been taken over

by the government so completely. But most Christians are glad for
human suffering to be relieved in any way possible. Help given by
the government and other groups frees the church to discover new
ways to relieve human suffering and to minister to human needs.

CHECK YOUR UNDERSTANDING

1. How has the church tried to relieve human suffering?
2. How do government and other organized groups help relieve
   suffering?

The Church Faces Social Issues

The church also serves God by proclaiming God's will for
human life and community. Prophecy, as you probably know, has to
do not so much with the prediction of things to come as with the
proclamation of God's will for human life now. A brief review of the
book of Amos will show what is meant by a prophetic ministry.
Amos, you remember, called upon his nation, his society, to obey
the will of God. He saw the judgment of God falling upon Israel for
her sins. (Read Amos 1 and 5:4–24.)

The demand for justice which Amos voiced is also found in the
writing of Micah. Religious ceremonies and rites are no substitute
for justice. (Read Micah 6:6–8.)

One of the great services which the church renders today is
keeping alive a Christian conscience. The church does this in many
ways. One is through the Christian conscience of members of the
church. They live as Christians as they conduct their business, as
they vote, as they swim or play tennis, or as they talk over coffee
cups. Sometimes all that is needed to change the outlook of a group
of youth or adults is for one Christian with courage to state his or
her convictions.

Another way the Christian church keeps alive a Christian conscience is through preaching. The preaching which goes on in
thousands of pulpits influences public life far more than most of us
imagine. Think of the sermons which you have already heard, and
see if any of them likely influenced the society in which you live.

A third way in which the church keeps alive a Christian conscience is through public statements on questions which are before society. Your minister may be able to provide you copies of recent statements for your study. There have been statements on such issues as gambling, war, and race relations.

It is important to note that Protestants believe that no statement of the church on any issue is perfect: all that human beings do contains error. These statements are simply declarations of what the church believes is the will of God in this time. But if we take the statements seriously and study them, we may find that they help us to see God's will more clearly.

We must continually remind ourselves that proclaiming God's will is an awesome responsibility and also a very hazardous task. There is always the danger that we shall confuse God's will with our own wills. As a great American theologian once said, our causes are never as righteous and our participation in them never as devoid of self-interest as we think they are. We have to learn to combine confidence in proclaiming God's will with the humility which knows that our understanding of God's will is always corrupted by our own self-interest.

CHECK YOUR UNDERSTANDING

1. What is meant by a prophetic ministry?
2. How does the church keep alive a Christian conscience?
3. Consider items 12–14 under "For Action" on page 170.

The Church Suffers

The church also serves by suffering. This sounds strange to us. Not many of us have ever suffered very much because of being members of the church. Some of us *may* have found that it was not popular to act as a Christian in certain groups and in certain places. But we cannot call this real persecution.

Yet the church has been called to suffer. Even today, it is called to suffer in many places. Young people who participate actively in the life of the church in some Communist countries are being persecuted. They may not be allowed to go to the school they wish to attend. They may not be given the job which they want and which they would get if they were not Christians. Their future may be endangered by their being Christians.

Certainly one of the greatest services which the church in such countries can render today is to suffer. Of course, there is no guarantee that, if the church suffers, it will finally win out. It is possible that the church in a particular place will be destroyed. But over and over again the church which has suffered has finally won the day. Time after time, the very fact that the church has been willing to suffer for her Lord has won the loyalty of other people to God.

And, as best we can, we need to enter into the sufferings of fellow Christians around the world. They are bound with us in faith to Christ, and what they suffer matters to us. Paul wrote to the Christians at Colossae, ". . . I rejoice in my sufferings for your sake, and in my flesh I complete what is lacking in Christ's afflictions for the sake of his body, that is, the church . . ." (Col. 1:24). Is the note of suffering being sounded in our service of Christ today?

CHECK YOUR UNDERSTANDING

1. How is suffering a service to the world?

The Church in the World

The church serves by being what it is, the church of Jesus Christ in the world. W. A. Visser't Hooft of the World Council of Churches has said that the great task of the church in our day is to show to the world that the church exists. We render our greatest service by simply being the church. It is easy for the church to become another club, another organization. It is easy to become like all other organizations. Only that church which is truly the church serves the purposes of God for the world.

Someone may protest, "But the church can always be clearly seen." In some senses this is true. The building is always seen. The members of the church can always be seen doing things with one another. The church as an organization is always seen. But the church as the people of God, as the people who trust God and who live humanely—can we be sure that the church in this sense is always seen? The Westminster Confession of Faith says the church is sometimes more visible, sometimes less visible (chapter XXVII). This is true of every church, isn't it? Isn't the church as the people of God sometimes more, sometimes less visible in your own congregation? The church serves by being visible.

We sometimes talk about going from the church to the world. Or we talk about coming out of the world into the church. When we talk this way, we may have fallen into the habit of thinking that the church somehow is outside the world. But when we really think about the matter, it becomes clear that *the church is in the world.* There is nowhere else for it to be. And this, we believe, is where God wants it to be.

For one thing, the church is where church members are. If a Christian is on the playground, the church is there. If a Christian is in the schoolroom, the church is there. If a Christian goes to a party, the church is there. The people are the church; and wherever they are, there the church is.

One of our great temptations is to divide life into compartments. Here is the church in one compartment, and there is the world in another. We refuse to mix the two. While we are in the one, we live piously. While we are in the other, we live according to the standards of the playground, the party, or the crowd we are in. Sometimes we limit the church to the realm of mystery. Religion has to do with those areas which we do not fully understand. It has to do with the origin of the world and with what happens after death. But some people seem to think it doesn't have anything to do with those things that we know more about. Life cannot be so completely divided into compartments, can it?

We serve God not simply when we say our prayers or think about the great mysteries of life. We serve God also when we study science or read history or decide what we are going to do tomorrow or plan for courtship and marriage. Jesus Christ is Lord of all of life, and Christians are called to serve him in all of life.

Of course, it is possible for the church to be worldly in a bad sense. This false kind of worldliness is what Paul had in mind when he wrote to the Christians at Rome, "Do not be conformed to this world . . ." (Rom. 12:2). This is the kind of worldliness which makes the church just like any club or just like the world. This is the worldliness of church groups which have non-Christian views on justice and on fair treatment for all people and on our need to help those who are in need. This is the worldliness which trusts money more than God, which regards social status as more important than faith and love, which thinks that having a good time and living a comfortable life are the highest ends of human existence. Church offices and organizations can be just as worldly as business offices and organizations. We have too much of this kind of worldliness in the church, don't we?

But there is another sort of worldliness, a holy worldliness. This is the worldliness which believes that this world is God's world. This is the worldliness which believes that God wants us to serve him in the world. This is the worldliness which believes that Christian faith is important in science, in politics, in courtship, in marriage, in daily work, and in every area of life. This is the worldliness which believes that Christian faith is important, not simply when we are dying or when we are praying in private or in the church, but also in the most public and worldly places of our life. This is the worldliness that belongs to the church that serves its Lord in every area of life in the world.

CHECK YOUR UNDERSTANDING

1. Is the church always visible?
2. What is the false kind of worldliness? What is holy worldliness?

Explore and Undertake

For Discussion

1. How does the careless way in which some Christians live handicap the church in its work of evangelism?
2. Do you think that if we are Christlike, others will want to be Christians? Why are *some* people repelled or made angry by Christlike acts?
3. What do you think members of new churches in Asia and Africa have to tell us about the Christian faith?

4. How can you help your church school do a better job of teaching the Christian faith?
5. Why is it important to think as a Christian? How does your church help you think as a Christian?
6. What are the needs in your community which your congregation could meet? Are there new opportunities for the church to serve in your community?
7. Have you heard of people in the United States who are being called on to suffer because of their faith? Do you sometimes risk being rejected by the group in order to be true to what you believe?
8. What would you do if you lived in a land where Christian worship was outlawed?
9. Is your church sometimes invisible in your community?
10. Is the church too much like other organizations?
11. Can you keep religion separate from some areas of life? Should you try?
12. Can you find both false and holy worldliness in your life? In your congregation?

For Action

1. Study Matthew 25:31–46. What does this passage say about how we may best serve Christ?
2. With the help of your pastor, find out if a new congregation or congregations has been established in your presbytery or classis in the past five years. Put in your notebook a brief account of the progress they have made.
3. Find out what your denomination is doing in the field of national (home) missions. Your pastor could give you the name of the board or agency equipped to help you do this.
4. Find out through your denomination's board of world missions what your church is doing in the field of world missions. In what countries is this board at work? What services is it rendering?
5. Write out in your notebook a biography of William Carey or Adoniram Judson. There is material about Carey on pages

189–191 of Langford's *Fire Upon the Earth* and on pages 174–179 of Bowie's *Men of Fire;* and of Judson, on pages 179–184 of Bowie's book. Who are some of the great missionaries of your denomination? Of your own congregation?

6. Learn by contacting your denomination's missions boards the type of workers that are now needed in the church's work in missions. Look at yourself, your own abilities and interests, in the light of what you have learned. Is there a place in the church's missions program for you? Keep this in mind as you approach the time of decision about your lifework.

7. Look at one of the following filmstrips: "Adoniram Judson (America's First Missionary)"; "Frank Laubach (The World's Reading Teacher)"; "Albert Schweitzer (Jungle Missionary)"; or "Toyohiko Kagawa (God's Man in Japan)." Act out in the group a scene included in the filmstrip, and discuss the meaning of the work each of these missionaries did.

8. Find out from your pastor if there is some project, related to your denomination's work in world missions, your group might undertake.

9. Make a list of persons serving in your church school. Let members of your group write a letter to each one of them, expressing appreciation for their work and recognizing its importance.

10. Does your congregation take part each spring in "One Great Hour of Sharing," a program related to the work of Church World Service? "A Matter of Fact" and "On the Move" are filmstrips that tell the story of CWS's ministry to human need. View one of them and talk about the importance of CWS's work.

11. How does your congregation relieve human suffering? your denomination?

12. Study Amos 1 and 5:4–24 and Micah 6:6–8. What do these Scriptures teach about what God expects of us?

13. Memorize Micah 6:8.

14. Secure from your pastor information on pronouncements given in recent years by the General Assembly or General Synod of your denomination on each of the following subjects: race

relations, marriage and divorce, alcoholism, gambling and vice, war and peace, capital punishment, Lord's Day observance, and church-state tensions.

15. Study the hymn, "Where Cross the Crowded Ways of Life." How is it related to the service of the church?

CHAPTER IX

The Church Hopes

The church confesses its faith, worships, obeys, and serves. The church also hopes. Hope, in fact, is one of the great words of the Christian faith. It is one of the words that sets our faith apart from all other religions and faiths. Nowhere else in all the world do we find the hope which we find in Christian faith.

Hope plays a part in the lives of all normal people. Yet many of our hopes are short-ranged and limited. We hope that tomorrow will be better than today. We hope that tomorrow we shall have the money to buy what we do not have money to buy today. We hope that tomorrow we shall have better health or a better job or more friends. But sooner or later these limited and temporary hopes play out. We know that one day we shall die. We know that some problems have no possible solution. And the long-range prospects for human society and for our universe do not appear to be good.

Is there any hope? Christian faith affirms that there is hope. The basis for this hope is the resurrection of Jesus Christ. It is not surprising that the great place of hope in the Christian life is clearest after the disciples had witnessed Christ's resurrection. In raising Jesus Christ from the dead, God demonstrated a power and a mercy greater than death. Here was a power and a mercy strong enough to undo what wicked men had done to Jesus Christ on Good Friday. Read Romans 5:1-5 and 1 Peter 1:3-8 and 21.

The New Testament does not promise us that tomorrow will

necessarily be better for us than today. It *does* assure us that the last fact in the world will be the power and love of God who raised Jesus Christ from the dead. It does assure us that God cares for us. For this reason we trust God with great hope in life and in death. Study carefully Romans 8:28–39.

Hope for a Better World

Let us begin by saying that we hope for a better society, a society in which there is more knowledge of God, more justice, and more love. Christians have always hoped for a better world. This hope, in fact, has been the inspiration of some of the finest lives in the history of the human race. Yet sometimes this hope for a better society has been more enthusiastic than at others.

We now live in a time when human hope for a better world is rather low. Can you think of any reason for our low hopes? Why are Christians not more hopeful of a better world? World War I and World War II, the armaments race and the Cold War, Vietnam, the energy crisis, the mounting birth rate and the scarcity of food in some sections of the world—these facts affect our hopes.

During the first decades of this century people were quite optimistic about the future. This optimism is reflected in such hymns written then as "Thy Kingdom Come, on Bended Knee." You may want to study that hymn. But the hopes then shared were crushed by World War I and by the great depression. People are now more cautious in their hoping. One reason some were disappointed is that they trusted too much in what people themselves could do and were hardly aware of the evil which even good people do.

Christians are not sentimental or utopian about human possibilities. Neither are they cynical, despairing of human goodness. They know that bad people have real possibilities of good in them, and they know that good people are capable of serious evil. Christians strive to be perfect as the Father in heaven is perfect, but they know they always fall short. Christians neither despair of people or problems, nor do they overestimate the goodness of people and the ease with which problems can be solved. Knowing that their salvation rests in God's mercy, they strive as best they can to win the victory by God's grace in their lives and in society. They are glad for progress along the way and for partial solutions to problems that defy final solutions. They know that life is a series of renewals and acts of repentance. Yet real progress can be made in individual life and in society. Christians are realists, taking human sin seriously but not too seriously.

The false grounds of hope have been demolished. It is important that we now build our lives on the sure grounds of Christian hope. This hope is based finally upon what God has done and will do. Almost two hundred years ago Christians despaired of telling all people of the good news of God in Jesus Christ. The modern missionary movement is dated from a sermon which a young man named William Carey then preached on the theme: "Expect great things from God. Attempt great things for God." William Carey knew all of the weaknesses of man, but he knew the power of God in the lives of people. Out of this great hope there developed the missionary movement of the nineteenth century, the really great century in the story of the world mission of the church. Kenneth Latourette, a prominent church historian, has told the story of Christian missions in seven large volumes.[1] Three of the seven are devoted to the missionary movement of the nineteenth century. This story could never have been told if Christians had not hoped, if they had not been optimistic about what God could do in and through the life of human beings.

At the end of the nineteenth century the Student Volunteer Movement, shared in largely by American college students, had these slogans: "The evangelization of the world in this generation" and "All should go and go to all." Of course the world was not evangelized in that generation. But the hope that inspired the students' dream is largely responsible for the fact that the Christian community became the first truly world-wide fellowship and that it exists today all over this planet.

The fact that some of our hopes for a better world have not been fulfilled must not keep us from rejoicing in the hopes which have been in part fulfilled. Certainly we cannot set limits on what the power of God's grace can do in a human life and in human society. Those Christians who have set no limits to what God can do in and through people have been the ones who have done the most to make this a better world in which to live.

Our Christian hope is based upon the power and the love of God. For this reason we dare not set limits on what God can do in an individual life. Some very unpromising people have become great servants of God. We dare not set limits on what God can do in and through the preaching and the witness of the church. The great missionaries always dared to hope what ordinary people were afraid to hope. We dare not set limits on what God, working through dedicated men and women, can do for justice and love in society. Christians of great hope have cleared slums, improved institutions for the mentally ill, abolished child labor, and done many other things that faint-hearted people are afraid to try.

Let us now move from what Christians have hoped for to what *we* hope for. Ask yourself these questions: What do I hope for in my life? What kind of person do I want to be a year from now? Ten years from now? Thirty years from now? Gordon Allport, a prominent psychologist, has said that the most important thing that you can know about a person is that person's intentions for the future. People have a way of becoming what they really want to be. There are few questions which you can ask yourself which are as important as this one: What kind of person do I want to be one, ten, thirty years from now?

Our hopes for society are also important. They shape, in some measure, the kind of world in which we and our children shall live. What do *you* hope for in the church? What do you hope for in your congregation?

CHECK YOUR UNDERSTANDING

1. What is the basis of the hope of the Christian?
2. By what events have the false grounds of hope been demolished?
3. On what is our Christian hope based?

Hope for Resurrection and Christ's Coming

No matter how optimistic our hopes may be for the manifestation of God's grace in human history and on earth, there remains the stark fact of death. All people die. In addition, evidence seems to indicate that there will come a time when the earth will no longer exist. Thus those who take hope in the fact that we live on in those who come after us have to face the fact that death is the end of everything upon this planet. The final day of doom may be a long time off, but it is surely coming.

One test of any faith is this: How does it meet the problem of death? How does Christian faith meet this problem? What does Christian faith have to say in the face of death?

The answer of Christian faith is the hope that God will raise the dead. As the Creed puts it, we believe in the resurrection of the body. As we have already seen, "body" here refers not so much to the chemistry of the body as it does to the person who lives in and expresses himself through a body. It means very much what we mean when we speak of "somebody."

The important points to note are these:

(a) In our belief in the resurrection of the body, we express the hope that our individual, historical lives will be fulfilled, judged, and completed beyond death. We do not hope for some vague, indefinite existence which really is not a continuation of the actual lives which we live now.

(b) We hope for life with God. Someone once commented about his friend on the occasion of his death, "Well, he won't like God." Being in heaven and not liking it — that would be something like hell, wouldn't it? If the resurrection of the body means life with God, then quite clearly some things which may be important to us now will not be important beyond death. It is also quite clear that we hope for a new quality of life as well as the continuation of life. Read and study 1 Corinthians 15.

(c) We hope that God will raise us. As Christians we know that we do not have the power to overcome death. But we believe that God has the power to destroy death and to raise us from the dead.

Christians believe that Jesus Christ will come again at the end of history. We do not know exactly how he will come. It is clear that those who get greatly involved in the details of how he will come always end up in confusion. The important point is that he will come and manifest himself as the Lord of history. But some may protest that this point is not so important. Most of us who are Americans find it difficult to believe that anything is important that is not happening right now. *Why* is the second coming of Jesus Christ important?

It is important because it tells us something about human history. It tells us that history is not going to end in defeat for God. At the end of history, God will still be God. The Jesus who was crucified has been raised from the dead, and he will stand at the end of history as its triumphant Lord and Judge. In other words we know how history is going to come out. When Soviet premier Nikita Khrushchev said that the Russians would bury the Americans, he was expressing his faith that he knew what was going to happen in history. As Christians we believe that Khrushchev was wrong. The final word in history will be the word of Jesus Christ.

Members of the resistance movements during World War II tell us that the promise of the Second Coming meant a great deal to them. It assured them that Hitler did not have the last word in history. They also tell us that they knew that the day would certainly come when Hitler would be defeated. Their experience helped them to understand the meaning of the Second Coming of Christ. Christians, having seen Jesus Christ come in history and win the battle against the forces of evil then, know that when the end comes he will return in triumph.

Belief in the Second Coming of Christ is like being at a ball game and knowing in advance the final score. You have seen the scoreboard. You do not know exactly how the game will be played. You don't know who will make the touchdowns. You don't know who will be in the lead at any particular time. All you know is the final score.

We do not know how history is going to develop. We do not know what is going to happen to the United States or to Russia. There is much that we do not know. But we do know how history is going to end up. We have seen Jesus Christ, and we know that he stands at the end of all history as its Lord and Savior.

Our final word must be the word of Paul. As he thought about the meaning of life, he affirmed his faith in Romans 11:33-36. Read the passage, noting this affirmation: "For from him and through him and to him are all things. To him be glory for ever. Amen" (Rom. 11:36).

CHECK YOUR UNDERSTANDING

1. What is the answer of the Christian faith to the fact of death?
2. What does "the resurrection of the body" mean?
3. Why is the doctrine of the Second Coming of Christ important?
4. With what confidence may we look forward to the end of history?
5. Consider questions 6-10 under "For Discussion" and items 3-7 under "For Action" below.

Explore and Undertake

For Discussion

1. What factors that are currently a part of the life of this country and of the life of the world lead us to despair instead of hope?
2. What basis is there for hope for a better life in this country a generation from now? In what does a better life consist?
3. What basis is there for hope for a better life in the world a generation from now?
4. Name some of the achievements of the modern missionary movement.
5. What are your hopes for your life? for the life of your congregation? for the life of the church in the world?
6. Does a person's beliefs about what happens after death have a bearing on life?
7. What is the difference between the Christian view of history and the Communist view?
8. Suppose that tomorrow a nuclear war were to begin and were to result in the destruction of all human life in the world. Would that be the end of you? of the church?
9. Would you want to sing such hymns as the following at the funeral of a friend? Why? "Praise Ye the Lord, the Almighty"; "A

Mighty Fortress Is Our God"; "Now Thank We All Our God";
"How Firm a Foundation"; "Thine Is the Glory"; and "Come,
Christians, Join to Sing."
10. What do you consider the most important insights you have
gathered in this course?

For Action

1. Study the hymn "God Is Working His Purposes Out." What
encouragement does this hymn give for the working out of
God's purposes in history?
2. Write an essay on the subject, "If Christ Had Not Risen from
the Dead." Put it in your notebook.
3. Using an encyclopedia, find out what Buddhists, Hindus,
Mohammedans, and Communists believe about life after death.
In parallel columns, answer the following questions about each
way of viewing the meaning of life: (a) Do persons of this faith
hope for life after death? (b) If not, what to them is the goal of
life? (c) In what way may individuals achieve the goal of life? (d)
Will individual personality continue?
4. What kind of country would you like the United States to be
twenty-five years from now?
5. Let each member of the group prepare and put in a notebook an
essay on the subject "My Church," including in it the main insights received in the study of this course in the Covenant Life
Curriculum.
6. Study the belief of your denomination about life after death.
The following references may help you: for members of the Associate Reformed Presbyterian Church and the Presbyterian
Church in the United States, chapter XXXIV of The Westminster Confession of Faith and questions 37-38 of The Westminster Shorter Catechism; for members of the Cumberland
Presbyterian Church, sections 118-121 of the Confession of
Faith and questions 39-40 in the Catechism; for members of the
Moravian Church of America, question 40 in the Catechism;
and for members of the Reformed Church in America, question 1 in The Heidelberg Catechism.
7. Memorize Romans 8:38-39.

APPENDIX

A BRIEF STATEMENT OF BELIEF*

ADOPTED MAY, 1962, BY THE GENERAL ASSEMBLY OF THE PRESBYTERIAN CHURCH IN THE UNITED STATES

GOD AND REVELATION

The Word of God

The living and only true God has made himself known to all mankind through nature, mind, conscience, and history. He has especially revealed himself and his purpose for man in the variety of ways recorded in the Old and New Testaments. The Bible, as the written Word of God, sets forth what God has done and said in revealing his righteous judgment and love, culminating in Christ. The Spirit of God who inspired the writers of Scripture also illumines readers of Scripture as they seek his saving truth. The Bible calls men to an obedient response to the Gospel and is the supreme authority and indispensable guide for Christian faith and life.

God

God has revealed himself as the Creator, Sustainer, and Ruler of all that exists. In the exercise of his sovereign power in creation, history, and redemption, God is holy and perfect, abundant in goodness, and the source of all truth and freedom. He is just in his dealings with all the world; he requires that men live and act in justice; and he visits his wrath on all sin. He is gracious and merciful and does not desire that any should perish. Both his judgments and his mercies are expressions of his character as he pursues his redemptive purposes for man.

*© Stated Clerk of the General Assembly of the Presbyterian Church in the United States 1965. Used by permission.

God is personal and he reveals himself as the Trinity of Father, Son, and Holy Spirit. It is the witness of the

Trinity

Scriptures, confirmed in Christian experience, that the God who creates and sustains us is the God who redeems us in Christ, and the God who works in our hearts as the Holy Spirit; and we believe that this threefold revelation manifests the true nature of God.

MAN AND SIN

God created man in his own image. As a created being, man is finite and dependent upon his Creator. Man

The
Image
of God

can distinguish between right and wrong, and is morally responsible for his own actions. He reflects the image of God insofar as he lives in obedience to the will of God. A unique creature standing both within nature and above it, he is placed by God in authority over the world. It is, therefore, his responsibility to use all things for the glory of God. Although made in the image of God, man has fallen; and we, like all mankind before us,

Original Sin

sin in our refusal to accept God as sovereign. We rebel against the will of God by arrogance and by despair. We thrust God from the center of life, rejecting divine control both of human life and the universe. From this perversity arises every specific sin, whether of negligence, perfunctory performance, or outright violation of the will of God.

Sin permeates and corrupts our entire being and burdens us more and more with fear, hostility, guilt and

Total
Depravity

misery. Sin operates not only within individuals but also within society as a deceptive and oppressive power, so that even men of good will are unconsciously and unwillingly involved in the sins of society. Man cannot destroy the tyranny of sin in himself or in his world; his only hope is to be delivered from it by God.

CHRIST AND SALVATION

God, loving men and hating the sin which enslaves them, has acted for their salvation in history and espe-

The Gospel:
Incarnation

cially through his covenant people. In the fullness of time, he sent his only, eternally begotten Son, born of the Virgin Mary. As truly God and truly man, Jesus Christ enables us to see God as he is and man as he ought to be. Through Christ's life, death, resurrection, and ascension, God won for man the decisive victory over sin *and* and death and established his Kingdom among men. *Atonement* Through Christ, bearing on the cross the consequences of our sin, God exposed the true nature of sin as our repudiation of God. Through Christ, bearing on the cross the guilt of our sin, God forgives us and reconciles us to himself. By raising his Son from the dead, God conquers sin and death for us.

God has an eternal, inclusive purpose for his world, which embraces the free and responsible choices of man *The Sovereign* and everything which occurs in all creation. This pur- *Purpose of* pose of God will surely be accomplished. In executing *God and* his purpose, God chooses men in Christ and calls forth *Election* the faith which unites them with Christ, releasing them from bondage to sin and death into freedom, obedience, and life. Likewise God in his sovereign purpose executes judgment upon sinful man.

Man cannot earn or deserve God's salvation but receives it through faith by the enabling power of the Holy *Justification* Spirit. In faith, man believes and receives God's promise *by Faith* of grace and mercy in Christ, is assured of his acceptance for Christ's sake in spite of his sinfulness, and responds to God in grateful love and loyalty.

In repentance, man, through the work of the Holy Spirit, recognizes himself as he is, turns from his sin, and *Repentance* redirects his life increasingly in accordance with God's *and* will. The Christian life is a continuing process of growth *Sanctification* which reaches its final fulfillment only in the life to come.

THE CHURCH AND THE MEANS OF GRACE

The true Church is the whole community, on earth and in heaven, of those called by God into fellowship with him and with one another to know and do his will. As the body of Christ, the Church on earth is the instrument through which God continues to proclaim and apply the benefits of his redemptive work and to establish his Kingdom.

The Church in the world has many branches, all of which are subject to sin and to error. Depending on how closely they conform to the will of Christ as head of the Church, denominations and congregations are more or less pure in worship, doctrine, and practice. The Presbyterian Church follows scriptural precedent in its representative government by elders (presbyters). These elders govern only in courts of regular gradation. The form of government of a church, however, is not essential to its validity. The visible church is composed of those who profess their faith in Jesus Christ, together with their children.

The Form of the Church

Through the Church, God provides certain means for developing the Christian mind and conscience and for maturing faith, hope, and love. Primary among these means are the preaching, teaching, and study of the Word; public and private prayer; and the sacraments.

The Means of Grace

The Bible becomes a means of grace through preaching, teaching, and private study, as the Holy Spirit speaks to human needs and reveals the living Word of God who is Jesus Christ. It illuminates man's thought and experience as it provides an occasion for the Holy Spirit's work of redemption and as it testifies to the working of God, but it is not intended to be a substitute for science and inquiry. In preaching and teaching, the Church proclaims and interprets the mighty acts of God in history and seeks to relate them to every phase of human life. The prayerful and diligent study of the Scripture guides the Christian in his relationships with God and his fellow man, and in his personal life.

The Bible

Christian prayer is communion with God in the name of Jesus Christ through the inspiration and guidance of the Holy Spirit. In prayers, alone or with others, we acknowledge God's greatness and goodness, confess our sins, express our love to him, rejoice in his blessings, present out needs and those of others, receive from him guidance and strength, and joyfully dedicate ourselves to his will. To pray in the name of Christ, our Mediator, is not to repeat a formula, but to trust his redemptive work, to ask for his intercession, to depend upon his presence with us and to desire what he has taught us to value and believe.

Prayer

Christ gave to the Church through his apostles the

The
Sacraments

sacraments of Baptism and the Lord's Supper as visible signs and assurances of the Gospel. Baptism sets forth, by the symbolic use of water, the cleansing and regenerating love of God through the work of the Holy Spirit; in this sacrament we and our children are assured that we are members of the covenant family of God, and are publicly accepted into fellowship with Christ and his Church. The Lord's Supper sets forth, by the symbolic use of bread and wine, the death of Christ for our salvation; in this sacrament we have communion with the risen Christ, who gives himself to us as we receive in faith the bread and wine for the nourishment of our Christian life. Being assured of his forgiving and sustaining love, we renew our dedication and enjoy fellowship with the whole people of God. The Lord's table is open to members of all churches who have publicly professed Jesus Christ as Saviour and Lord and who come in penitence and faith.

CHRISTIAN LIFE AND WORK

Vocation

Each Christian is called to be a servant of God in all of life, so that we must seek God's will for the work we do and for the manner in which we do it. Christian vocation may be found in any work where our own abilities and interests best meet the legitimate needs of God's world. The Church is charged under God with the obligation to seek out the most responsible and effective Christian leadership. It is the special role of the ordained ministry, including elders and deacons, to perform particular services in the life of the Church and to strengthen every Christian in the discharge of the responsibilities of the priesthood of all believers in the Church and the world. For the Christian, all life becomes significant as he does his daily work with dedication and diligence out of love for God and for his neighbor.

Social
Responsibility

The range of Christian responsibility is as wide as human life. The Christian must recognize, but not accept as inevitable, the world as it is, distorted and torn by sin. Christians as individuals and as groups have the right and the duty to examine in the light of the Word of God the effects on human personality of social institutions and practices. As servants of the sovereign will of God, Christians are under obligation to their fellow men and to unborn generations to shape and influence these institutions and practices so that the world may be brought more nearly into conformity with the purpose of God for his creation. The Church's concern for the reign of God in the world is essential to its basic responsibility both for evangelism and for Christian nurture.

Providence and Suffering

We believe that our destiny and that of the world are not subject to chance or fate, but to the just and loving sovereignty of God. In this assurance we face the problems of suffering and evil. Faith in the purpose and providence of God assures us of his presence in suffering and of his power to give it meaning. We are confident that no form of evil can separate us from the love of God, that God works in all things for good, and that evil will ultimately be overcome. Therefore, while we cannot fully understand the pain and evil of the present world, we can offer ourselves as active instruments of God's will in their conquest.

JUDGMENT AND THE LIFE TO COME

Eternal life is the gift of God. We are assured by the promises of the Gospel, by our relation to Christ, and by his resurrection that death does not put an end to personal existence, but that we too shall be raised from the dead. Those who have accepted the forgiving love of God in Christ enter into eternal life in fellowship with God and his people. This new life begins in the present world and is fulfilled in the resurrection of the body and the world to come. Those who have rejected the love of God bring upon themselves his judgment and shut themselves outside the fellowship of God and his people.

Resurrection

Return of Christ and God's Triumph

As Christ came once in humility, he will return in glory for the final judgment and for the consummation of his universal Kingdom. The work and promises of Jesus Christ give assurance that the age-long struggle between sin and grace will in God's good time have an end; all the power of evil will be destroyed, and God's holy, wise, and loving purposes will be accomplished.

Bibliography

General

John H. Leith. *Introduction to the Reformed Tradition.* Atlanta: John Knox Press, 1977.

John T. McNeill. *The History and Character of Calvinism.* New York: Oxford University Press, 1967.

I. The Church in the Bible

R. Newton Flew. *Jesus and His Church.* London: The Epworth Press, 2nd Edition, 1943.

II. The Church Particular and Catholic

Claude Welch. *The Reality of the Church.* New York: Charles Scribner's Sons, 1958.

Emil Brunner: *The Christian Doctrine of the Church, Faith and the Consummation.* Philadelphia: The Westminster Press, 1962.

———. *Revelation and Reason.* Philadelphia: The Westminster Press, 1946. Excellent chapters on Christian faith and religions.

III. The Church Protestant

John S. Whale. *The Protestant Tradition.* Cambridge: University Press, 1955.

IV. The Church Reformed and Presbyterian

G. D. Henderson. *Presbyterianism.* Aberdeen: The University Press, 1954.

V. The Church Confesses Its Faith

J. N. D. Kelly. *Early Christian Creeds.* New York: David McKay Company, 1971, 3rd Edition.

Gordon Allport. *The Individual and His Religion, a Psychological Interpretation.* New York: Macmillan, 1950.

VI. The Church Obeys

Bernard S. Childs. *The Book of Exodus.* Philadelphia: Westminster Press, 1974. Excellent discussion of the Ten Commandments.

Eduard Schweizer. *The Good News According to Matthew.* Atlanta: John Knox Press, 1975. Commentary on Matthew 5—7 and excellent summary of views on Sermon on the Mount.

Amos Wilder. "The Sermon on the Mount" in *The Interpreters Bible,* Volume VII. Nashville: Abingdon, 1951.

Joachim Jeremias. *The Sermon on the Mount.* Philadelphia: Fortress Press, 1963.

James Gustafson. *Can Ethics Be Christian?* Chicago: University of Chicago Press, 1975.

VII. The Church Worships

James H. Nichols. *Corporate Worship in the Reformed Tradition.* Philadelphia: Westminster Press, 1968.

VIII. The Church Serves

Hendrik Kraemer. *A Theology of the Laity.* Philadelphia: Westminster Press, 1958.

Karl Barth. *Church Dogmatics* IV, 3,2, pp. 830–901. Edinburgh: T. and T. Clark.

IX. The Church Hopes

Daniel Day Williams. *God's Grace and Man's Hope.* New York: Harper, 1949.

John Baillie. *And the Life Everlasting.* New York: C. Scribner's Sons, 1933.

John Macquarrie. *Christian Hope.* London: Mobrary, 1978.

Audio-Visual Resources*

OTHER RELIGIONS

Films: *The American Experience: Religious Diversity.* BFA Educational Media, producer, 1976. Released by Materials Distribution Service, Atlanta. 18 min., col., sd., $22.00. Through this film, we meet young people involved in seven of America's major religious groups, and viewers will be able to observe some of the differences and similarities that exist within America's religious diversity. (Junior High, Senior High, Adult)

Four Religions. National Film Board of Canada, pro-

---

*This list of audio-visual resources was compiled by Eleanor Godfrey.

ducer, 1962. Released by Materials Distribution Service, Atlanta. 54 min., b/w, sd., $10.00. Basic origins and beliefs of Islam, Hinduism, Buddhism, and Christianity are presented through live action, artwork, architecture, and literature. (Senior High, Adult)

Major Religions of the World. Encyclopaedia Britannica Films, 1954. Released by Materials Distribution Service, Atlanta. 20 min., col., sd., $10.00. Presents an objective survey of origins, rituals, and symbols of Buddhism, Christianity, Hinduism, Judaism, and Islam. (Senior High, Adult)

The Long Search Series. British Broadcasting Corp., producer. Released by Time-Life Multimedia, 1977, 52 min. each, col., sd., $100.00. (Check your public library.) No. 1 Protestant Spirit USA; No. 2 Hinduism: 330 Million Gods; No. 3 Buddhism: Footprint of the Buddha—India; No. 4 Catholicism: Rome, Leeds and the Desert; No. 5 Islam: There Is No God But God; No. 6 Orthodox Christianity: The Rumanian Solution; No. 7 Judaism: The Chosen People; No. 8 Religion in Indonesia: The Way of the Ancestors; No. 9 Buddhism: The Land of the Disappearing Buddha—Japan; No. 10 African Religions: Zula Zion; No. 11 Taoism: A Question of Balance—China; No. 12 Alternative Life Styles in California: West Meets East; No. 13 Reflections on the Long Search. (Youth, Adult)

Filmstrip: *Comparative Religion.* Time-Life Multimedia, producer, col., guide, $7.00 each. Part I—Hinduism, Part II—Buddhism, Part III—Confuciansim and Taoism, Part IV—Islam, Part V—Judaism, Part VI—Christianity. (Youth, Adult)

Tape: Marty, Martin E. *The New Religions.* 1 cassette. Thomas More Associates, 1973.

CHURCH AND SOCIAL DIVERSITY

Films: *Faith in Action.* Johnson-Nyquist Productions, producer. Materials Distribution Service, Atlanta, distributor, 28 min. col., sd., $25.00. Television documentary presenting the testimonies of a variety of people from widely different walks of life, relating the relevance of their faith to their daily activities. (Junior High, Senior High, Adult)

Film: *Roadsigns on a Merry-Go-Round.* CBS News, producer, 1968. Mass Media Ministries, distributor, 56 min., col., sd., $25.00. An intricate course is steered through the vast and complex thought forms of Martin Buber, Teilhard de Chardin, and Dietrich Bonhoeffer with their writings poetically rhapsodized in a beautiful statement of ecumenical faith, while a modern day husband and wife struggle to find answers to doubts and perplexities that characteristically interfere with a sense of wholeness in the 1960s and 1970s. Rich collages of scenery from the NOW world provide exciting visual contrasts and mind-blowing points of linkage to the theological visions being explored. Youth, the poor, the minorities, the starving, the aged, the distressed, and the boiling pot of modern urban society play their parts in this cinematic panorama. (Adult)

These Four Cozy Walls. TRAFCO, producer, 1968. Mass Media Ministries, distributor, 54 min., b/w, sd., $20.00. The story of what the Casa View Methodist Church of Dallas, Texas, does to update itself should be appreciated as part of the churchmanship training of every active member of the Christian community. Surrendering the opportunity to be a large white prestige suburban parish, they put their energies into pioneer types of inner city ministries, ones that often necessitate economic, civic, political, and social service involvement. The story of a church congregation engaged in worship and work in many varied forms, necessitating a split and withdrawal of many conservatives. (Youth, Adult)

Church in the World. Paul Keller, Kairos, producer and director. Materials Distribution Service, distributor, 20 min., col., sd., $20.00. Imaginative use of modern cinema technique shows the beauty and squalor of the world as it really is and applies the gospel to the needs of the world. (Youth, Adult)

CHURCH CONFESSIONS/CREEDS

Game: *A.D. 325.* John Washburn, producer. Simulation Games Center, 221 Willey Street, Morgantown, WV 26505, distributor, $2.00. A simulation of the Council of Nicea. Participants produce a creed. (Youth, Adult)

Filmstrip: *The Council of Nicaea.* United Church Press, producer, 1964, 111 fr., col., record, 26 min., script, $17.20. Augsburg Publishing House, distributor. A documentary providing background, personalities, and decisions of the Council. (Senior High, Adult)

CHURCH HISTORY

Film: *The Presbyterians.* ABC-TV News and United Presbyterian Church, U.S.A., producers, 1974. Presbyterian Film Distribution Centers, distributor, 28 min., col., sd., $5.00. Through rare filmclips and photos in settings historic and modern, this film ties together four centuries of ministry and mission. The post-1861 period focuses on the UPCUSA. (All ages)

Filmstrip: *A Family Portrait: We the Presbyterians.* Joint Committee on Presbyterian Union, 1974. Materials Distribution Service, distributor, 99 fr., col., cassette, 15 min., $5.00. The story of the Presbyterian Church from its early days to the divisions with a look at some of the work Presbyterians are doing together today. (All ages)

Game: *Covenanters.* James H. Adams, producer and distributor, 9443 Brett Lane, Columbia, MD 21045, 1975, instruction sheet, playing board, six tokens, 1 history paper, 1 numbers page, $2.00. Provides resources for learning Presbyterian history and history makers such as John Calvin, John Knox, Francis Makemie, Charles Briggs and the Westminster Assembly, the American Synod, First Assembly, schisms, and doctrines. (Youth, Adult)

Filmstrip: *Journey from Our Beginning.* Explorations into Faith Audio-Visual Kit, Geneva Press, 1977, 47 fr., col., cassette, $10.00. Materials Distribution Service, Atlanta, distributor.

PRESBYTERIAN POLITY

Filmstrip: *Presbyterian Polity Filmstrip Set.* Part 1: Road Map 45 fr., col., cassette (7½ min.), script. Part 2: But, What Makes It Tick? 44 fr., col., cassette (6½ min.), script. TRAV, Presbyterian Church, U.S., Heritage Series, 1977, $6.00. Presentation of Presbyterian form of church government as distinguished from other forms and a description of a local church government with special emphasis on the qualifications and duties of church officers. (Youth, Adult)

SACRAMENTS

Film: *Eucharist.* Franciscan Communications Center, 197?, producers and distributors, 1229 South Santee Street, Los Angeles, CA 90015, 10 min., col., sd., $15.00. Illustrates that faith is not only a belief in the presence of Christ in the symbols of the liturgy, but also in inner realization of Christ's incarnational and redemptive presence in every aspect of human life. (Junior High, Adult)

Film: *Baptism.* Family Films, producer, 1976. Materials Distribution Service, distributor, 17 min., col., sd., $16.00. Tracing the 2,000-year-old Christian rite back to its biblical beginnings, the film explores the mode and meaning of Christian baptism as practiced in five different Protestant traditions. (All ages)

Filmstrip: *The Sacraments.* Explorations into Faith Audio-Visual Kit, Geneva Press, 1977, 46 fr., col., cassette, $10.00. Materials Distribution Service, Atlanta, distributor.

Filmstrip: *The Last Supper.* Bauman Bible Telecasts, 3436 Lee Highway, No. 200, Arlington, VA 22207, producer and distributor, 1975, 104 fr., col., cassette (20 min.), script, $24.50. Uses 30 classic paintings of the Last

Supper by da Vinci, Velazquez, Dali, Rubens, and others. (Youth, Adult)

PERSONAL FAITH

Film: *Do You Ever Wonder?* Johnson-Nyquist Productions, producer. Materials Distribution Service, distributor, 11 min., col., sd., $15.00. Provocative illustrations of four contemporary songs to explore personal relationships. Who am I? Who am I with others? Who am I with Christ? A discussion-starting film. (Youth)

Film: *In the Son Again.* Family Films, producer, 1976. Materials Distribution Service, distributor, 50 min., col., sd., $42.00. A compelling true-life story of how Christian popular composer/singer/entertainer Verne Bullock struggled to make his personal commitment to Jesus Christ real and authentic. (Youth, Adult)

Film: *From Whom All Blessings Flow.* United Presbyterian Church U.S.A., producer, 1976. Materials Distribution Service, Atlanta, distributor, 12 min., col., sd., $6.50. A film to help you think anew about the meaning of praising and giving as seen in the lives of five members of five congregations. As they drop their offering in the plate, you will see them involved in other activities in their lives which are also ways of praising God and giving of themselves. (Youth, Adult)

Tape: *Young Culture Lifetime Cassette Service.* Bill Wolfe, director. Discipleship Resources, P. O. Box 840, Nashville, TN 37202, distributor. Current information regarding those persons and issues that are influencing and shaping youth, particularly music personalities, their music, philosophies of life, and religious commitments. $5.25 each for Nos. 3 through 28 cassettes or bulk rates. (Youth)

Tape: *Recycle Youth Series.* Dennis C. Benson and Marilyn J. Benson, producers and distributors, P. O. Box 12811, Pittsburgh, PA 15241, $36.00 a year subscription. "Life Style Model" section offers interviews with personalities talking about philosophies of life, theological perspectives, and styles of commitment. (Back issues of the Bensons' *Quest* contain same material) (Youth)

CHURCH CATHOLIC

Film: *Household of Faith.* Broadcasting and Film Commission, National Council of Churches of Christ, U.S.A., producer, 1960. Materials Distribution Service, distributor, 28 min., col., sd., $8.00. Stresses ecumenicity while exploring foreign mission theme—"Into All the World Together." Photographed in India, Africa, and Thailand. (Junior High, Senior High, Adult)

Film: *Behold . . . All Things New.* Lanritz Falk, director. Swedish Television and John Taylor, producers, 27 min., col., sd., $20.00. Mass Media Ministries, distributor. A documentary on the 1968 World Council of Churches Assembly at Upsala, Sweden. Mingled with many leading voices heard there is the overwhelming turmoil, spectacle, fascination, puzzlement, and challenge that the international scene continues to be in the focus of world mission. The impact of media on the Christian Church in "the global village" is dealt with as well as poverty, war, hunger, racism, politics, and universal justice. (Senior High, Adult)

Filmstrip: *The Churches in the 70's.* Alba House Communications, producer and distributor, 1970, 2 filmstrips, col., record, guide, $25.95. Presentation of the Christian faith and worship of representative denominations: Eastern, Roman Catholic, Lutheran, Presbyterian, Episcopal, Methodist, and Baptist Churches. Contains historical data and analyzes the many things they share in common while underscoring their distinct differences. (Junior High, Senior High, Adult)

CHURCH IN THE BIBLE

Game: *Who Can Belong?* New Testament—8 Simulated Activities, No. 6. Jack Schaupp and Donald L. Griggs, producers, 1974. Griggs Educational Service, P. O. Box ⸱362, Livermore, CA 94550, distributor, out-of-print.

(Check Church Resource Centers.) A problem from Acts regarding Gentile converts, pp. 59–76.

Game: "The Council of Jerusalem," pp. 153–162, *Using Biblical Simulations,* Vol. 1, Donald E. Miller, Graydon F. Snyder, and Robert W. Neff. Judson Press, 1973. A simulation based on Acts 15. $4.00. (Youth, Adult)

Games: "The Silversmiths of Ephesus," pp. 187–204, and "The House Church," pp. 205–222, *Using Biblical Simulations,* Vol. 2, Donald E. Miller, Graydon F. Synder, and Robert W. Neff. Judson Press, 1975, $4.00. A simulation based on Acts 19 and a simulation based on the Book of Philemon. (Youth, Adult)

Filmstrip: *Stories of the Early Church.* The Story Our Bible Tells Series, No. 4. Family Films, producer, 39 fr., col., record, 8 min., guide, $13.00. God's redemptive purpose at work through New Testament accounts of the early Christian church, including the ministry of Peter, John, and Phillip, Saul's conversion and some of Paul's missionary adventures.

Filmstrip: *Paul and the Early Church.* Roa Filmstrips, producer, 197? 8 filmstrips, col., 4 records, 8 guides, $160.00. Relates stories of the early church from Pentecost to Paul's imprisonment in Rome.

Filmstrip: *Life of St. Paul.* Cathedral Films. 2 sets, 6 filmstrips each, 6 records each, guides, $59.00 each set or $10.50 per filmstrip. Augsburg Publishing House, distributor.

WORSHIP

Film: *In Breaking Bread.* United Presbyterian Church, U.S.A., producer. Materials Distribution Service, distributor, 16 min., col., sd., $5.00. Designed to facilitate discussion on the use and adaptation of the "Service for the Lord's Day" in the *Worshipbook,* the participation of children, laymen, and women in worship, new and old styles of worship. (Youth, Adult)

Kit: *Worship/Liturgy.* Locke E. Bowman, producer. National Teacher Education Project, 6947 E. MacDonald Drive, Scottsdale, AZ 85253, distributor, 1969,

$10.00. 2 tapes — "The Meaning of Reformed Worship," 27 min.; "How Liturgy Comes into Being," 28 min.; "Liturgy and the Life of the Congregation," 25 min.; "Problems of the Worshippers," 27 min.; 11 transparencies, 9 charts, 10 copies Strasbourg Rite of Geneva, guide.

Kit: *Program on the Sacrament of Baptism.* National Teacher Education Project and Niobrara Presbytery Teacher Tape Task Force, 1971, $8.95. 1 tape, 1 instruction sheet, 10 study sheets.

Kit: *Program on the Sacrament of the Lord's Supper.* National Teacher Education Project and Niobrara Presbytery Teacher Tape Task Force, 1972, $8.95. 1 tape, 1 instruction sheet, 10 study sheets.

Notes

Chapter I

1. G. D. Henderson, *The Scots Confession* (Edinburgh: St. Andrews Press, 1960), p. 62.

Chapter II

1. Catechetical Lectures, XVIII, 23.
2. *The Book of Church Order of the Presbyterian Church in the United States,* p. 23.

Chapter IV

1. James Moffatt, *The Presbyterian Churches* (London: Methuen & Co., Ltd., 1928), p. 2.

Chapter V

1. Dorothy L. Sayers, *Creed or Chaos?* (New York: Harcourt, Brace and World, Inc., 1949), p. 23.
2. Donald Baillie, *God Was in Christ* (New York: Charles Scribner's Sons, 1948), p. 184.

Chapter VI

1. W. H. Auden, *For the Time Being* (New York: Random House, 1944), pp. 123–124.
2. Arthur Koestler, *Darkness at Noon* (New York: The Macmillan Co., 1941), p. 261.
3. J. Edgar Park, *The Interpreter's Bible* (Nashville: Abingdon Press, 1952), Vol. I, p. 989.

Chapter VII

1. *The Book of Church Order of the Presbyterian Church in the United States,* 1963 edition, p. 123.
2. Raymond Abba, *Principles of Christian Worship* (New York: Oxford University Press, 1957), p. 6.
3. Karl Barth, *The Teaching of the Church Regarding Baptism* (London: SCM Press, 1948), p. 60.

Chapter IX

1. Kenneth Scott Latourette, *A History of the Expansion of Christianity* (New York: Harper & Row, 1937–1945).

There was a ho... institution—a h... country beyond.

Little Mike found the hole first—and Pat McGarry followed him through it, an uninvited stranger in Mike's secret world.

That was the beginning of the daily hikes they took together . . . over obstacles that challenged every quality of mind and heart, and through setbacks that came close to destroying all they had gained . . . climbing toward the final dangerous, glorious height that Mike could never hope to reach alone . . .

Here, in a man's caring words and a child's unforgettable drawings, is one of the most moving stories ever to teach you the meaning of triumph. . . .

A SOLITARY DANCE

"Sensitively, poignantly well-written . . . I was immediately caught up . . . I found it difficult to put down."
      —Dr. Carole Carlson,
        Clinical Psychologist and author of
        Your Child is Asleep: Early Childhood Autism

ROBERT LANE, long fascinated by human behavior, received his Ph.D. from the University of Wisconsin, Madison, and worked as a clinical psychologist in various mental institutions and treatment centers in the Midwest. Dr. Lane is now on the faculty of the University of Wisconsin, Oshkosh.

A SOLITARY DANCE

A Novel by

ROBERT LANE

A SIGNET BOOK

NEW AMERICAN LIBRARY

————ACKNOWLEDGMENTS————

My deepest appreciation to my best friend, Mary, who has been nothing short of superb throughout this endeavor; to Ted Solotaroff, a gently supportive editor who lent his considerable skills as this story took shape; and to my six-year-old niece Shelby, who was kind enough to help me with the illustrations.

I am grateful to them, and to the many others who contributed along the way.

———A NOTE ABOUT THIS STORY———

There are thousands of children such as I have described here. Living in groups, homes, treatment centers, mental hospitals across the land, they are called by many names—schizophrenic, emotionally disturbed, autistic. Yet beneath the symptoms that contribute to such diagnoses, one often finds a common denominator: an exquisitely sensitive, confused, lonely youngster. A child who longs not only to be loved, but to be able to love in return.

This story is for each of those special children, and for the people who care for them. It was written with the hope that it will help others have a better understanding of the emotional disorders of childhood.

What I have tried to do is to capture the essence of my experiences, both as a psychotherapist and as a supervising therapist and teacher. Because of that, the story rings true. All of what I have written here, though, is fictitious—the end product of a very active imagination. Hence, any resemblances to real individuals, situations, or institutions are pure and simple coincidence, and nothing more.

*And in the sweetness of friendship let there
be laughter, and sharing of pleasures.
    For in the dew of little things the heart finds
its morning and is refreshed.*

KAHLIL GIBRAN

—————— *chapter one* ——————

Destinies have a way of intertwining, sometimes taking extraordinary turns when least expected. On Michael Harris's fifth birthday, he was committed to the children's unit of a psychiatric hospital. He was still there three years later when I arrived as an intern in clinical psychology. That's how our paths crossed.

Merrick State Hospital is probably the most picturesque of any of the institutions run by California's Division of Mental Hygiene. It lies in a remote mountainous area north of Santa Barbara, straddling a line between the dark fertile hills and valleys of citrus groves that flow down to the coast and the rugged mountains that rise up to the east. There the terrain is desolate enough that only the wiry manzanita brush can survive.

The entrance to the hospital grounds is through two stone pillars set imposingly on each side of the macadam road that curves innocuously back among the hills. Except for the brass plaques inscribed Merrick State Psychiatric Hospital, there is no evidence of an institution.

My first reaction to Merrick was that the site had been chosen by people who regarded mental disorders as something to be hidden from public view. Unless you worked there, or were a patient or visitor, you would hardly suspect that tucked into such pretty countryside were hundreds of mental patients, all of them sufficiently disturbed to be committed and some of them so dangerous that they were kept in a maximum security wing.

The buildings that finally came into sight had high walls of dull yellow brick and red-tiled roofs that created a dramatic contrast to the rolling lawns and blue sky. Yet despite the very tasteful architecture, the manicured grounds and abundant shade trees, the picnic tables and other amenities, the impression lingered that I had entered a modern-day leper colony whose principal function was to quarantine undesirables. Everything appeared to go on indoors. Though the parking lots were filled with cars, there was hardly anyone to be seen. At each intersection white signs with neat black lettering indicated the numbered dormitories, the food service building, a general hospital. It was like a medium-sized college campus. Except that the lack of any visible activity, the silence, were eerie.

At the last intersection, the road left the main hospital grounds and followed a series of bends that led into an off-shoot canyon and the Children's Unit. This was made up of a circle of a half-dozen cottages, plain and functional. There were noticeably more signs of life here—a few youngsters darting about, then a football arching up, only to land on a cottage roof, accompanied by shouts of dismay. On the far side of the quad, beneath the branches of a live oak, a group was gathered around a teacher. From a distance it could have been an ordinary class in any elementary school. Nearby was a small school building, its playground surrounded by a cyclone fence sagging with fatigue. Everything seemed quite commonplace.

The name on the open door matched the one written on the moist paper I was tightly grasping. Not wishing to startle the man who was intently studying a large packet of papers, I knocked lightly on the doorframe. Dr. Scott, the chief psychologist of the Children's Unit, glanced up, his eyes crinkling with a welcoming smile.

"Patrick McGarry, is it?" I nodded and reached for the extended hand. "Call me Scott," he said. "It serves nicely as both my first and last names."

Right away I liked him—a trim man in his middle years with short gray hair brushed haphazardly to one side. He was low-key and informal, his feet resting in a small clearing of an otherwise overflowing desk.

"And how is Warfield, the old warhorse?"

"Fine, he sends his regards." Dr. Warfield, my advisor at Cal State, had arranged for me to spend my yearlong internship on the Children's Unit. He and Scott were old friends; I had heard many stories about their escapades.

After talking for a time, Scott suggested taking a walk around the unit so that I could get my bearings. The warm and direct manner was soon put to the test by a crowd of children who trailed after him as we strolled about the grounds.

"Hi, Dr. Scott—lookit me, lookit me!"

"Hey, Dr. Scott, got any gum?"

"Dr. Scott, Dr. Scott, can I go home this weekend? *Pleeeeeze*? It's my friend's birthday and I'm invited to his party, and I've done all my assignments, and my folks say it's okay with them, and everyone says I've been good all week, and . . ."

He was steadily besieged by youngsters requesting favors, hanging onto him, tugging at his coat, grabbing his hands. With each one he stopped, talked, joked around, once tousling a curly mop to see who was under it and suggesting sheepshears. He listened attentively and patiently to each child and gave firm, unevasive

4

answers—not always the ones the kids wanted to hear, but they seemed to accept even the negative ones. As I watched, my respect for him grew rapidly.

After the first wave of children had been dispatched, Scott motioned to one of the larger cottages and we started across the lawn toward it.

"You know," I said, "I can't help being surprised. For kids who are supposed to be so deeply disturbed that they need hospitalization . . . well, they're not at all what I expected. They don't seem that much different from ordinary kids."

Scott nodded. "They're not . . . generally. But just now you've seen the ones who relate fairly well, the ones who've figured out who signs the home passes and grants other privileges. And they can be pretty good kids if there's something in it for them. But don't let your guard down for a minute. Or be inconsistent with them. That'll set them off every time."

By then we had reached the entrance and Scott turned. "This is the autistic children's ward. Let's go in for a few minutes—I want you to see some of our more difficult cases. Probably more like what you expected."

He flipped through a huge key ring, opened the door, and motioned me in.

Instant, unbelievable chaos.

Scattered about a large tiled room were some

twenty-five children, each in his or her own singular frenzy, but collectively creating a state of pandemonium. Some were spinning like tops, careening recklessly around the room. Others sat on the floor rocking back and forth in awkward, jerky kinds of motions, while others jumped or ran, hurling themselves across the room like unguided missiles. Still others crouched alone in different corners, babbling to themselves or waving splayed fingers before their faces.

A few of the children wore padded mittens and football helmets. They looked odd at first, until one little girl suddenly hit herself on the side of the head five or six times and shrieked, "No, no, NO, *NOOOO!!!*"

Then she ceased as abruptly as she had begun.

Scott touched me on the shoulder and as I turned, a youngster sprinted by me, running full tilt.

"Got to watch yourself here," Scott said.

Then another small boy, no more than five, walked up to me and wrapped his arms around my leg. As I bent down to talk to him, another came and put his arm on my shoulder, trying to burrow his face into my hair.

I tried to talk to the two children, but there was no intelligible response. I recalled reading somewhere that a conversation with an autistic child is like talking to the walls. It's worse. And more unnerving. They just stared right through

6

me. Finally I had to untangle the encircling octopus arms of my new friends. They resisted at first but then moved away, each returning to his own isolated activity.

"These are the really tough ones," Scott said as we left. "The ones we can't seem to reach. You'll be putting in a bit of time here."

Doing what, I wondered. I just couldn't comprehend how young, physically healthy children could act in such grotesque ways. Of course, I had read about infantile autism, but nothing had prepared me for the reality of the actual children—kids who battered themselves, or chewed their lips bloody, or sat immobilized in stiff, awkward postures.

What had life become for them? And what, if anything, could anyone do for them? The realization began to seep in that I would be expected to come up with something. And then a sinking feeling came in an icy wave: It seemed like such a hopeless task. What if I couldn't hack it?

Scott seemed to sense my misgivings and we walked along in silence while I tried to sort through the jumble of images and reactions. For years now I thought I had known what I was going to be getting into. But in my practical experiences at the university clinic, the children had all been capable of interacting on some level at least, and none had been so severely disturbed.

Just as I had begun to regain my composure, Scott slowed, then pointed toward a slight figure standing behind a bush near an adjacent cottage. "Let's go over there, Pat. I want to show you a rather classic example of childhood schizophrenia."

He approached the boy, who was propped rigidly against the brick wall, staring down at the ground.

"Hi, Danny, how're you doing?"

Danny, who looked to be eight or nine years old, slowly raised his head. His dark wavy hair was parted perfectly, each hair fastidiously in place. But it was his deepset eyes that captured my attention; they were a soft moss green, and incredibly remote. Glazed, too, perhaps by an antipsychotic drug. Thorazine, or Mellaril? His eyes turned toward us in a blank stare. Then his arm moved ponderously, almost in slow motion like a robot's, as he withdrew a dirty sheaf of papers from his pocket. In a steady monotone that reminded me of a rocketry engineer's discussion of critical orbital calculations, Danny began to tell us about the mathematical computations that covered some twenty smudged pages. His child's voice seemed strangely incongruous.

"This is the X factor; if you multiply four billion, 300 million, 500 thousand by three hundred and sixty-five you get this figure, and if then for each day you subtract this constant of six million, it will give you the latitude and

8

longitude you need for the computation of the Y factor . . ."

Danny droned on, using familiar words and concepts, but stringing them together in a litany of uncontrolled imagination. Meanwhile he leafed through the pages, some of which were refolded so many times they had the look of parchment. Scott listened for a time, as patiently as if it were their first encounter. None of what Danny was saying made sense but, following Scott's lead, I nodded my head occasionally while glancing at the intense little boy running his ink-stained, pudgy finger across the pages of numbers. I tried to decode the reasoning behind his calculations, but it seemed totally simulated. Such a conspicuously bright youngster—what could have happened to him?

"That looks fine, Danny," Scott finally broke in. "But come on, let's go spend some time with the other children, too, okay?"

He put his arm around the youngster's shoulders. Danny put up no resistance, allowing himself to be guided from the bushes to a group of children sitting on the lawn not far away. Silently he took his place in the circle without seeming to be aware of the others.

As we moved away, Scott said, "Danny came here just six months ago. As you can see, he's very delusional. I wish we could've gotten him sooner—we might've been able to do more for him. . . ."

I looked back at Danny, who had folded his grimy little papers along their familiar creases and was stuffing them back into his pocket. I was suddenly struck by the terrible isolation he must feel; the calculations seemed to be his only conduit to people—and yet no one could understand them.

Scott broke into my thoughts.

"Cottage 4 over there is where we house the younger schizophrenic kids, like Danny."

I glanced at the long low building. It looked like all the others. At the far end, though, the large metal door stood propped open. Scott stopped, rubbing his chin thoughtfully.

"That's odd, the—"

Suddenly, a small hunched figure dashed from the cottage and disappeared behind a low wall.

"What on earth was that?"

"Ah, yes, that explains it," Scott nodded, his gaze sweeping along the wall. "That," and he sighed, "is Merrick's very own feral child. Mike?" he called out.

The top of a head peeked over the wall.

"Hi, Mike—I thought that was you. How are you?"

The head vanished.

I tried to focus on this new shock. "A feral child?"

"Well, it's not much of an exaggeration. He's eight years old, been here for three years, and goes into a frenzy if an adult comes within twenty-five feet of him. Watch him eat sometime. He just wolfs down his food, grunting and making weird sounds—like a wild animal. And I guess every chance he gets, Mike roams the hills back there. We've given up trying to contain him—he can always find a way out." Scott nodded toward the high boundary fence that encircled the compound. Behind it brush-covered hills thrust steeply upward, saw-toothed and scarred by countless rock slides. It looked like formidable terrain.

Just then, out of the corner of my eye I saw another fleeting movement. A head of wildly chopped blond hair appeared, and a pair of intent glistening eyes, alert as a lynx's, were inspecting us again.

I waved.

Once again, the head vanished.

"We're being observed and followed," said Scott. "That's why we call him the Little Shadow. But he never comes any closer. That's what's so frustrating. He'll follow at a distance—you can sense he wants to make contact—yet the minute you try to approach him, he's off like a shot."

I scanned the length of the wall while we stood there a few minutes longer, but the child didn't reappear. Something about his eyes seemed vaguely familiar to me, though. A "feral child"— it seemed fantastic in this century. By the time we reached the administration building, Scott had told me everything he knew about Mike.

*　　*　　*

The next day Scott showed me some diagnostic test reports and outlined my responsibilities. "We'll be rotating you around to the various cottages so you'll have some contact with nearly all of the youngsters and will be able to get a feel for the kinds of treatment programs we have here. There'll be diagnostic reports and progress notes and all the bureaucratic paperwork that the state requires. And later on you'll be doing some admission interviews. For now, though, I want you to give some thought to working with one of the children."

I knew this would be coming eventually, but Scott had caught me by surprise. After what I had seen yesterday, I wasn't at all sure I was ready for it. Suppose I were assigned to one of those autistic kids in the football helmets?

As though reading my mind, Scott said, "You seemed quite interested in Mike, our Little Shadow. Do you think you might like to try working with him? Or would you rather wait a bit until you get to meet some of the other youngsters?"

"I don't know . . ." I began.

But then, I did know. There had been something very intriguing about that goofy little kid scooting around, stalking us, furtively poking his head out at intervals. I'd found myself thinking about him on the drive home last night, wondering what had happened to him, how one

might begin to reach him. He had dimly reminded me of some other people I'd known
and felt close to—a solitary beach rat named
Charlie I'd philosophized with during my surfing years, and Lars, a deeply reclusive odd-jobs
man I'd become friendly with during the win-
ters when I was a ski bum. Both of them had
had a special air of desolation, a quality that I
recognized even then as an extension of my
own solitariness. I sensed something similar in
Mike, although his was certainly a far more
extreme version.

"You know, I guess I might like to have a go
at him. What do you think?"

"Well, he'll be a tough one. For one thing,
Mike's been here for quite a few years now and,
as I told you, no one has been able to make a
dent so far. It'll take a lot of work and patience—
and you may not get much in the way of results.
It often takes a long time to get anything going
with these kids, but with Mike . . ."

"That's okay," I said as confidently as I could.
"That's why I'm here."

Scott smiled noncommittally. "I had a hunch
you'd want to take him on." He handed me a
heavy folder, jammed with institutional records,
case history, progress notes, school reports.

Later, back in my office, I sat and stared at
the enormous file. It represented a person, a
child—eight fragile years of life distilled into a
three-inch-thick mass of papers. I felt vaguely

repelled, not really wanting to scrutinize it, to be guided by the reams of words that had been dictated, typed in triplicate, initialed, and dutifully filed. The whole process seemed too impersonal and futile. Finally, however, my curiosity got the better of me and I began to thumb through the pages.

———— *chapter two* ————

ADMISSION NOTE

Name: Michael Harris
Age: 5 years, 0 months
Diagnosis: Schizophrenia; Childhood Reaction
Psychiatric Impairment: Maximal
Prognosis: Poor

This five-year-old child is quite psychotic, autistic, and hyperactive; he is ritualistic and regressed in both speech and movement, seemingly paying no attention to people in his environment; speech behavior ranging from muteness to jabbering in a singsong voice that is marked by a severe speech impediment; thinking disorganized and judgment, insight,

15

and reasoning very defective; he is intensely fascinated with running water, fires.

Parents report child is unable to attend school, unable to get along with other children or people, and needs constant supervision because of starting fires, wrecking things, and stuffing paper up his nose.

According to the case history, Mike was the only child of a woman who had been hospitalized several times for what was described only as a "nervous breakdown." Mrs. Harris was twenty-eight when Mike came to Merrick and she was said to be unkempt and "thin as a rail," a highly emotional and unstable person with so little confidence in herself that she was almost totally reliant upon her husband. Tom Gazarro, the psychiatric social worker who did the intake interview, felt she was a borderline psychotic. It was difficult for him to get an accurate history, but it seemed that shortly after Mike was born, Mrs. Harris had become very depressed and began to believe that her son was exposing her to an onslaught of "germs." She handled him as little as possible, convinced that Mike would make her sick if she spent too much time with him or got too close to him. Contact was limited to giving him a bottle or changing his diapers.

Responsibility for Mike had rested mainly with the father; he was described as a rather slight, volatile man—"a bantam rooster"—whose conversation was laced with quotes from the Bible. He ignored his wife's bizarre ideas and behavior, acting as if she were as sane as the next person. An assembly line worker, Mr. Harris had boasted of his recent election as a shop steward, but he acknowledged that his long working hours prevented him from spending much time with his son.

The parents could not remember clearly at what age Mike had sat up, crawled, walked, talked, been toilet trained. About all they could contribute was that he was a "fussy baby," sick a lot, and that his strange behavior began when he was about three. Evidently that had been when Mike moved toward schizophrenia, filling the vacuum in his life with fantasy figures, routines, and communications until, at the age of four, his teeming imagination and profoundly frustrated feelings began to overwhelm him.

And then I hit the shocker. The pediatrician who had referred the family was convinced that Mike was trying to commit suicide. . . .

I leaned back in my chair and thought about *that* one. How is it even *possible* for a child that young to comprehend committing suicide? But, according to the parents, about eight months prior to his admission, Mike had begun to hold his breath and, shortly thereafter, to stuff paper, cloth—whatever was handy—into his nose and mouth. He would gag and roll around on the floor in apparent attempts to stop breathing.

The pediatrician had even observed one of these incidents.

I could only speculate how Mike's four-year-old mind might have been operating: When you don't breathe, you feel weak, dizzy; it's as if you're going to pass out, become unconscious, die. But in his naiveté he could not know that breathing is an autonomic function; when you pass out the body automatically breathes, a built-in survival mechanism. But it is conceivable that Mike surmised that restricting his breathing was a way of killing himself.

Finally, whether out of sheer desperation for attention, or in angry retaliation toward his parents, Mike began to light fires in the house. After the draperies had been charred and a large hole burned in the living room rug, the Harrises at last sought professional help. They apparently had no understanding of Mike's behavior other than that it was "God's will . . ."

Fortunately, the pediatrician sized up the situation, realized that Mike needed to be removed from the home, and advised the parents that immediate psychiatric treatment was imperative. He referred them to a mental health center and, after the admission interview two weeks later, Mike became Merrick State Psychiatric Hospital Patient No. 65433-CU.

On admission Mike must have been virtually psychotic, his speech a regressive and incoherent word salad, accompanied by tirelessly choreographed movements: left arm forward, right arm back, one step forward, one step back, arms swing out, two steps forward, two steps back, then right arm forward, left arm back, one step forward, one step back. . . . During the intake interview Mike was like a wound up toy, and he totally shunned the group.

After leaving him at the hospital, his parents then completed their abandonment of him. Since his admission they had never visited and had resisted every effort by the staff to make contact with them. From the start, Mike had been one of the few children in the unit who never went home—even at Christmas, when it was especially tough to be confined to the hospital.

In the three years since his admission, little had changed. He always fled from people, particularly adults. This stemmed partly from an incident that occurred not long after Mike came to the hospital when a group of aides cornered him and, holding him down, washed and cut his hair, which was outlandishly long and matted. Evidently though, it was an exercise not to be repeated. He had been like a ferocious little weasel—fighting, biting, and scratching. And it must have been a sharp reminder of his life at home because that night Mike had tried to hang himself with his belt.

About two months after the enforced haircut a teacher had come upon him in a classroom, snub-nosed, paper-cutting scissors in hand, snipping and sawing huge chunks of his hair, which was growing long again. Ever since, Mike had been allowed to do the job himself as best he could, which explained the uneven straw-blond swatches and cowlicks that gave him the appearance of a short-circuited scarecrow.

On the whole Mike had survived by becoming as self-contained as a turtle. And as he had grown, so had his shell. He never related to the staff or the other children, preferring the company of his own ritualistic gestures and meaningless monologues. He would obey simple commands if only to ensure that adults kept their distance. His antennae were always out sweeping, and if an adult came near, Mike skittered away sidelong like a little beach crab, watching guardedly for any sign of an imminent threat.

His days were spent sitting listlessly in the dayroom, staring out the window, or attending classes but never participating. Every chance he got, he wandered the grounds restlessly like some caged animal and, as Scott had noted, from time to time Mike was seen roaming the hills above the hospital. Occasionally when a belligerent child would pick a fight, Mike would react in a primitive fashion: he would run away if he could, fight if there was no place to run, but never seek protection from an adult.

Over the years various therapists had tried to reach Mike and win his confidence. One had sought to entice him into the play therapy room with bowls of ice cream, his favorite food. But Mike had spurned her attempts. Another therapist, obviously in the throes of frustration, had written that he considered Mike to be "organically paranoid" and hence, "absolutely untreatable."

It was a devastating story. And it all sounded pretty hopeless. Mike had clearly never even had a shot at learning the means and mechanisms of relating to other people. Instead, he was locked into a way of life that was as barren as it was rigid. And, with each passing year, it was becoming more difficult for him to break out of it—or for anyone to break into it.

At home that night I went through my textbooks and notes from psychopathology seminars to review what was known about childhood schizophrenia. The theoretical notions and research materials were familiar, but now they took on added interest when brought to bear on an actual child.

I sifted through a wide variety of explanations about what caused schizophrenia in childhood. Several pointed the finger of blame at the parents, with the most severe indictment directed at the omnipotent and domineering mother who had been observed often enough to have earned a label—the *schizophrenogenic mother*. Literally, one who produces schizophrenia by choking off growth, adaptation, integration. She does this by pyschologically whipsawing the child—giving such contradictory messages and interactions that no matter what the youngster says or does, he's wrong, and this becomes grounds for vindictive criticism and punishment. It's the classic double-bind, no-win situation.

Other researchers had identified a relentlessly possessive type of mother who refuses to nurture the individuality of her child, preferring instead to foster such a smothering and intertwined relationship that the youngster cannot distinguish himself from her. In time, this ego suffocation leads to such a profound degree of dependence that any hint of separation from the mother is generally sufficient to propel the child into an absolute panic, if not psychotic frenzy. From what I could gather from the case history, though, Mike's family did not appear to conform to either profile.

The pattern they came closest to was that of the "refrigerator mother" who operates in tandem with an absentee father. Neither provides any form of emotional sustenance to the offspring. These types of parents often neglect even basic physical care: feeding, changing, and bathing are erratic at best. In time such acute rejection and isolation effectively warp the psychological development, leaving the child incapable of experiencing reality in a meaningful and goal-oriented way. The result—a major structural defect in personality.

That explanation matched Mike's situation, along with the solid evidence that persons from families with a higher incidence of schizophrenia are more vulnerable than persons from nonafflicted families. The research had shown that 12 to 14 percent of children with a schizophrenic parent develop the disorder. In cases where both parents have schizophrenia, the probabilities jump to 35 percent. Perhaps there was a predisposing factor; Mike's mother had been hospitalized for emotional problems, although nowhere in the record could I find a reference to her diagnosis.

This research in genetic determinants was also related to various hypotheses that suggested a physiological basis for schizophrenia, that some agent—a biochemical anomaly, a breakdown in the ability of the brain's neurotransmitters to filter and assimilate information, even a vitamin deficiency—was responsible for setting the symptoms in motion.

It was all rather confusing; obviously no one knew for sure. But there could be no doubt about one conclusion: Schizophrenia, especially in its childhood form, is the most devastating of emotional disorders, ravaging the orderly process of growth, wreaking havoc with the most intricate component of humanness—the personality. It severely disrupts that most crucial of developmental tasks, the ability to relate and attach to other human beings.

Parental abuse and neglect play a prominent role, with the hapless child unable to ward off the onslaught of fear, anxiety, and eventual despair. Such psychological torment is exhausting. Finally, in a desperate bid for survival, the child withdraws, slowly throttling his feelings until they gasp, sputter, and ultimately lapse into dormancy.

That is the break with reality, the splitting off, the retreat from others and into oneself, with a progressive reliance upon a reverie of distorted thoughts and fantasies to provide a protective, if highly limited, mode of survival. For Mike, though, even the relative protection offered by his craziness had been insufficient to shield him from the acute pain—so he had sought to end his life. Fortunately that period had passed; with the understanding he had come to with the staff, there were no further suicide attempts. Just three years of apparent oblivion.

I closed my notebook and sat back, staring into space. Here I was in my first professional position, about to take on a patient whose pathology had, so far, consistently defied treatment. And yet, as inexperienced as I was, I still felt confident. More so than was justified, really. Perhaps it was a function of my determination, but . . .

The more I thought about it, the more I sensed some connection with my past. Like Mike, I had been something of a loner myself, although I had most definitely never known the privations he had. On the contrary, I had come from a sensible, caring, middle-class background, growing up in a suburb of Los Angeles. But I was a kid who was overwhelmed by the big city—the masses, the noise, the confusion. My reaction had been to rebel, to go against the grain. I dropped out of college and then spent the next few years drifting, ski-bumming the High Sierras in the winter, migrating in the summer to the surfing beaches of Southern California.

During those years, I came to understand that the nomadic existence was a means of escape, a way of protecting my sensitivity. It also allowed me to counter the fear of what others thought of me. I had felt that I didn't belong, and so I placed myself on the fringe of society, where there was much less risk, less pressure to conform. I was even more comfortable with those on the outer fringe of the fringe, like the two men who had come to mind when Scott mentioned working with Mike.

Charlie was a lapsed businessman who lived from day to day dragging a screen frame over the public beaches early each morning. Several hours' work usually resulted in a few dollars' worth of coins and an occasional ring or watch. He spent the rest of the time drinking muscatel and reminiscing about a life turned sour. I could listen for hours to Charlie's rough-and-ready knowledge of the rat race that he now despised. But I couldn't help but notice the terrible sadness of his eyes, gleaming at me through puffy slits of flesh, and separated by an enormously bulbous red nose.

The other extreme case of alienation that I had encountered was Lars. He lived deep in the Sierras in a small hand-built cabin, where his only company was a pair of woodchucks. Though Lars was avoided by most of the others who frequented the ski lodge, I knew at the time he wasn't any crazier than I was. He was just one of the most profoundly lonely people I'd ever met and come to befriend. I could still picture the dust-covered, beautifully-made snowshoes he had crafted for his wife, who had left him some twenty years before—a rejection from which he apparently had never recovered.

People like Lars and Charlie touched a deep chord in me. Even then I had tried to understand the twists of fate that accounted for their bad fortune. They seemed so desolate and yet there appeared to be nothing they or anyone else could do about it. That was the way things had turned out for them, as each would have been the first to admit. Yet in my youthful optimism and concern, I kept thinking of alternatives for them, ways that might get them out of their ruinous ruts.

It was also true, as I came to realize, that niggling away in some remote corner of my mind was the fear that what had happened to them could also, given the right circumstances, happen to me. . . .

I spent the next few days sounding out the professional staff who knew Mike, delving for any clues that might suggest a starting point. I first tracked down Jody Fletcher, who was head nurse at Mike's cottage. A small, pretty young woman who laughed easily, she was younger than most head nurses, but I soon understood why she was in charge; what she lacked in age and stature, she made up for in authority.

We were joined by Chuck Benson, a psychiatric aide who had known Mike since his admission three years before. Chuck was a heavily muscled ex-marine in his late thirties whose arms were covered with tattoos. He shook my hand self-consciously and insisted on addressed me as "Doc."

"We were just talking about Mike Harris, Chuck. Maybe there's something you could add," Jody said.

"What do you want to know about him, Doc?" he asked, and I could hear the rasp of a marine drill instructor in his voice. "There's not much to tell—" He glanced at Jody.

"That's true enough," Jody agreed. "We've really drawn a blank on Mike. He's definitely not been one of our success stories. We've tried just about everything to draw him out, but so far he's resisted us. Still, there's an appealing quality about him that makes us sense that if we could just find the right approach, he'd respond."

"What makes you say that?"

"For one thing, it's the way he follows us. You know, it's very unusual for a kid as disturbed as Mike to show any interest at all in other people. I've never seen it happen before to the degree it has with Mike. But the minute we acknowledge he's there, that's it. At first we thought that once he felt he could trust us, he'd relent and let us help him. But it's never happened."

"What kinds of things have been done so far?"

"Oh, over the years different therapists have tried to get him involved in toys or games, stuff like that. But there's never been even a flicker of interest. Most of us have just worked toward gaining his trust by doing little things for him and by not pushing him or making demands. We've come around to allowing him to set his own rules with the hope that eventually he'll initiate some kind of interaction."

"Which, unfortunately, he's never done," said Chuck. "You know, usually a kid will soften up and begin to relate, but Mike's just so closed off he won't even let you come near him—twenty-five feet, that's the limit."

"Not even any of the other kids? No one's ever observed anything like that?"

"Nope, nothing." Chuck shrugged. "From what

we've seen, Doc, Mike just doesn't talk or inter-
act on any level except to do what few simple
things we ask—take his meds, go to school, meals,
things like that. And that's just to get along and
avoid being hassled."

"It's an accommodation of sorts," added Jody.

Chuck nodded. "Yeah, and it's worked for
him so far. We're deadlocked, and I'm afraid
everyone else around here is going to tell you
exactly the same thing. . . ."

He was right. Cecile Stevens, Mike's middle-
aged teacher, could add only that Mike's time in
school was spent staring out the window. "I've
made so many attempts to attract his attention
through books, drawings, colors—even cartoon
movies, which the other kids love. But—" She
shrugged. People did a lot of shrugging when it
came to Mike.

And then there was Tom Gazarro, Mike's social worker, who had interviewed the parents
on the day Mike was admitted. Tom's one-word
description of them was "weird!"

"They've never answered my letters, apparently don't have a phone, or else it's unlisted.
What it amounts to is that they've simply abandoned Mike, virtually disowned him. They evidently want nothing more to do with him, or
with us. It's a damn shame! And it shouldn't be
tolerated, but under the circumstances, what do
you do?" He paused for a moment. "You know,
I could understand that attitude more easily

with some of the other kids here; a few of them work pretty hard at alienating the people around them and it takes real grit to put up with them for any length of time. But Mike—well, he just got a bum deal."

The chief psychiatrist, Mark Conable, seemed as baffled as everyone else about Mike. He admitted candidly that all he had been doing was prescribing a maintenance dose of an antipsychotic tranquilizer, and that there had been little change over the years. On a few occasions he'd decreased or discontinued the medications altogether to see what would happen, but Mike then became more overtly psychotic, unable even to get dressed or go to school. Otherwise, Conable's contacts with him had been infrequent, although he too had been followed by Mike from time to time.

What it all came down to was that Mike was as much a mystery to the people who had been around him for years as he was to me.

That first week I also wrote to Mike's parents informing them that I was going to be seeing him in therapy and that I very much needed their assistance in my efforts. Would they please call me—collect. Two weeks later I still had not heard from them, though from what Tom had said that didn't surprise me. I tried once more, sending a follow-up letter saying it was urgent that I talk with them about Mike. There was no response to that either.

In the meantime, Scott was keeping my days busy. He would observe me testing a patient, then meticulously check my scoring of the Wechsler Intelligence Scale for Children and the Rorschach Inkblot Test. Together we would go over the hypotheses I had drawn from them, along with those from the Bender-Gestalt, the Children's Apperception Test, and the Draw-a-Person Test. Then he would drill me on translating the information into the cohesive psychodynamic description of the child that formed the basis for our treatment recommendations.

Whenever I had a chance, though, I observed Mike from his prescribed distance. What I saw was a grubby little ragamuffin in a misbuttoned faded flannel shirt, patched blue jeans, and tattered sneakers. But under that disheveled veneer was a slender body with the sleek gliding motion of a potential athlete. There was even an odd grace to the ritualized steps he seemed compelled to do throughout the day.

But it was his face that fascinated me. His expression was always the same—a somber, unyielding mask—and I had never encountered one quite like it. His impoverished existence was painfully reflected in the pinched narrowing of his deep-set hazel eyes, the unmistakable constraint in his thin, tightly compressed lips, and the tension of preparedness with which he carried himself. Constantly on guard, alert for danger, he resembled a small, vulnerable creature in a thicket of predators. In many ways Mike seemed old, even wizened, a world-weary eight-year-old.

Finally, I told Scott I was as ready as I would ever be. When he asked me about my therapy plan for Mike, I started out with the notes and ideas I'd been developing. I mentioned the psychoanalyst Bruno Bettelheim, who has written several books advocating love and understanding as the best possible treatment for childhood schizophrenia. Another analyst, Melanie Klein, suggests climbing into the psychotic shell of the youngster and leading him out. "But she doesn't say exactly how to do it . . ." I stole a glance at Scott and retreated to safer territory.

The psychotherapist I had read most avidly was Carl Rogers. His position is that the success of psychotherapy is dependent upon the attitudes communicated by the therapist; he stresses the importance of empathy—sensing what the disturbed person is feeling—and of accepting that person with unconditional positive regard. Most important, the therapist must be open and guileless. All of these attitudes form the basis for trust, and thus facilitate growth and change. So far, my experience at the university clinic had convinced me that this approach worked. Also, the concepts were consistent with my own view of the nature and worth of human beings.

I considered myself to be a "Rogerian"—a client-centered therapist.

Virginia Axline, another psychotherapist who specialized in working with troubled children, had written a book in which she incorporated Rogers' ideas into play therapy, but her approach, as did his, depended upon a certain degree of cooperation.

"And then there's operant conditioning. A lot of people have had success using behavioral techniques in the treatment of schizophrenia. But that's so controlling. You're really just programming the kid, using rewards to train rote behavior. Besides, I'd have to catch Mike in a net to get him hooked on M&Ms or Fruit Loops as reinforcers. I wouldn't know where to start.

Scott nodded. Then he smiled. "You seem to be running out of theorists . . ."

"Not quite. I know she's out of style, but I've always been impressed by the writings of Frieda Fromm-Reichmann. She speaks of how important it is for the therapist to help the person with schizophrenia discover that life with others can be bearable and even rewarding. That there are ways to get along, that people don't have to live in a world of irreality and delusions. Problem is, her neo-analytic approach is also dependent on being able to get near the child." Warming to the task and somewhat impressed with how much information I had memorized, I rattled along, parroting all the wisdom I had gleaned from my readings.

Scott listened, drawing reflectively on his pipe. Finally he raised his hand and I ground to a halt.

"You've got all the jargon down, haven't you? But let's get practical now. What exactly is your plan going to be?"

"I really don't know what will work—or even what approach I should try first. I thought maybe I'd just experiment, cast about."

"Do you think play therapy is feasible with Mike?"

"I doubt it, particularly if I can't get closer to him than twenty-five feet. Besides, others have tried that and no one's gotten to first base."

"So what *are* you going to do?"

"I guess I'll just go over to the cottage and explain to Mike that we're going to be spending some time together and then take it from there. I'll just have to play it by ear."

Scott looked dubious. "That doesn't sound very professional. We usually try for a bit more structure than 'playing it by ear.' What about all that stuff you were quoting from the books a minute ago?"

"I don't know. None of it seems to fit right now. I guess I just won't know until I see how Mike reacts to me."

Scott looked doubly dubious, but then his face relaxed into a rather disconcerting smile. He seemed amused.

"So you're going to wing it. Well, that should prove interesting—for you as well as for Mike."

———————— *chapter three* ————————

The next afternoon I set out to see Mike for the first meeting. I was clad in a brown corduroy coat, button-down shirt, striped tie, beige denims, and loafers. The ensemble had been carefully selected to reflect casual professionalism. I had also been cultivating my warmest, most patient tone of voice; a gentle, understanding smile; and a pipe—generally unsmoked, but always available as a suitable prop.

When I reached the cottage door I pushed the buzzer, stepped inside, and within a few moments Chuck, the aide I had talked with a few days earlier, joined me. Together we located Mike in a corner of the dayroom, staring out one of the heavily screened windows. He sensed our approach and darted away.

"Hi, Mike." I poured my most empathetic manner into the two words.

No response.

"Mike, my name is Pat. You've seen me around the hospital—I'm the one who waves at you, remember? And from now on you and I are going to be getting together regularly and doing things. Whatever you want to do, okay?"

Still no response except for Mike's eyes, which swept back and forth from Chuck to me and back again.

I tried again, though already I was beginning to hear strain in my voice. "Mike, is there something you'd like to do with me today?"

From over my shoulder came Chuck's gravelly voice. "Forget it, Doc, he doesn't talk to people."

I glanced back at him and in that instant Mike saw his opportunity. He shot past us, out the dayroom door, and down the hall—as far away as he could go.

"Look, Doc, that kid's been here three years and, like I told you, none of us have ever been able to get him to talk to us, much less come near us. If we want him to go somewhere, into a room or outside, then we tell him it's okay and walk away from the door. That's the deal we have with him. We stay away from him, and he does what we say. It's as simple as that."

I nodded, trying hard to appear to take what he said in stride. One professional to another.

"Okay, let's let him out."

Chuck ambled down the hall, unlocked the door leading outside, and blocked it open. Then he turned to Mike, who was standing near his room, tense and vigilant.

"Okay, Mike, you can go out with the Doc here, but you stick with him and you come back when he tells you to, okay? You understand that, Mike?" Chuck backed away from the open door.

As he slipped toward it, Mike continued to watch us. Then, flashing one quick glance at me, he vanished.

Chuck turned toward me with a shrug of his shoulders. He'd probably seen a slew of interns like me over the years, fresh out of graduate school, full of newly absorbed facts and ideas, primed with fantasies of rescuing people.

I nodded a thanks to him and walked quickly to the center of the quad; Mike was nowhere to be seen. After searching awhile, I caught a glimpse of a small figure lurking in the bushes near the twenty-foot-high boundary fence. From a measured distance, I talked into the bushes.

"Mike, you can run all day, but we could be doing something that's fun."

The chain link fence rattled, and suddenly Mike emerged on the other side of it. He turned abruptly then, and began to walk along a narrow, overgrown path leading into the hills.

Scrambling through the bushes, I discovered a well-concealed hole, just large enough for a person to squeeze through. I eased into the opening, hooking my coat in the process, and by the time I clambered through, Mike was nearly out of sight. Half running, I chased him up the slope. When I was about fifty feet behind him, though, he began to walk faster, so I dropped back, panting and out of breath, allowing him to set the pace. He stayed well ahead of me, every so often turning to be sure I was keeping my distance.

After another fifteen minutes or so of climbing, the trail broke out onto a plateau covered by a well-maintained citrus grove. Mike ran immediately to the nearest tree, picked a large lemon, and began to eat it—skin and all.

I couldn't believe it! Even from where I stood, my mouth puckered in protest. Yet Mike's expression had not changed. How could he *do that*?! And then it occurred to me that the fruit was probably sprayed. I shouted to him to stop, that the lemons might be poisonous and they might make him sick.

Mike kept chewing.

I moved in to take it away, but he was too quick and scuttled off before I was even close. Changing my strategy, trying for a more authoritarian voice, I said,

"Give me that lemon!"

Mike continued to take huge bites, all the time keeping a wary eye on me.

"Look, we don't want you to be sick, do we?"

In response, he stuffed the last wedge of lemon into his mouth, reached up, and plucked off another.

As he devoured the second lemon, I sagged against a tree. What the hell would Carl Rogers do in a spot like this, I thought. Fantasies began running through my mind of my first patient becoming critically ill, maybe even dying. How would I explain to Scott that Mike had eaten a bunch of pesticide-coated lemons up at the citrus orchard and now they were (a) pumping his stomach, (b) doing an autopsy on him, (c) considering filing negligence charges against me, (d) all of the above . . .

Meanwhile, I watched Mike pick yet another lemon. This time, eating it slowly and calmly, he turned and started up the trail again, then stopped to look back at me. I obediently followed.

That's when it struck me that Mike, unable to tell me what he wanted to do, was trying to show me—he wanted to hike. We climbed on, eventually reaching a line of rocks that marked the top of the ridge.

Oblivious of me, Mike chanted some unintelligible words and sidestepped with a swaying motion. Perhaps, I thought, expressing his satisfaction at reaching the crest. Or maybe that was just my projection—I had hardly anticipated this kind of treatment situation.

As he rocked slowly, gazing out over the valley, I realized that he must have come here many times before. Sitting down on a small boulder, he continued the swaying motion, totally absorbed in whatever was going on inside his head.

I commented on the beauty of the spot and thanked him for letting me tag along, but he ignored me. Finally we both sat in silence—the required twenty-five feet apart—and listened to the wind.

As we trudged back, my loafers dusty and scratched, my coat dangling from my shoulder, I had to smile at how ill-prepared I had been. Mike ran on ahead, his nonsensical singsong drifting back to me. Occasionally the words sounded familiar, but they were so looped and jumbled together as to defy interpretation.

Other times his mutterings were just that: "Ka-ka-jah-bah-bow-boooo-gah-bah-jah-kaaaa." The most frequent version was a repetitious, lilting hum, like the chant of a mantra:

"Ahooooooommmm-ahooooooooooommmm-*ah-ooooooooooommmmmmm* . . ."

From time to time Mike turned to check the distance between us. Perhaps he was establishing with me the same understanding he had with the aides and nurses: If you come no closer, I won't run away.

When Mike reached the cottage, he rang the bell and disappeared inside before I had a chance to say anything to him. I was beat—in more ways than one—and with a desultory wave to Chuck, I turned and hobbled slowly back to my office.

Two days later I was ready to give it another go. It was a beautiful, warm summer day and this time I was prepared—I had exchanged my suit for hiking boots and Levi's. Mike was in the dayroom again, rocking back and forth and staring out the window, arms clasped around his knees.

"Hi, Mike. How about another hike today?"

I was standing far enough away so that I wouldn't startle him, and was concentrating so hard on him that I was unaware of anyone else in the room. Suddenly a number of other children materialized at my side, jumping up and down and pulling on my sleeve.

"Me too, me too!" . . . "I wanna go on a hike!" . . . "Take me, too!"

I hastily explained that Mike and I were going to be seeing each other regularly and doing things together. Just as they did with their social workers or with one of the doctors.

"Yeah, but they never take *us* on hikes!"

"Well, ask them to sometime. I'm sure they'd take you if they knew you really wanted to go."

42

I was more sure I'd hear about this later from the staff.

During all this Mike had continued to stare intently out the window.

"C'mon, Mike, let's go."

Without a glance in my direction, he slid from his chair and walked toward the outside door. I followed, amazed that he could appear so withdrawn and yet respond immediately when he wanted to. Obviously there were times when he was attuned, well in touch with reality. What was baffling was that it was impossible to tell from his expression or posture when he was out of contact. And although it was evident that he was alert to certain things going on around him, could comprehend at least some of what others said to him, he had apparently lost, or perhaps never mastered, the ability to communicate with them in return.

We left the cottage, Mike setting a brisk pace as he headed directly for the hole in the fence, again ignoring my attempts at long-range conversation. After the first hike, I had checked with the rancher, who assured me that the lemons in the orchard were safe. In fact, he had often seen Mike walking through the grove, calmly chewing a lemon.

As before, Mike reached the summit well ahead of me. When I cleared the last rise, he was already perched on the same rock as the last time, swaying gently, lips moving in some silent conversation.

Going as close as I dared, I tried repeatedly to elicit an intelligible response, or at least some reaction, but none was forthcoming. Apparently he'd convinced himself that he had nothing to fear from me, and now was behaving as though I weren't there. His solitariness remained absolute.

For some time we sat in silence. It was a relief to get away from the Children's Unit with its institutional routine. The incessant noise and confusion were beginning to wear on me. Here the air was sweet, the landscape spacious, the rolling hills giving way to the rows of citrus trees that stretched across the valley. Recalling my own years in the mountains, I could well understand why Mike liked to visit this spot.

It intrigued me that there was no mention of these hikes in the nursing notes. How long had Mike been coming up here? Was this a recent interest, or something he had been doing for a long time? I glanced at my watch and realized I had to be in a staff meeting in forty-five minutes.

"Time to go back, Mike."

Remarkably, he looked over at me. For a moment his face relaxed slightly and I thought I caught a brief glimpse of the little eight-year-old who was under the layers of wariness and isolation. Then the curtain dropped again, the fixed expression returned, and he was on his feet, nimbly picking his way along the rocky path.

As usual Mike was far ahead of me all the way back, ringing the bell and disappearing into the building as I rounded the corner. I managed to call, "Bye, Mike. See you Monday," as the door closed behind him.

That night I wondered whether I had actually seen up in the hills what I thought I had. Maybe his momentary unguardedness was just wishful thinking on my part; I wasn't sure. By now I wanted so much to reach him.

But that's how it began, the series of skirmishes and truces that were to characterize the relationship between the novice therapist and his veteran opponent.

chapter four

The next several months were virtually a stand-off. My fantasy of Mike's responding dramatically to my warmth and sincerity soon crumbled as the forces of unconditional positive regard, acceptance, and empathy did not liberate him, did not open the world of reality to him.

Repetition compressed time to the point where it felt as if I had been seeing Mike forever, each meeting a carbon copy of the previous one. Several times a week I would dutifully appear at the cottage after Mike was out of school, prop the door open while he sidled out, and then follow after him, slipping through the familiar hole in the fence and up into the high country. But I enjoyed it anyway, even though there was

46

never any progress. It was therapeutic for me just to get away, to smell the fresh, pungent sage and then, from the top of the hill, to stare out toward the gray haze of the channel islands.

It took me back to my days on the ski patrol at Mammoth Mountain. There I had prized the first runs of the crisp mornings when I would often sweep to a stop and look back, contemplating the meandering doodle of curves I had inscribed on the light, fresh powder. I recalled again the freedom and exquisite beauty, the massive stillness of the frosted mountain broken only by the soft running of skis. During those aimless years, that tranquillity alone had been enough. Now it seemed a long time ago . . .

It was impossible to know how Mike regarded what we did. Frequently he hiked along the trail silently and mechanically, looking either straight ahead or down. If I called his attention to a swooping hawk or a dart-tongued lizard, he ignored me. At other times he catapulted into craziness. He would become echolalic, his voice a shrill monotone as he repeated sounds to himself, reeled off strings of nonsense syllables, or phrased sentences that had psychotic overtones.

One day just outside the fence, Mike began to slap one hand with the other and to shriek: "Mi-koe baahd boy! . . . Mi-koe BAAHD BOY!"

At first, because of his peculiar pronunciation, I couldn't understand him, but after a time it dawned on me that he was saying bad—"Michael is a *bad* boy!" And at that point I had to agree with him. The strident babbling was beginning to set my teeth on edge, and I couldn't fathom what had precipitated the outburst. I tried to counteract his frenzy by declaring, "Michael is a *good* boy. Michael is my friend."

It was a pretty absurd spectacle, a boy and a man twenty-five feet apart, each shouting opposing statements over and over as though baying to the gods, while they climbed single file into the hills. If I needed anything to underscore my sense of futility, this exchange of contradictory and repetitive messages certainly did the trick. Moreover, nothing seemed to subdue him; the ranting continued until we reached the crest. By that time Mike's voice was a rasping wheeze. Mine wasn't much better. The contest had gone on for nearly half an hour—and then the wailing ceased as abruptly as it had begun.

I wondered where Mike could have picked up the phrase, and whether it was connected to some recent event. But when I inquired later, none of the aides or nurses or his teacher recalled saying anything like that to him.

I related the incident to Scott. He said that Mike's verbal seizure was fairly typical of kids like him, that in all likelihood this was material that had been stored in his memory for years, probably going back to when he was still living with his parents. It would doubtless continue to emerge sporadically.

I was moved by the thought that these were the words he remembered most from his early childhood. It was another moment when I sensed the child inside the patient, and I redoubled my determination to help him.

There were other times during those first months when I couldn't relate to Mike's behavior at all. For example, his movements and posture would become stiff, his stride resembling that of a blue heron. He would pick up one leg and step rigidly forward, appearing to freeze in space while he carefully scanned the ground before completing the step. These gestures had a ceremonial, superstitious quality to them, as if he had taken seriously the sidewalk game of "step on a crack—break your mother's back." Once begun, Mike seemed compelled to continue this way of walking as though to ward off some terrible thing that might happen if he stopped, or perhaps only to assure some degree of order to a world that he felt was threatening to overwhelm him.

His most frequent mode of ritualistic behavior was to spin in slow circles, hands outstretched, humming monotonically and rocking to and fro like a slow-motion disco dancer. I called these movements his solitary dance, an eerie blend of self-stimulation and magical symbolism, its source unknown and perhaps inexplicable.

One day I noticed that Mike's tennis shoes

were completely worn out. I mentioned this to Scott and he suggested checking the donated items at the hospital's Clothes Corner. I did and was elated to discover three pairs of children's hiking boots that might fit. That afternoon I took them to the cottage and set them on the lawn near the door. When Mike came out, I pointed to them and urged him to try them on.

After hesitating a few moments he approached them, staring suspiciously while I kept my distance and awaited his verdict. At first I thought he was going to reject them all; but then, selecting the nicest pair, he tentatively shoved his feet into them. Fortunately they seemed to fit, and he clomped around looking at them and scuffing the toes against the ground. Then he mumbled something and charged off toward the fence without bothering to see if I would follow.

As we climbed to the crest of the ridge, Mike kept stopping to check his boots. Perhaps, I thought, to be sure they were still there. Several times he also loosened the laces, adjusted the tongue, and painstakingly retied them. I watched, fascinated. Mike's method of tying his laces was quite involved—an intricate series of knots that ran right to the end. When he was finished it looked like a pigtail—obviously a system that he had devised himself.

His behavior toward me remained the same, but from then on Mike wore his boots everywhere, even on days we wouldn't be hiking. I took it as a sign of something positive, a straw to prop up my morale.

Another incident occurred about the same time. As we were returning from the hills one afternoon, I asked Mike if he would like an ice cream cone.

As usual, he didn't respond directly; he simply veered around and marched toward the canteen. I followed, amazed as always by the awareness that coexisted with his isolation. Because he was so noncommunicative, one could easily overlook how adaptive he was, how much on top of things he was in his own way. But I wondered whether he would be willing to enter the canteen with me.

When Mike reached the building he stepped cautiously inside, pausing near the door to check out the room. Then, with a glance that clearly indicated I should stay away, he walked up to the counter and pointed mutely to the container of chocolate ice cream.

He nodded tersely when the counterman held up a large cone, his eyes tracking every move as the man scooped out the ice cream and pressed it into the cone. The man said something and laughed but Mike did not respond, keeping his eyes firmly fastened on the cone. Reaching back into the freezer, the man added another generous dollop. He smiled, asked Mike his name, while holding the cone tantalizingly out of his reach. Mike suddenly seemed on the verge of

51

panic, anxiety clearly etched on his face. Seeing this, the man relented, set the cone on the counter, and stepped back. Mike promptly snatched it and fled the room.

"He's a strange one, that kid," the counterman said, shaking his head. "But then, out here I guess they all are, aren't they? Sure is rough when they're that young."

"Yeah," I agreed. "Mike's a very lonely and frightened kid."

"Too bad," he said, still shaking his head. "Makes you wonder what happened to him, don't it? Mike's his name, huh? I'll remember that."

"By the way, thanks for giving him a little extra. Even though he couldn't say anything, I'm sure he appreciated it."

"Oh, I do it for all the kids. Geez, you know, you feel so sorry for them, that young and all, and stuck in this place . . ."

I nodded. I did indeed know how he felt.

As I left the canteen, though, I was encouraged. Another tiny glimmer of hope. Mike had again acknowledged something I had said and had even allowed me to do something for him by accepting my offer of an ice cream cone. And in the process he had inadvertently revealed that he *was* listening to me—at times, anyway—and that he could understand and relate to me in his own constricted way.

Still, the silences and distances between us were frustrating, to say the least. By nature we are communicative creatures, and being with someone as intensively as I was with Mike, without a response from him for weeks at a time, made me feel so futile. Our relationship seemed unreal at times. As, indeed, it was. Although Mike tolerated me, we hardly had what could be considered a reciprocal relationship. And the frustration was building; after three months I was impatient for results.

It was Scott who kept me glued together during that period. Several times a week I would sprawl in the big leather chair next to his desk and, more often than not, recount my latest stalemate with Mike. One day he had had enough of my glumness and let me have it with both barrels.

"Beginning therapists like you are always in such a hurry, always expecting immediate success. You're so ingrained with the American ethic of quick results for little effort—of instant change when it suits you—that you can't stand the thought of little or no progress, no overnight success stories like in the movies!

"It takes *time* to build a relationship, Patrick, to gain an understanding of the patient's psychodynamics, to earn his trust. It's taken little Mike eight years to get to where he is now. How can you expect him to change it all in a few months? Especially when you're clambering over the mountainside for only four or five hours out of each week? If it were truly that simple, don't you think somone around here would've stumbled on that solution and helped Mike long ago?"

Still, in spite of Scott's lecture, I was rapidly approaching my wits' end. Three months in the trenches were getting to me. All that time I had been chasing that kid, and he still wouldn't come a jot closer, talk to me, or for that matter, even recognize that I was any different from one of the rocks he liked to rest on. Except that he'd get close to *them* . . .

"Well, at least you're getting into shape," Scott commented.

"I'm afraid that little guy has really got my number, but good."

"Want to give up? Try one of the other kids? Lots of other possibilities around here—"

"Of course not! I'm just getting started. I can be just as stubborn . . . no, *more* stubborn, than Mike. But what I haven't been able to figure out yet is how to break the pattern—how to get him to relate to me."

"Maybe it's time you went back to square one."

"What do you mean?"

"Perhaps you should begin to put some of your knowledge of psychology to use: instead of allowing Mike to call all the shots, you start calling some of them."

"I still don't follow, Scott. I've been trying to do that all along, and I can't think of any other way than I've already tried."

54

"What exactly have you been doing up to this point?"

"Well, I've been trying to do what Rogers advocates—provide unconditional positive regard, acceptance, empathy. The emotional symptoms and distress are supposed to subside as the innate forces within the person strive for psychological balance. That's the theory, anyway. And it seems to work for Rogers . . ."

Scott smiled. "Have you seen any evidence that it's working with Mike?"

"No, not really. Maybe a look from him here and there, but I can't even be absolutely sure of that, especially at a distance of twenty-five feet."

"Okay, now. Are you ready to consider the notion that perhaps one theoretical approach is just not enough to cover all therapeutic situations? That there is no one method of therapy that is going to be applicable to every single patient we encounter?"

"I suppose." It was a grudging admission for me. Scott had broached the subject before, without much success.

"Boy, you're not kidding when you say you're stubborn! Patrick, do yourself a favor and ease up a bit. You've admitted that several months of work with Mike have gone nowhere, so you've got nothing to lose by considering other possibilities, have you?"

"I'm not sure. What do you have in mind?"

"You know how I feel about Rogers' approach.

It's an excellent attitude to have toward the people you work with, but there may be some patients who need much more than an interested, supportive listener. I suspect Mike is one of them." Scott gave me a wry smile. "As a fellow humanist I can wholeheartedly agree with the sentiments behind Rogers' ideas, the fact that his concepts are based upon a deep respect for the person and his or her life situation, and that the therapeutic relationship is then constructed upon that premise. But remember, self theory falls far short of being a universal explanation of human behavior."

"What's the alternative, then?" I said, sensing what was coming. "You don't think behaviorism is the answer, do you?"

"Not entirely. But the principles of learning and conditioning have been demonstrated very nicely in studies, especially those by B.F. Skinner. Behaviorism does have its uses and some very good techniques. In spite of what you might think. Of course, it has its limits of usefulness, too, like any other theory. But we know that in certain situations positive and negative reinforcement work extremely well in changing specific types of behavior patterns. So you don't want to disregard learning theory simply because it may be anathema to your humanistic notions.

"Psychoanalysis, too. Many of Freud's concepts— such as the unconscious, the defenses— have certainly withstood the test of time. The empirical data may not have supported some of the major hypotheses of his theory, but the fact remains that many of the psychodynamic constructs, as well as the therapeutic techniques, have proven extremely useful."

"Scott, it's our same old argument!" I broke in. "I'm a dyed-in-the-wool humanist because I can't buy either the behavioristic view of people as mechanized creatures of reflex or the analysts' notions of unconscious motivation, that behavior is ruled by base instincts. I really believe in the integrity of the individual, and that each person has a choice. *Anyway*, I'm familiar with the principles of the various theories you've mentioned—that's the easy part. The problem is that I can't apply the techniques of *any* of these theories to a little buzz bomb named Michael Harris who runs up and down hills like a mountain goat and won't let me near him!"

"All right," retorted Scott. "The problem is that you have yourself prematurely committed. There are no absolute applications of any of the theories yet—that's why they're still theories. Psychology as a science is, to put it mildly, in diapers. We have a lot of promising leads, some well-conceived studies, some good data, and the start of a body of knowledge. But we are a long way from fully understanding human behavior, much less predicting it with one-hundred-percent accuracy."

"That's for sure. I'm beginning to wonder why I spent so much time in graduate school."

"Well, it's not as hopeless as it may sound. But when you make the jump from the rudiments of science to applied work you have to stay loose, flexible, and accept the fact that you're not always going to be perfectly on target. What the theoretical framework does is increase your chances; it allows you to be objective, to plan, even to predict what *should* happen during the course of psychotherapy. What I'm advocating you do with Mike—with anyone you work with professionally—is concentrate on understanding him and assessing the situation. And be open to using any of the theories that might seem appropriate. So when you first start working with a person, begin by picking out the theory that seems to fit the individual's dilemma best, whether that theory is called self, behaviorism, psychoanalysis, whatever. Use those explanations, but be ready to look elsewhere when they don't seem to account for what's going on. Or when there doesn't seem to be any progress. Stay loose, flexible, open to anything.

"That's what sets true professionals apart: they draw upon their knowledge of science, using their skills to objectively evaluate what is needed, and then they choose a course of action. It's rarely very clear precisely what that should be; sometimes several treatment alternatives would be appropriate. One simply has to make a choice and, if things don't work out, be prepared to switch to another approach.

"And remember, Pat, all the while the patient may very well sense what is best: the Wisdom of the Mind, if you will. Some people, for example, *need* to dig back into the trauma of their formative years and work through unresolved issues and long-buried troublesome feelings—as the psychoanalysts advocate—while others simply blot out the past and deal with learning a more adaptive style of living that is future-oriented. More along the lines of a behavioral approach. But most, the majority I would say, want a combination. You have to learn to mold yourself, to shape yourself to whatever will best help your patient—an accommodation between what *you* sense they need, and what you think *they* sense they need, and what therapeutic approach will be most suitable for that purpose."

I was shaking my head by this time, but Scott pressed on.

"What I'm suggesting therefore, Pat, is that you be more eclectic. Be aware of the value of trying different things instead of being locked into one theory and approach. Mix a little Rogers with some Skinner and maybe add a dash of Freud. Okay?"

"At best I *think* I see what you're getting at, Scott. But I still don't see how using a goulash of theories and techniques is going to help me know what to do with my particular little id kid."

Scott grinned his roguish smile and leaned back, drawing long and thoughtfully on his pipe. When the last thin wisp had emerged, he watched it gyrate toward the ceiling and then he turned to me.

"You like challenges—that's another one for you. Think about what I've said, then try to put it to use."

—————————— *chapter five* ——————————

So I had to come up with another plan, the sooner the better. And then one afternoon a notice appeared on the department bulletin board. Ivar Lovaas, a UCLA psychologist, was scheduled to present a workshop on developments in the treatment of childhood schizophrenia and autism. I knew that Lovaas was a behaviorist who for some time had claimed considerable success in using operant conditioning techniques with severely disturbed children, but that was all I knew about him.

Scott encouraged me to attend, saying, "What have you got to lose?"

Very little, I had to admit. At this point I was willing to listen to anyone, try anything.

ROBERT LANE

Lovaas showed filmed accounts of the treatment program he had devised for schizophrenic and autistic children. All were extreme cases, exhibiting a wide range of self-stimulating behaviors that precluded interaction with others—gazing at light through flapping hands, being mesmerized by spinning objects, or parroting nonsensical speech in an echolalic fashion. In each case specific conditions were set up whereby the child had to produce an appropriate form and level of performance. Using a variety of rewards or "primary reinforcers," the therapist taught simple words, initiated cooperative play, encouraged personal hygiene habits. The idea was that the youngster performed some act—pulled a wagon with another child in it, identified his nose, buttoned a button—and was immediately rewarded with food, especially candy, and "secondary reinforcers" such as the therapist's emphatic *"Goooood!"* accompanied by a smile and a nod. A toothy Lovaas, with his Norwegian accent, managed to string out the word "good" until it was almost an aria. After a short time the child made the connection between the pleasurable reward and the smiling therapist who provided it. The systematic creation of a new behavior pattern also had an unexpected and remarkable side effect: the psychotic mannerisms began to drop away.

More drastic measures were called for with children who engaged in self-stimulating and

62

autistic behaviors. Negative reinforcement could be a sharp "No!," a painful slap, a squirt of lemon juice, and sometimes physical restraints. On occasion, mild electric shocks were used to break up physically self-destructive behavior such as self-hitting and self-biting.

A particularly striking example of this involved a four-year-old girl who for over a year had been gouging her arm with her teeth. Every conventional approach had been tried—including a plaster cast and a pint-sized straitjacket. But as soon as she had access to her arm, the biting resumed. With her arm ulcerated once again, electric shock was applied to teach the child that every time she hurt herself, she could expect an unpleasant jolt. Now the inflicted pain was no longer under her control, and almost immediately the procedure began to "shape" her behavior as she understood the link between injuring herself and the extremely aversive electric shock. Within three weeks the self-mutilation was elimination—or "extinguished," as the behaviorists say.

Lovaas maintained that of all these intrusive methods, delivered in a consistent fashion, offered the best chance of success in counteracting long-standing psychotic and self-destructive behavior patterns.

I had to agree. It was evident that these techniques had brought about some remarkable changes. Without exception, the before-and-after films were very impressive, showing child after child coming around under the uniform, systematic treatment. And the whole process took only weeks. A sharp contrast to the time needed by the more traditional therapeutic approaches. As Lovaas made clear, the children still had a long way to go, but they were unquestionably more amenable to treatment than they had been before.

I returned from the presentation intrigued by what I had seen, excited by the implications, but also troubled. I couldn't help but compare their success to the absolute frustration I was feeling after months of sparring with Mike. On the other hand, learning theory had always seemed to me too remote, too dehumanizing. Fine for pigeons and rats, but too manipulative and unfeeling for human beings. But I couldn't deny that the techniques appeared to have an amazing effect on children very much like Mike.

And when I began to analyze the interaction between Mike and me in terms of Lovaas's ideology, it became very clear who was getting all the positive reinforcement: Mike was going hiking, having ice cream cones, and doing generally what he wanted to do, all the while forcing me to go by the rules he had established. And it was just as evident who was getting all the negative reinforcement: I was still no closer to Mike, there had been no change in his overall behavior, and nothing to indicate that I was learning to be an effective therapist. No wonder I was frustrated. All my idealistic notions and rescue fantasies were being "extinguished," thwarted by an eight-year-old boy who had done a beautiful job of "shaping" my behavior.

Still, there remained, for me, certain ideological and personal problems with behavior therapy. In particular, the emphasis on minimizing, virtually eliminating, the trusting relationship between therapist and patient—and substituting one that seemed more like that between a trainer and an animal—was completely counter to my training and philosophy. And I was bothered by the aversive procedures and the use of punishment. Shouting "No!" at Mike, or if he were to hit himself during one of his "bad boy" episodes, conceivably having to shock him—all of this seemed terribly insensitive and went against everything I believed in.

I was becoming a psychotherapist to help people, not to inflict physical pain on top of psychological pain. I wanted him to learn how to enjoy closeness, and that seemed a strange way to do it. I just couldn't imagine how Mike, or any child for that matter, would ever be able to trust the adult who zapped him like that. If an association were made between candy and the therapist who gave it, would not just as strong an association be made between the therapist and the shock he delivered? If negative reinforcement were used at all, it needed to be somehow combined with reward. Was there a way of doing that?

The more I thought about it, the more I realized that my resistance to these methods was deeply embedded in my own temperament and background, as was my decision to work with Mike in the first place. My convictions were also closely linked with the personal changes that had brought me out of the wilderness of my own solitude.

Soon after I had decided to return to college, I landed a job as a playground director at a school for blind children. There I worked closely with some twelve youngsters, helped them to build models, took them on trips to the zoo and the park, even managed to produce a circus with them. Nothing in my life until then matched driving down a busy city boulevard with a car-load of inquisitive blind children who kept calling out, "What's that noise?" ... "Why did you slow down?" ... "Is that a bus?" ... "When's the tunnel?" ... And when we reached the tunnel, they would recognize the change in light and a chorus of voices would exclaim, "Tunnel. TUN-NELLLLL!"

The children's adaptiveness to their handicap, and in some cases several handicaps, continually moved me. They were so venturesome, appreciative, and positive that it was a joy to be around them and to share things with them. For the first time in my life I felt I was doing something that was indisputably worthwhile, and it was evident to me that I needed and responded to them as much as they needed and responded to me. Helping people seemed to bring out the best in me, and the most confident and purposeful side of my character.

From that revelation evolved a sense of direction that led me back to college and a psychology major. That was how I met Dr. Warfield, who became my adviser. He encouraged me to become a psychologist and indelibly exemplified for me just what it meant to be a psychotherapist.

The most remarkable illustration of Dr. Warfield's skill was provided the first time he took our undergraduate class to visit a nearby mental hospital. We assembled in the one-way observation room where he first briefed us about the different people he'd be interviewing and related their diagnoses to concepts we had studied.

When Dr. Warfield and the first patient entered the group therapy room on the other side of the one-way glass, we were all struck by a dramatic change in him. Gone were his classroom antics; his theatrical lecture style was replaced by a quiet voice and gentle manner. He communicated empathy that reached even the most disorganized and delusional patients, and then coaxed each of them down his or her particular path to reality.

The last one was an attractive woman in her

mid-thirties. Her expressive Mediterranean face oozed boredom and derision as she sat chain-smoking and ignoring Dr. Warfield's comments. But her taut expression, coupled with the jerky gestures as she tapped ashes or ground stubs into an ashtray, betrayed an underlying vortex of rage.

Finally the strain became too much and she exploded in a torrent of lurid curses and obscenities that shocked our small group. I had never seen or heard such vehemence—at one point I thought she might even attack Dr. Warfield. But he took it calmly and his voice remained soothing and accepting. The woman tried to light a cigarette, but her hands were shaking so badly that she couldn't. Dr. Warfield lit one for her, then sat back in silence while she regained her composure. Suddenly she broke down in waves of sobbing: "I don't know what came over me, Doctor. I just can't control these feelings any longer—they *haunt* me." Then she slowly began to share the anxieties and fears that were tormenting her. Dr. Warfield skillfully drew her out, gaining her trust with his supportive gentleness. It was the most remarkable performance I'd ever witnessed, and it had remained until now as the main model for what I wanted to do as a therapist.

My quandary now was whether there might be a middle ground for me somewhere between the humanistic concerns of the self theorist and the harsh logistics of the behaviorists. The more I thought about it, the more certain I became that even if the theories themselves were intellectually incompatible, they could share equal time in a practical sense. All it would take would be a little bending of the techniques to fit the situation.

It wouldn't be a very elegant approach—the kind that made for sophisticated scientific presentations—but if it worked, who cared? And if it didn't, I'd just have to come up with another angle. It was at least worth a try. With some chagrin, I realized that I had come around to precisely what Scott had been suggesting: Be flexible. . . . Pick and choose. . . . Anything that might work with a youngster—with anyone—is fair game. . . .

In the previous four months Mike's and my routine had been fairly well established. I would go up to the cottage after school, find Mike, and we would set off on a hike or a walk around the hospital grounds, with an occasional stop at the canteen for a treat.

But at our next session, as Mike stood poised, waiting for me to open the door so he could catapult himself out, I put up my hand and motioned him into the empty dayroom. He backed in, eyeing me, keeping as much distance between us as he could.

"Mike, I'd like to try something different from

now on. Each time I come, I want you to tell me what you want to do. Okay?"

Silence.

"You look as if you're ready for a hike today, so before we go, I'd like you to tell me that. Say 'hike.' Okay? Do you think you can say that for me? 'Hike.' "

Mike sat across the room, his face cupped in his hands, staring out the window. There was no indication that he had heard me, but I knew he had.

I tried again. "Mike, all you have to say is 'hike.' Then we'll leave right away."

No response.

I slowed it down, enunciating clearly. "Mike, look at me. Say it like this: 'Hiii-ka.' That's all you have to say, Mike. Then we'll go. 'Hiii-ka.' "

Mike turned and looked at me, his face expressionless. Then he swung halfway around and gazed impassively out the window again. His face seemed to become more set then, and I wondered how he was interpreting the new condition—as punishment, rejection, an unreasonable demand, a trick? There was no way to tell, but I was determined to wait it out, to see what his reaction would be.

We sat for fifteen minutes. Every now and then I would repeat what he had to say, but Mike paid no attention. He had retreated to somewhere deep inside himself. Finally I decided to tantalize him a bit to see if I could provoke a response.

"You know, Mike, we're missing a beautiful afternoon of hiking; I bet we could see clear across the valley, maybe even see the ocean today. C'mon, let's get out of this crummy cottage for a while, and get away from the hospital. Those lemons up in the orchard are really tasty. One would taste *sooooooo* good while you're sitting on your favorite rock at the top of the hill, wouldn't it? C'mon, Mike, all you have to do is say 'hike.' That's not so hard, is it?"

Silence. Mike continued to stare remotely out the window.

Another five minutes dragged by, then ten. Maybe this wasn't going to work after all. Lovaas had sometimes used punishment to force interaction in such a situation, but I had elected to try a more positive approach. Still, if Mike didn't want to hike badly enough . . . maybe it was too much to expect of him. Asking him to speak to me was a big step. Perhaps I should have tried for something easier initially.

Thirty minutes had now passed. I gave it one more try. "Mike, it really is a super day out there." I stood up as if I were about to leave. "Look at me, Mike. Say 'hike.' That's all. C'mon, just try it."

When there was still no reaction, I sat down again, prepared to wait the rest of the afternoon if necessary while I pondered my next tactic. Sometime later I was about to repeat my instructions when I noticed a very slight shift in Mike's shoulders.

Then, with a distinct sigh, his towhead swung in my direction and he stammered a couple of barely audible, unintelligible words.

"What was that, Mike? I'm sorry, I couldn't hear you. Please say it a little louder."

Several more moments passed in silence; then, staring at the floor, he said in a subdued but discernible tone something that sounded like, "Hi dugfahs."

Because of his odd enunciation, it was very difficult to understand what he was saying. It sounded, though, like "Hike" something. What could he be saying? Hike what?

At the moment it didn't matter; it was close enough.

"That's great, buddy! I knew you could do it! That was very, *very good*. Okay, you lead the way!" I smiled and nodded enthusiastically, the pent-up positive reinforcers tumbling out.

Once out the door, Mike was off like a wild mustang. We hiked the rest of the afternoon, but although I watched for a reaction—possibly even a repetition of the words—there was nothing different in his manner. He seemed to have completely forgotten our earlier confrontation. Later, as he disappeared through the door of the cottage, I praised him one last time for talking to me, hoping that it would carry over to the next day.

I went immediately to tell Scott the news. Charging into his office, grubby and bedraggled, I found him on the phone. When he saw me he couldn't help but chuckle. Hanging up the receiver, he said, "You look like the proverbial cat—"

"I got two words out of him! One I understood— 'hike'—but the other I couldn't make out. He held out a long time and I was just about to give up when he finally came through! I can't wait to see what happens tomorrow . . ."

"Sounds like a start. But remember—be patient. And don't expect too much."

The next day I had changed into my hiking clothes and was waiting for Mike at the cottage when he returned from school. I ordinarily wouldn't have seen him again until later in the week, but I couldn't wait that long. He seemed unusually reluctant to follow me into the dayroom; if possible, he was more withdrawn and hunched over than ever. He chose the same chair that he had sat in the day before and resumed his familiar staring out the window. So we would have the dayroom to ourselves again, I locked the door behind us and then turned to Mike.

"Okay, shall we decide what to do today? If

you want to go hiking again, tell me like you did yesterday. Just say 'hike.' "

We sat in silence for several minutes and then, as I began to think I should repeat my instructions, Mike's lips moved as if in rehearsal. Then he whispered, "Hi," and the elusive word again.

"Mike, please speak a little louder—I can't quite hear what it is you want to do."

"Hi dugfahs."

"Try it once more, Mike. Say the whole word. 'Hiii-ka.' "

For a few tense moments I was afraid he'd clam up again, but at last he muttered, "Hike dugfahs."

"Good, Mike! Great! You said it right that time. That's just fine. I'm really glad you could tell me what you want to do. Going for a hike—" and here I paused, trying to approximate what he had said, "—'dugfahs' is fine with me, too. Let's go!"

Over the next several meetings, Mike quickly adapted to saying the required words on cue. I couldn't believe it. He was being so cooperative that a couple of weeks later, when we were cutting back to the Children's Unit by way of the canteen, I decided to try for a little more.

"Mike, if you want to stop for a Coke or an ice cream cone, we can. All you have to do is say, 'I want Coke' or 'I want ice cream.' "

Mike acted as if he hadn't heard me, but when we passed directly behind the canteen, he looked over longingly. So did I. After the dryness and dust of the hike it seemed like an oasis. He slowed, obviously undergoing an intense internal battle. Finally he stopped, scuffing his feet in the dirt, head down. His voice barely carried back to me.

"Geh Coooke."

Two words. I decided to push my luck. "Almost, Mike. Now say, 'I . . . want . . . Coke.'"

The familiar faraway look returned. Then he repeated, "Geh-Coooke-now! GehCOOOKE-NOWWW!" His voice became an insistent yowl.

I stood my ground. "No, Mike. Say, 'I . . . want . . . Coke.'"

His face controted, he screamed, "CAHN'T SAYEE THAAHT!" Then abruptly he wheeled and ran off in the direction of the cottage.

When I next encountered Scott, I reluctantly explained to him what had happened. The incident seemed disastrous to me, a major step backward, but Scott again reined me in.

"I wouldn't worry about it. Actually, it's a good sign. He's really dealing with you, that's the important thing. At least he told you off, and that's a good indication that you've gotten a toehold on his psyche. Remember, this is a kid who hasn't expressed a feeling or said anything to anyone for a long time. Now he's relating— and that's progress, Pat!"

I wasn't totally convinced that there wouldn't

be some negative carry-over from the incident, but I was determined to follow my plan to make demands on Mike. It seemed the only thing to do. I let a couple of days slide by so that he could think things over. Then I called his teacher and asked her to tell Mike I'd be up for him after school that afternoon. He was sitting in the dayroom when I arrived, and I gestured toward the open door, then followed him outside.

"It'll be quieter and easier this way to plan what we want to do today, Mike. Now I'd like you to tell me again what you want to do, but say it loud enough so I can hear right away. Okay?"

Mike was looking down, intently studying the tangle of knots that topped off one hiking boot.

"Say it loud now, Mike, and then we'll be off."

He raised his head slightly but did not look at me. "Hike dugfahs," he muttered, quickly glancing down again.

"Good, Mike. I heard you fine that time. And if that's what you want to do, that's what we'll do. We'll hike 'dug-fahs.' That was very, *very* good!" Abruptly, an idea crossed my mind. "Mike, is 'dugfahs' what you call the hill where we hike? Is that a name?"

An all-but-imperceptible nod. Then Mike gazed off in the direction of the bluff. "Dugfahs ... Dugfahs ... Dugfahs ..." he whispered, almost as if it were a force pulling him.

I tried again to understand. "Dugfahs ...

76

Dugface . . . *Dog*face? Is that your name for the hill—*Dogface*?"

Again, eyes down, the faint nod.

"Well, that's great, Mike; that's a very good name. Let's go hike Dogface."

chapter six

The rocky outcropping that rose up behind the Children's Unit bore no resemblance that I could see to a dog's face or head; the name Mike had given it had apparently emerged out of sheer fantasy. "Dogface" was part of a range of jagged hills, blanketed with rough bushes that scraped your legs as you walked along the narrow animal trails. There were gravelly washes of decomposed rock, and here and there gigantic sets of boulders clung together as if for support against their common enemy, the elements.

Near the top, the terrain became almost inaccessible. The millenia of weather had worked their magic, combining with volcanic nuances to leave a series of deep cuts on the high rock faces. Mike's little spot was a relatively easy climb that circumvented the more difficult heights. But sometimes he had sought out different routes and over the months I came to recognize the challenge and the allure that hiking on Dogface held for him.

Since some verbal communication was being established, I was primed for the next step. Even though Mike still kept his distance, there were times now when he yielded a bit. It had taken over four months, but on occasion I was finally permitted to draw within ten feet or so before he became antsy. I was learning to deal in fractions. Since his consuming interest was in "hiking Dogface," I began to think about how I could increase communication by devising another task that would be within reach and at the same time help to strengthen our relationship.

Seeing some of the other children coloring pictures one day gave me an idea, and the next time I went up to the cottage I took along some drawing paper and crayons. Mike's eyebrows arched slightly when he saw me beckoning him to come into the dayroom, and his eyes narrowed as he spotted the drawing materials next to the chair where he usually sat. He hesitated a few moments, then went to the window and looked out, his back toward me.

"Mike, what would you like to do today?"

"Hike Dugfahs," came back, a flat monotone glazed over with suspicion.

"Good, Mike, that's very good; but first I want you to do one thing—draw a picture. Will you do that? Then we'll be off for Dogface, okay?"

Mike continued to stare out the window, steadfastly ignoring the paper and crayons. I settled in for a marathon session, watching him closely and trying to read something from his expression. It was impossible, though, to tell whether his noncompliance was stubbornness, or whether he was withdrawing again, retreating from me.

For a full half-hour Mike sat in stony silence, never moving except when he blinked. Every so often I would try to goad him, but again it seemed as if a battle of wills were taking place between us.

Another ten minutes elapsed and I was getting fidgety. Maybe I had gone too far again, pushing for too much. But progress had to come sometime; if I didn't press for more, we wouldn't get any further.

Finally I said, "Mike, if you don't draw a picture soon, it's going to be too late for us to hike up Dogface. I have to be back for a meeting and we've got only an hour left. C'mon, draw the picture so we can take off."

No response. If anything, I detected a stiffening of the shoulders—and the resolve. We sat in silence until I felt the point of no return had been reached.

"Okay, Mike, I guess we'll just have to miss our hike to Dogface today. That's too bad; I know it's hard for you, but you think about it—think about drawing that picture for me next time and then we can hike. I'll see you tomorrow, buddy."

Mike didn't move as I unlocked the dayroom door and walked down to the nursing station to tell them we wouldn't be leaving. I talked with the nurse on duty for a few minutes and when I returned to the dayroom, Mike was gone.

The paper and crayons, untouched for over an hour, were now scattered all over the floor. . . .

The next day there was a message for me from Cecile, Mike's teacher. All morning he had been jumping up and down, pacing, and jabbering, and she wondered whether his behavior was a result of something going on in therapy. I showed the note to Scott.

"That's another good sign; maybe not on the surface—usually we're more apt to feel like we're making progress when a child *isn't* disruptive— but Mike's really struggling with some issues, and he may begin to act out like this now and then. Talk with Cecile so she understands what's happening and ask her to let you know whenever Mike does something unusual. You'd better also tell the cottage staff to expect some misbehavior, but not to punish him. Encourage him to work it through."

Right after lunch I met with Cecile and filled her in, then compared notes with the nurses and aides at Mike's cottage. Later, as soon as classes were out, I strolled back up there, crayons and paper tucked under my arm. It was a perfect day for a hike, with lacy cirrus clouds strung delicately across the azure sky. I knew that wouldn't be lost on Mike and I hoped it would provide an impetus for cooperation.

I found him looking a bit sulky, curled up in his regular chair near the window. As I greeted him, I pushed the paper and crayons down the table to him.

"Boy, is it ever *beautiful* out there, Mike! What do you want to do today?"

"Hike Dugfahs."

"Okay, fine. But you know what you have to do first. Did you think about drawing that picture for me? Can you do that today, Mike?"

Silence.

"Please give it a try, Mike. Then we'll take off for Dogface."

Several moments passed, then there was a hesitating movement. Finally Mike turned and straightened the paper. His shoulders sagged as he halfheartedly picked up a crayon and scribbled a stick person. Then he stopped to await my verdict.

"Goooooood, Mike!" I was amazed at how well this was working and even caught myself drawing out the "good" as Lovaas had done. "That's great, Mike. Okay, let's be on our way. . . ."

* * *

Two days later I was back again. This time Mike went obediently to the table and quickly sketched another stick figure, then dropped his hands to his lap.

"Mike," I said as gently as possible, "that's fine, but I need a little more—you can draw a better picture than that. Please try."

He sighed and picked up the crayon again. Then other crayons. He drew two more stick people, faces blank, and a grid of lines that made them appear to be in jail, behind a dark, forbidding door. Once more he stopped.

"Goooood! That's a fine picture. What is it, Mike? What did you draw?"

"Heah," he mumbled, his voice barely audible.

"Ah, that's your cottage here, where you live?"
A slight nod.

"Okay, Mike, very good. Now what shall we do?"

"Hike Dugfahs *nowww!*" came out emphatically. He was poised on the edge of his chair ready to spring for the door.

"Sure, Mike, that's great! You're really doing fine!"

The picture he had drawn seemed to characterize aptly his perception of the hospital—kids barricaded in, imprisoned by the always-locked door. I couldn't help but wonder what it was like for him, as he took these first steps toward reality.

At our next meeting I laid the crayons and paper down on a table and moved away. Mike glanced at the materials, went to the window for a brief look, then turned and sat down beside them. It was as if he needed to remind himself that what was to come would be worth all this trouble.

"Will you draw another picture for me, Mike, so we can go on our hike?"

Mike contemplated the paper and then he abruptly reached for the crayons. Again the stick figures with no discernible features, standing alongside what I guessed to be a tree.

As he moved away from the picture, I walked over and examined it more closely. "That's very good, Mike, but why don't the people have faces?"

I retreated from the paper and Mike walked back, stared briefly at the page, then swiftly pushed it away.

"Hike Dugfahs NOW!"

"Okay, Mike. You've done everything I've asked of you. You deserve a hike—and maybe a double-decker chocolate ice cream cone, too."

He looked over at me, and for an instant his expression softened at the prospect of a treat. But a second later the spontaneity was gone, and the veil of flatness descended once again.

Yet later that afternoon, as we were returning from Dogface, Mike did something that astonished me. We were approaching the canteen when he suddenly blurted out,

"We geh ah-eese creeemcone!"

I stared at him. Had I heard him right? Did he say *we?* Hearing Mike talk about doing something with me was perhaps a small step. But then I was learning, as Scott had said, that there would be no miracles, just tiny gains reflected in a word here, a look there.

Later, Scott went over the pictures with me. He was impressed. "This is a good start. A child, and especially one who is disturbed, can tell you so much about his inner dynamics with a drawing. In fact, sometimes you can get information it would be difficult to get any other way. You know, there are some good signs here."

"Where?" The pictures looked pretty bleak to me.

"Well, the first thing is that he drew people, so people are a part of his world. Or are starting to be. He said 'we' today, and that's pretty consistent with what he's done here. I think all your time and work with Mike may be starting to pay off." He paused for a moment. "The blank faces are interesting, aren't they?"

"I asked him about that, but he didn't answer. What do you make of the rest?"

Scott looked thoughtfully at the drawings spread out before him. "Well, we've got some primitive stick people, a rather barren tree, a cottage with everyone locked in. It's about what we might expect from someone with Mike's background. The darkened tones would perhaps indicate some depression, but that'd be understandable, too. Mike hasn't had much to be happy about."

"Yeh."

"Did you ask Mike if he's in either of these pictures?"

"No. Should I?"

Scott nodded. "Try asking him. See if you can get some descriptions. Start working him toward telling you stories about what he draws. It might be very revealing."

"Okay."

"Then begin dating these and keep them in order. They may come in handy and be even more helpful as therapy progresses. I'd have him draw on a regular basis. Encourage him to use colors, open himself up to the world. Mike's beginning to use you as the go-between to a world he's never known, but you're going to have to be the one to lead the way."

chapter seven

It was more of an impulse than anything else. I had attended a weekend workshop in Santa Cruz and, while planning my route back to Merrick, I saw the name Reidsville. I remembered that that was where Mike's parents lived. Since I hadn't been able to reach them any other way, why not drop in? Maybe I could find out why they had never answered any of my letters, and perhaps even learn something about Mike's early years. Besides, I was curious.

Fortunately, Reidsville turned out to be quite small. I stopped at an old service station to ask where the Harrises lived. The teenager who filled my tank told me and added, with a smirk, "You can't miss the shrine."

He was right. In the front yard, standing on its partially buried end, was an enormous old white enamel bathtub. This bit of recycling wizardry served as a shelter for a child-sized statue of the Virgin Mary. Plaster-of-Paris sheep lay at her feet and a half circle of small whitewashed stones and bright plastic flowers completed the tableau.

The house was a rambling one with an air of perpetual renovation. It had several additions, all of which seemed to have been built with whatever was available at the time. Two different shades of blue aluminum siding overlay one wall, a patch of redwood ran up to some exposed tar paper on another, and even the roof sections were two colors of shingle. Bricks, lumber, and odd lengths of aluminum siding lay here and there. Mr. Harris was evidently an accomplished scrounger.

At the end of the driveway stood a rusty Cadillac Fleetwood that I guessed to be ten or eleven years old. Its massive hood was open, a small figure draped over the fender as if in the process of being swallowed by a gigantic lizard.

"Mr. Harris?"

I approached the car and peered into the cavernous inner workings.

"Yeh." Irritated at being interrupted, he blinked at me through the sweat and grease that had seeped into his eyes. He buried his head in a sleeve for a moment, then gave me a sharp look. "You better not be selling something on a Sunday—"

"No, no. I'm Patrick McGarry, Mike's therapist from the state hospital."

"Oh . . ." Mr. Harris's head descended back into the engine.

"I was up at a meeting in Santa Cruz and thought I'd stop by and see you and your wife, let you know how Mike is doing. Is Mrs. Harris here?"

"Yeh, but she's not feeling too well today. And stuff about Mike upsets her."

"I see. Well, do you suppose it would be too much of a strain on her to hear about Mike? Actually, he's been doing fairly well lately."

Mr. Harris was very intent on tightening something. His face twisted as he bore down on the ratchet, then unexpectedly the bolt broke and his hand plunged against the radiator. Leaping back, he cursed, slammed down the hood, and turned on me. "You coulda just sent a letter, you know. You didn't have to come all the way out here and bother us."

So Mike's progress was a "bother" to them . . . "I've never been too sure my letters have gotten to you. Besides, I thought you might like to know about Mike firsthand."

Mr. Harris grunted; his eyes narrowed as he studied me. "Why'dya hide your face behind a beard? Only hippies and commies wear beards."

I just shrugged and smiled. Mr. Harris's jowly

jaw looked as if it had been shaved with a straight razor. I remembered from the case history that he was only a year or two older than I, but he seemed already middle-aged, worn down, his slack shoulders gravitating toward a small paunch.

Abruptly he swung toward the side door of the house. "Wait here," he said. After a few minutes he returned. "Don't talk too much in there now. My wife gets upset very easy. She's not a strong woman."

I followed Mr. Harris through the kitchen and into the living room. The furnishings were shabby but everything was clean and neat, a noticeable contrast from the mess outside. I guessed that Mrs. Harris took care of the interior, but then I wondered if she was capable. Although the hospital record had painted a dismal picture of Mike's mother, I was still startled by the emaciated woman who sat cowering in a rocker, a Bible clutched in her hands. When she saw me, she cringed.

"You're . . . you're not going to take me back to the hospital, are you?" Her fingers began making little fluttering movements as they ran up and down the edges of the Bible.

"No, Mrs. Harris. I'm Patrick McGarry. I'm from the Children's Unit at—"

"There's no need to worry, Mother," Mr. Harris interceded. "He's not from *that* hospital. He's from Merrick, where Mikey is. No need to get upset now." He moved near her and put his hand protectively on her shoulder.

Mrs. Harris relaxed somewhat, but her expression now was one of bewilderment. "Mike?" she asked, as if the name were new to her. "Mike?" she repeated. She raised her eyes beseechingly toward her husband.

"That's okay, dear," he responded and then glanced uneasily at me. "My wife has spells. She's a little confused today."

Suddenly recognition flooded her face. "Oh yes, *Michael*. Michael, the Archangel . . ." She smiled sweetly at me, as if pleased to make the connection.

What the hell was going on here? "No, Mrs. Harris, Michael your son. He's almost nine years old now, goes to school, and loves to hike in the hills behind the hospital . . ." My voice trailed off as I realized that she wasn't listening. She was mumbling under her breath, forming silent words and twisting a handkerchief back and forth in her hands. Her face had a familiar vacant look. I remembered the social worker's observation that Mrs. Harris was probably a borderline psychotic. No longer borderline, I amended to myself.

Abruptly Mr. Harris leaned over, plucked the Bible from his wife's lap, and began waving it in front of me. He was suddenly flooded with energy. "We've always known what was wrong with our Mikey. I don't know why you people can't see it! It was Satan who got hold of him. Demons possessed him just like the Bible says—it was God's punishment for our sins, our misdeeds. Somewhere along the way we broke God's Law and, in His Almighty Wisdom, He saw fit to punish us through Mikey. The Power of God demonstrated once again!"

I kept looking at Mrs. Harris, whose fingers were now wearing a groove in the arm of her chair. She had hunched over as though lashed by her husband's words and I thought she was crying.

". . . the Power of Prayer," Mr. Harris thundered on. "Let us bow our heads in prayer!"

I looked at him questioningly. What had I gotten into?

"Bow your head!" he demanded. "We're going to pray for salvation." He glared at me until I complied. "Our God in Heaven . . ." he intoned, Bible held high in the air.

I kept my head down, staring at the pattern in the worn rug until it began to swirl. Occasionally I peeked at Mrs. Harris, who now had her hands clasped in fervent prayer. A look of beatific bliss played across her face. Mr. Harris prayed for twenty minutes straight and I was rocking on my heels by the time he wound down to a hoarse, "Amen." I mumbled a heartfelt one myself.

Mrs. Harris raised her arms longingly toward heaven and I noted a remarkable resemblance between her and Mike; it was not so much a matter of features as of the same reflexive flinch that I had seen so often in her son, an alertness and guardedness as though she expected momentarily to be struck. As she gazed at the ceiling, I could tell from her varying expressions that she was in some kind of religious ecstasy, or maybe hallucinating. Then her eyes settled back down on me and she smiled benignly. We regarded each other for a few moments and I felt genuinely moved. She was a gentle as well as frightened creature and I could readily understand why her husband was so protective of her. I recognized, too, that she was once again in contact with reality, so I pressed on with my message.

"I just wanted you both to know that Mike is fine. He and I spend a lot of time together hiking in the hills behind Merrick. Mike's grown to be quite a little mountain climber. And he's growing like a weed—you wouldn't recognize him . . ." My voice faded as I realized the import of my words.

But Mr. Harris didn't notice. "Does Mike still have those spells? Those awful screaming fits?"

"Not really. But then he doesn't come near people yet, either. As long as he isn't pushed, and we don't expect too much of him for the time being, he's pretty quiet and cooperative. He's talking a little now, and is learning to ask for things. He likes chocolate ice cream cones—"

I broke off as Mrs. Harris's head slowly sank and the mumbling resumed. She seemed to be losing her fragile hold again. I looked questioningly at Mr. Harris and he pointed toward the door. Nodding, I bent over and said, "I have to be going now, Mrs. Harris. It was nice meeting you . . ."

The trance persisted and I straightened to find Mr. Harris beside me. We both tiptoed quietly from the room. When we reached the driveway, he paused and asked, "Do you believe in the Power of Prayer?" His manner was almost friendly now. My participation in the marathon prayer had apparently mollified him.

"Well, yes, sort of . . ." I hedged. Then I summoned up my courage. "I'd like to ask you to do something, Mr. Harris."

"What's that?"

"Get some professional help for your wife. Take her to the community mental health center. For her sake, and yours, too. I know she'll probably be frightened, but just tell them that before you take her in and they'll understand. Perhaps they can prescribe something so she doesn't have so many spells, as you call them. It's terrible for her to be in such a state, Mr. Harris. Something could happen to her while you're at work. And that could be avoided. There are things that can be done."

"She gets along okay."

All I could do was shake my head. He still

ecognize how disturbed she was, any
han he had appreciated a few years ago
mperative it was for Mike to get into
therapy. "Mr. Harris." He looked up at me and
our eyes met. "She needs professional help. Please
get her some."

"Well, Mr. McGarry, I suppose you mean well.
But I reckon we'll just stick with our own ways.
We get along okay."

"What about your son, Mr. Harris?"

"Our minister has told us to stay away from
him, because of the demon possession. He says
Michael is no longer ours, that he's been taken
over—"

"Well, he *is* yours," I interrupted. "Mike is
still your child even though he's seriously disturbed. He's a very sensitive kid, Mr. Harris,
and you shouldn't just write him off."

He dropped his eyes. "What're his chances?"

"I honestly can't tell you. I'm trying to help
him, but I just can't say how far he'll be able to
come. No one at Merrick can. But we do know
we need your help. You can contribute, especially if Mike continues to make progress."

"You know, I never thought there was much
anyone could do; leastways that's what the minister says. I dunno. Could I maybe come out and
see him sometime?"

Boy, I thought, I'd sure like to square off
with that minister. "Of course, Mr. Harris. But
first I'd want you to take your wife to the men-

tal health center and get that help for her. She really needs it. I should think it would take a big load off you if she were in a better frame of mind."

We shook hands and though I never expected to see or hear from him again—nor was I hopeful that he would go to the mental health center—I was glad I had stopped in. At least I had tried . . .

Dismaying as my experience with the Harrises was, its net effect was to help me see—and perhaps more important, feel—Mike's problems in the context of that devastated family. My visit had given Mike a history. He was no longer just the little bundle of symptoms and fears and resistances I was trying to counteract, of potential resources I was attempting to mobilize. He now loomed in my mind as a child with a past, like any other. The child of that fanatical father and woebegone mother. And if I didn't understand his plight any better, I certainly felt it more keenly and toughened my resolve to do whatever I could for him. But I was concerned about something else—only six months remained in my internship, and I wondered just how much I could accomplish in that period.

Mike turned nine early in December, but when I tried to explain what his birthday meant, he simply looked blank. However, he didn't have

any trouble understanding the hot fudge sun-
dae I treated him to at the canteen.

Two weeks after his birthday, Mike was wandering among the cottage Christmas decorations.
But if he sensed any difference at all from the
rest of the year, it didn't show.

—————— *chapter eight* ——————

January and February were unseasonably cold
and rainy and, more often than not, we post-
poned our hikes. From his post by the dayroom
window, Mike kept a close eye on the elements.
Sometimes I'd prop the door open, but he would
refuse to leave. On other occasions, he might
venture out but would then abruptly turn around
and lope back to the cottage, having seemingly
had his fill of the blustery weather.

With the arrival of better hiking conditions, I
decided the first order of business should be to
get Mike to come physically closer to me. I had
tried various ways of coaxing him to do so, but
although he had reduced the distance somewhat,
he consistently maintained the boundaries of

his space. I had rarely been able to penetrate them—and then only for seconds.

I knew that this was pretty much an approximation of the psychological distance that Mike wanted to preserve. It was his way of protecting himself; he was still far from being able to take chances with me or anyone else. But this meant, in effect, that we had reached an impasse: Mike listened to me and did what I suggested if he were so inclined, but otherwise I remained simply an observer of his solitary activities.

It was apparent, then, that I had to think of a new tactic if I were to set things in motion again. One afternoon shortly after Mike and I had left the lemon grove, some vivid pictures from a magazine article I had recently read popped into my mind. The photographs showed two mountain climbers scaling a steep summit, and the text had stressed the importance of their teamwork.

Well, it was worth a try. I had done some climbing in the past and figured we could handle some of the ridges without too much danger. Ahead of me was a rock wall that Mike, trotting along up the path, had already passed. I called out to him, "Mike, let's try going up this way; we can get to the top quicker."

I scrambled up the draw, using the mesquite bushes as handholds. Then, when I reached the wall, I began creeping slowly up a narrow fissure in the granite face. Halfway up I paused, out of breath, and looked down at Mike, who was standing on the trail, intently watching me.

"Hey, this is fun," I yelled. "It's like mountain climbing. C'mon." I twisted along, inched through some loose shale and, pulling myself onto a ledge, I stood up. From here Mike was just a small figure.

"C'mon, Mike. This is great," I shouted. "But watch your footing—it's steep!"

Mike was gazing up at me and I wondered whether he'd follow. But then he began clambering through the brush to the wall. I coached him to place his feet carefully and to test the footing before shifting his weight. Within a short time he was just below me. As he neared the ledge, I knelt down and extended my hand.

"Here, Mike, let me help you." Then I added, "Hikers have to work together!"

Ignoring the outstretched hand, Mike circled around me. But I sensed a possibility—he had seemed intrigued as he picked his way up the wall. After that I began to search for more difficult and rugged terrain that was still reasonably safe. It seemed to be an adventure for Mike, because each time he would come immediately to the spot I had selected and then, after watching me ascend, he would follow. I noticed, too, that he often traced my steps and planted his feet as he had seen me do.

Mike was listening and learning, so I continued to offer climbing advice and encouragement and, although his expression remained distant and noncommittal, it was clear that he was eager to climb. I always went first so that at difficult spots or at resting points I would be waiting, my hand extended for a helping boost. As he'd get close, I'd say, "C'mon, Mike. Take my hand. It's okay—remember, hikers have to work together."

But he would have none of it, and after a few weeks of scaling various routes, I began to get discouraged again. There had not been the slightest inkling that Mike might accept my idea of working together; even on a narrow rock shelf, he managed to maintain as much psychological distance as before. Also, as Mike's prowess increased and we attempted more challenging climbs, I became concerned about the hazards. What if Mike fell? I had a professional as well as a personal responsibility for him. I had discussed this with Scott after the first climb and he had concurred that the possibility of real gain was worth the small risk. But with the risk increasing and no gain in sight, I was on the verge of giving up.

"Besides," I told Scott, "if reaching out hasn't worked yet, it's probably not going to. We should have seen something, some reaction, by now. I think it's just too big a jump for him."

Scott didn't reply immediately; then a slow smile crept across his face and he chuckled. "You know, I'd really like to see you guys up there sometime. I have this mental image of you swinging out on a cliff, dangling from a rock by one hand, and yelling, 'C'mon, Mike, hikers have to work togetherrrrrr!' "

I smiled, but I didn't think it was very funny.

"Seriously, Pat," he went on, "we know how much Mike loves to get up in the hills and now there's his new interest in climbing. Sooner or later he may just understand the importance of teamwork. Why don't you try it a few more times? After all, what else have you got?"

One day two weeks later Mike and I were on the march again. With over eight months of tramping the hills behind us, we were nearing the summit of Dogface from the back—the south side—which was much more precipitous than our usual routes. We had stopped many times before to scout the mottled rock wall, but had always gone on. It just seemed too difficult and dangerous to attempt. By now, though, Mike had become a surefooted and nimble little climber, and as we passed a gap he threw an appraising glance up the wall. So I challenged him.

"Shall we go for the top from this side, Mike?" I nodded toward the cliff. "I don't know. . . . It'll be a tough climb—think we can do it?"

He stopped and looked back at me, then up the ridge. After several moments of hesitation, he started back toward me and I took the opportunity to remind him, "Now Mike, this is the kind of climbing where hikers have to work together, help each other out. It's going to be hard. So if you need any help, sing out! Agreed?"

This time I really meant it, but he remained impassive, eyes riveted upon the ridge.

I began to climb. The first dozen yards to the wall were relatively easy going, but then as I hit a patch of gravel on rock, I was scrambling on all fours in an effort to make headway up the steep incline. Farther up, some roots protruding from the bank offered a temporary respite. While I rested I scanned the next stretch and then, planning the route to take from there, I noted where the granite seemed decomposed and likely to be brittle.

Mike stood motionless at the bottom, watching me.

"Well, this is it," I said under my breath, and pushed off from the bank. Swinging across the gully, I used my momentum to reach a narrow ledge, pressing hard against the cold rock face while I searched for safe handholds. When I'd found some, I began to climb again, selecting and testing my holds, then shifting my weight carefully, kicking away loose rocks. A little farther on I stopped again to assess my route and position, and to give Mike a progress report over my shoulder.

"This seems to be a pretty good way, Mike.

But watch the loose rock and be sure to get good handholds. Dig those boots in!"

Mike remained motionless, observing me intently.

But the next part was harder than I had anticipated and by the time I was halfway up the wall my arms were aching. Finally, after another ten minutes, I pulled myself into a large crevice in the rocks just below the crest of the ridge. Panting and gasping, I sagged against the opening. As soon as I caught my breath, I yelled down:

"Mike, forget it! It's too dangerous! Go around the other way and I'll meet you at the top. I'm going to rest here for a few minutes."

But I was too late. After making sure that I was not going to dislodge any more rocks, Mike had already started after me and the loose shale clattering down behind him drowned out my warning. All I could do was watch—and feel a growing concern. Maybe this time I *had* gone too far.

Mike traversed the bottom quickly and soon reached the steeper part. Now that he could hear me again, I repeated my earlier warning, urging him to go around the other way. But to no avail. He was bent on scaling that wall and there was nothing I could do to stop him. I could only watch as he crisscrossed the ridge, studying the route and wending his way along the ledges and cracks. When he was about halfway up, he disappeared behind a shelf that jutted out at an angle away from the cliff wall. Then there was silence; perhaps he had stopped to catch his wind.

"That's right. Take a rest, Mike," I counseled.

A few moments later the sound of dropping rock indicated he was moving again and then his head came into view some twenty feet below me. He was sweating and his face was streaked with dirt. I could see that he was scared.

I moved down near the edge and braced myself.

"Just a little bit farther, Mike. Carefully now— you can make it okay."

Pulling himself up hand over hand, he was concentrating hard on not looking down. He still looked frightened, but a strong sense of achievement seemed to be propelling him on. His expression was determined. For the last few yards between us the going was treacherous, the rock broken and slippery, and as he came across this last stretch I reached out toward him, extending my hand as before.

"Here, Mike, let me help you."

At precisely that moment his footing gave way and he began to slip sideways. In that split second pure instinct took over and, lurching forward, he grasped my hand. I pulled hard, practically yanking him off his feet and into the narrow gap where I had been waiting. Adrenaline pumping, we collapsed togther against the cliff—not a foot apart.

It wasn't the way I would have chosen to have it happen. He had slipped, and grabbed more out of desperation than anything else. But I was willing to take whatever I could get.

"Mike, you did some great climbing there— you're getting to be a real pro!"

He sat trembling beside me, arms clasped tightly around his knees, exhausted by the strain and fright of the climb. I could almost hear his little heart drumming away; it had been too close a call for him.

I reached over and rested my hand gently on his shoulder. "Hikers really do have to work together, don't they, Mike?" Then I took a moment to point out the importance of what had just happened—how much we both needed each other, depended on each other for help and support.

Mike was too wrung out to protest my touching him, much less move away. He just huddled there, still shaken by the exertion and shock. During the twenty minutes or so that we rested on that rock ledge I was physically closer to him than I had ever been. I felt good about that. Even though I knew he was just too spent to budge, I was thinking that what had happened once could more easily happen again. Gradually the color returned to Mike's face and he seemed to be recovering. Time to move on.

"Last one to the top's a monkey's uncle!" I challenged.

Mike gave me a quizzical look. Then, haltingly, he said, "Munng-key uhnn-koe?"

The little freckled face, all squinched up in an effort to understand, made me burst out laughing. For the first time, it was Mike who was puzzled—and showing it—and trying to comprehend something I had said.

"That's just a saying, Mike," I explained. "A monkey's uncle is just a funny expression. C'mon, you ready to go for the top?" I motioned toward the summit and Mike got up, still looking slightly perplexed and began to climb up out of the gap.

Later on that afternoon as we bushwhacked down through a steep talus field, I offered Mike my hand again, but he went on by. As I watched his heel-digging descent, I wondered fleetingly whether we would ever be as close as we had been earlier. In any event, I knew it was absolutely essential that I follow up on what had happened on the south face.

"Mike, shall we hike up Dogface again tomorrow?"

From twenty feet away his reply came quickly, without hesitation, "Hike up Dugfahs tumawah!"

"Okay, and I hope you'll let me help you again. Hikers really do have to take care of each other."

I sensed he was studying me and I glanced at him; but when our eyes met, he quickly looked away.

Mike was still drawing pictures before our hikes, and after grabbing my hand I hoped the experience would be represented in his next drawing. It wasn't. Taking the crayons, he painstakingly drew a house and a stick figure. He had drawn this same picture dozens of times, occasionally with different colors or with more figures. But the people were always the same, and always without faces.

So I didn't know what kind of impact our dangerous climb had had until we were on Dogface again the next day. After leaving the crayons and drawing at the nursing station, we headed for the hole in the fence, slid through, and tramped along in silence. I had in mind a particular escarpment that I thought would offer a safer climbing challenge. When I stopped, Mike also halted not far behind me, and I pointed toward the craglike ridge that rose before us.

"This is one we haven't climbed yet, Mike. Want to give it a try?" Without waiting for an answer I started forward, knowing that Mike would not be inclined to refuse. About halfway up, a ledge widened considerably and there, where powerful volcanic forces had heaved the wall, I could spot where the ledge reversed itself and changed direction. It was a somewhat tricky climb, and when I pulled myself onto the shelf, I realized it was the perfect setup.

"Mike, I'm going to stop here," I shouted down. "Why don't you come on up?"

He didn't have to be asked a second time. Rapidly he wound his way to the base and began the ascent. After five minutes of hard climbing, he ducked into a granite cleft not far below me.

"Take a breather, Mike. This next part is harder, so rest. And remember, hikers have to work together, so if you need a hand, say so and let me help you. Sometime I may need some help myself, and I'll certainly ask for it if I do, okay?"

Without giving any evidence of having heard me, Mike resumed the climb. He was careful yet sure in his movements and in a few moments was standing just below my position on the ledge.

Reaching out toward him, I said, "Here, Mike, take my hand. I'll help you up."

He squinted at my outstretched hand, studying it as if there might be an extra finger. Then he gazed across the cliffside and down, apparently retracing the course he had just scaled. He was clearly caught in a conflict, his darting eyes betraying uncertainty and anxiety. And then, as if remembering what had happened the previous day, he extended his arm to where I could just grab his hand. I drew him up the last few feet and he sank onto the terrace beside me.

"Great, Mike! That's the way—that's how hikers work together!"

We sat together in silence for a few minutes and then I pointed out a small lizard that had popped out from behind a rock to inspect the company. We watched it for a while, sprawled side by side against the rock, and Mike didn't seem to mind the closeness.

After a time I said, "Okay, Mike, ready for the top?"

His reply was immediate and emphatic.

"Hike top Dugfahs!"

I looked sharply at him. Edging into the monotone I was so used to, his voice carried the hint of excitement. A subtle inflection I couldn't be sure of, and yet . . .

We moved off the ledge and the surprises continued. Instead of reverting to his usual distance, Mike stayed close to me and, side by side, we climbed to the top of Dogface. I couldn't recall a time when I had felt more encouraged and rewarded as we sat beside each other on the crest. It had taken such a long time, but at last Mike was allowing me inside his magic circle.

Forty-five minutes later as we approached the cottage door, Mike was still walking near me. As I took out my keys to let him in, I said, "Mike, I want you to know how very proud of you, I am, and how happy I am that you gave me your hand so I could help you. I know it was hard for you, and that makes it a very brave thing that you did. Sometimes it's scary to take a chance and trust someone, but I'm glad you were able to do it again today, and I hope you'll do it some more. And Mike . . ." by this time he was shifting his weight impatiently from one foot to the other, "I also want you to know that it's just super to have my hiking buddy as close to me as you have been this afternoon. That feels very, very good to me, and I hope it does to you, too. You're really a good friend, and it's nice to do things together."

Mike was staring intently at the door. But when I opened it, he gave me one quick glance and our eyes met momentarily before he slid out of view. But that was enough. He had heard and understood what I said. I was sure of it.

During the following week, Mike alternated between coming near me and shying away, as if uncertain from moment to moment what his attitude should be. For my part, I didn't push it. Except for one occasion.

We were hiking down from the summit, playing a game I had taught Mike of jumping from rock to rock. When we cleared the boulder-field, I noticed that he was limping slightly. Catching up with him, I saw that he was holding his hand on the inside of his upper thigh, and walking fast, rather stiff-legged. When he saw my concerned look, he began hobbling even faster.

"Mike, what's wrong? Did you hurt yourself back there?"

He shook his head and stepped up his pace.

As I stood there watching him shuffle along, a memory circuit clicked. I had seen a gait like that before. And then it hit me: when we took the blind children on field trips, the rest rooms were always unfamiliar. Some of the kids, not wanting to contend with strange toilets, would try to hold back too long. As parents do, I quickly learned to anticipate such problems; it was always easy to spot a child in that distress. That's how Mike looked now, as though he was literally trying to hold it in. Suddenly it occurred to me that on all our hikes I had never seen him relieve himself. On a couple of occasions I had stepped behind some rocks, and I had assumed Mike did the same.

"Mike, do you have to go to the toilet?"

No reaction.

"Mike, if you have to pee, just walk over behind those rocks. You don't have to wait till we get all the way back to the cottage. Is that what you're trying to do? Mike?"

He slowed, and then stopped. He wouldn't turn to face me so I went around in front of him. Sure enough, he was holding his hand in the inimitable manner of small children when they *really* have to go.

"Mike, just go on over to those big rocks there. It's okay to pee."

He shook his head, still looking down.

"Why not? Why won't you?"

"Bahd."

"It's not bad, Mike. Who ever told you that?"

"Bahd," he repeated.

"No, it's not; it's a very natural thing. Peeing, going to the bathroom, is okay—just like eating and drinking. What goes in must come out!" I said it lightly, but Mike didn't make the connection. "It's okay for you to go out here, Mike. That's what people do when they camp, or when they go hiking and there's no toilet around."

He still wasn't moving, other than squirming

from foot to foot. And then I thought, What the hell, I sort of have to go too. I'll set an example.

"C'mon, Mike, I'll join you. Let's go over there." Sensing that Mike was shy, I added, "You take one side of that big rock and I'll take the other. C'mon, I don't like to see you hurting like this."

I wheeled in the direction of the large boulders at the base of the cliff and he reluctantly followed.

"You'll feel a heck of a lot better," I said, unzipping my fly.

Mike looked furtively around, then at me for one last signal of reassurance, and hastily opened his pants. Within seconds, the relief on his face was so evident I laughed.

"See, doesn't that feel a lot better?"

"Fews goooooood!"

"Right, I told you it would. There's no point in suffering like that, is there? From now on, whenever you're hiking and you have to go, just find a nice rock or a tree. There's nothing 'bad' about it."

Little of consequence happened with Mike over the next month. But in other ways, things brightened up a bit when Debbie Shaw, a clinical psychologist, joined the staff. Somewhere in her late twenties, she was extremely attractive, a healthy tan softening her distinctive features. She had deep brown eyes that followed your every word and a quick, sunny smile. I eagerly volunteered to show her around and Scott agreed, but then cautioned, "Don't come on too strong with the McGarry charm—she's going through a pretty rough divorce." Nevertheless, Deb and I hit it off immediately, and the kids really took to her, too.

It wasn't long, though, before I began getting impatient again. Mike continued to let me stay closer to him, taking my hand now and then when I manufactured a situation. But that was about it. Occasionally we exchanged comments; but generally he drew his pictures, then we hiked silently to the summit of Dogface, rested, and returned. Something more was called for. So one day, instead of letting him choose the drawing topic, I instructed him:

"Mike, I want you to draw a picture of us hiking on Dogface. Will you do that for me? He sat pensively and I wondered whether his uncertainty reflected an inability to draw a mountain. So I sketched a quick profile and handed it to him. "That's how a mountain looks. Kind of. Now you draw one, but don't forget us. Show Mike and Pat hiking, okay?"

He set to work then and the results were gratifying. It seemed as if he needed just a bit more structure at times. A little nudge now and then.

"That's a very good picture, Mike. Very good! Now, can you tell me a story about it?"

Puzzled, Mike stared at what he had drawn.

"Hike Dugfahs."

"Okay, Mike, but first, isn't there anything you can tell me about your picture? I see there are two people. Who are they? Is one of them you?"

A slight nod.

"Can you show me which one is you?"

Slowly, Mike moved his finger and placed it on the smaller figure.

"Good, Mike! Now, am I there, too? Where is Pat?"

117

The finger slid over a couple of inches and came to rest on the slightly larger form.

"Very, very good, Mike. That's excellent! What are we doing there?"

"Hikin' Dugfahs."

"That's right, we are, aren't we? And what's this?" I pointed to the house.

Mike shrugged. "Cahge . . ."

"Cottage? Your cottage here?"

A single nod. "Hike Dugfahs."

"Okay, Mike, very good. But one more question." I paused. "Why don't Mike and Pat have faces? Why don't we have eyes . . . and noses . . . and mouths?"

Mike turned away, staring out the window, where his refuge awaited. "Hike . . ."

I sighed. "Okay, Mike, you've done very well today. Let's go."

Two weeks later, Mike and I were advancing to the final approach to the crest of Dogface. I had suggested that we again climb the difficult rock face on the south side where Mike had slipped and almost fallen. We hadn't been back to that area since that day, but now Mike unhesitatingly agreed to give it another try. The rock formation was heavily pitted with cracks and, once again, the going was slow as we climbed, one of us on either side of a vertical rift. We went at a much slower pace than the first time, conserving ourselves, and whenever we stopped for a breather, I would tell him:

"Don't forget, Mike, hikers have to work together. So if you need help, let me know."

From time to time one of us would dislodge a rock and then both of us would stop, listening as it clattered and ricocheted to the bottom. It was a reminder that the rock could have been one of us. Then, more carefully, we'd begin climbing again.

Farther up I dropped back, intentionally allowing Mike to gain a lead, and as we neared the summit glimpses of the familiar crest stood out against the cirrus-clouded sky. High overhead a hawk drifted soundlessly, sliding from side to side on the warm air currents. Mike had just cleared the last ridge and without a backward glance was starting up the trail when I found the spot I'd been searching for. In a crevice shadowed by an immense overhang, I braced myself and called out sharply, "Mike! I need some help here—could you come back?"

In a few moments he returned. Kneeling, he peered down into the space where I was lodged.

"I got myself jammed in here somehow," I told him. "Take my hand, get a good grip, and pull hard, okay?" I reached up toward him.

Mike didn't respond immediately. Instead he knelt there, looking at me and at my outstretched hand. Then his head lifted and he gazed out above me, his eyes following the waves of rolling hills, the valleys with their ribbons or orchards melting into the haze, and the silvery ocean beyond. Again there was that lost look—the expression that I had begun to see more and more—an imprint of the confusion that was going on inside him.

Fortunately, I had placed myself in a fairly secure position, because Mike thought long and hard about what he should do. And, as always, all I could do was wait. As he looked back down at me again, I could see the turmoil of his decision, the misgivings mirrored in his eyes. And then, abruptly, he leaned out and reached down a trembling hand, which I quickly grasped tightly.

For once I dispensed with my "hikers" reinforcer—no words were needed this time.

As soon as I had clambered over the edge, Mike immediately stood up and resumed the short walk to the top, where he sought out his favorite rock. I hung back a while, sensing that he might need some time alone. At last I traced his steps and went over to sit beside him, putting my arm gently across his shoulder.

"Thanks for your help, Mike," I said softly. "That's what it's all about—hikers, people—working together."

I squeezed the back of his neck affectionately. Mike had seen me do this to other kids many times and they always squealed with delight when I did it. But for Mike it was different. He was like a young, wild colt, and I patted him reassuringly when I felt a couple of nervous shivers through his thin shirt. That seemed to calm him and we sat together, faces turned toward the warming sun, relaxing in the lingering breezes that meandered over the crest of Dogface.

I found myself thinking back to our first time up here. And how very much had happened . . .

—————— *chapter nine* ——————

After those extraordinary days on the summit of Dogface when Mike let me help him and then reached out and assisted me, some undeniable changes began to occur. Slowly the little boy—the child who had been imprisoned inside himself for so long—started to emerge. The transformation was quite subtle initially, reflected in a comment or request, a glance or expression. By now I was sensitized to the nuances, rare as they were. As in climbing the rock faces, each step toward trust was one of weighing the risk, testing the footing carefully, then stepping out—usually forward, but at times halting and backtracking. Still, once Mike made the commitment, as scary as it was for him, he persevered, just as he had on the south wall of Dogface.

The rest of that month was uneventful. Then one afternoon we were sitting in the dayroom, where I had just watched Mike complete a crayon drawing of his favorite theme: the cottage with two figures that represented us. The faces remained blank as usual; even Dogface had not been outlined.

For the two-hundredth time I inspected the scene and then turned to him.

"Okay, Mike, that's a fine picture, but before we take off for Dogface I want you to tell me why the people don't have faces. Why don't you ever draw any faces?" This time I was determined to get an answer.

Mike sat cross-legged, staring somberly at the paper.

"Do you want me to help you? Should I guess why there are no faces?"

Mike shook his head. He was studying the drawing, then he pushed it toward me and stole a quick glance at me before averting his eyes. I couldn't read anything from his expression, but his shoulders hunched slightly as he gazed solemnly at the floor. Sensing a certain thoughtfulness, I pressed as gently as possible, my voice lowered, trying to convey the concern I felt:

"Mike, I know it's hard, but is there a reason for not drawing faces? I'd really like to know—could you share it with me? Please?"

His lips moved, as if he were talking under his breath.

"Please, Mike . . ."

The voice that finally emerged was low, husky, the words tumbling out rapidly and strung together.

"Dey-aw-wuk-kin-uduh-way."

"Mike, I couldn't understand you—could you say it a little slower, please?"

A long, almost exasperated sigh.

"Dey aw wuk-kin uduh waaay."

"They're all looking the other way? Is *that* it, Mike—*all the people are looking the other way?!*"

A quick nod.

So that was it, the answer to the riddle of no faces. Ignored and rejected early in his life, Mike believed that everyone was, literally, looking the other way. He saw no faces; just the backs of people's heads.

I whistled a big sigh and Mike looked up at me, startled.

"Mike, what you've just told me really blows me away.... Now I understand better—much better—what things must be like for you. But I hope we can change all that for you, Mike, so you can be a happier person. One thing you can be sure of is that I'm not going to be like that. I'm not ever going to look the other way. Hikers—and best friends—have to help each other out, care for each other. And that's what we are, aren't we, Mike? We're best friends, right?"

While I was talking Mike had looked away again, but now his eyes searched my face.

"Munng-key uhnn-koe . . ."

"What? Monkey's uncle? Oh, boy."

Mike seemed to have latched on to that expression. I wasn't sure why. Maybe he just liked the sound of it, the catchy rhythm of the words. Or perhaps that was now his name for me. In any case, with Mike's incredible disclosure, we had rounded another significant corner.

I caught Scott later that same afternoon just as he was heading for the parking lot. "Got time for a bombshell?" I asked.

He set his briefcase down on the walk. "What's up?"

Showing him the picture, I related what had happened earlier.

"They're all looking the other way, huh?" Scott shook his head, studying the drawing thoughtfully. "That's really classic, Pat. The beautiful transparency of the young coming through, completely without guile. Once you reach a child and he begins to relate to you, to trust you, things do have a way of falling nicely into place."

"Still a long way to go."

"Oh sure. But you seem to have found the right key with Mike—it fits and it's opening doors. Now it's just a matter of time and seeing how far the little guy can go. You're starting to uncap some of that straight-arrow honesty that comes with trust, and as long as he begins to identify with you, and introject you—"

"He is, isn't he?"

"Sure he is. Mike is giving up the aloofness, the withdrawal. He's trying reality on for size—throwing in with you, in a psychological sense. Mike will be using you as a conduit in coming to terms with people and how he's going to get along with them."

"What happens next?"

"It's hard to know for sure. Mike may initiate the next step, but it's more likely that you'll have to do it again. Or he might go back and forth about it. We may want to try play therapy one of these days. But for now, trust your own intuition; you'll probably sense how much he can handle before you see it." Scott inspected the drawing again before handing it back to me. "They're all looking the other way. . . . Boy, it's tough to see that kind of stuff in kids." Scott's voice trailed off. After a moment he added, "You know, I think this little guy's going to make it."

"Of course he is, Scott! You had doubts?"

Scott fixed me with a baleful eye. "See you tomorrow, Pat."

Shortly after that I brought up with Scott the subject of my internship. It would be over in a couple of months and I was concerned about Mike. Scott cut me off in midsentence.

"I just assumed you'd stay on and collect the data for your dissertation right here. No need to move on to do that. Here are the papers and stuff I need you to sign, though, if you decide to stick around and take a staff position. It'll pay a little better, too . . ." He pushed the forms at me. They'd already been made out, except for my signature.

For once, I was speechless.

That evening I began to map out a program of expanding activities, finding things to do that would perhaps allow Mike to discover some of the childhood experiences that had so totally eluded him. A few days later, I pointed to the pair of gigantic water tanks perched high on a bluff overlooking the main hospital.

"Would you like to hike up to those water tanks today, Mike?"

His gaze followed my arm, but his face remained blank.

"Water tanks, Mike. See those big green things up on that hill? That's where all the hospital water comes from. It's stored in those tanks until you turn on a faucet to get a drink, or when you see the sprinklers going, that's where the water comes from. You know about water faucets," I said and winked at him.

Mike's head bobbed. "Waduh, waduh, have hahn-doe?"

"No handles, Mike, you know better."

He nodded; he did indeed know better. Handles were a no-no for our kids. Normal youngsters will watch with intense concentration as pieces of wood or plastic boats float in a bathtub or down a gutter, but the child with schizophrenia will turn on a water tap full-blast and sit for hours mesmerized by it. So all the outdoor faucet handles at the hospital were kept locked when not in use. Mike had a well-earned reputation for spotting the spigot with an over-looked handle, then turning it on until someone discovered him. That's why he was wondering if those huge tanks had handles. He was anticipating releasing all that water.

"Do you want to hike up to the water tanks, Mike?"

An affirmative nod.

"Okay, ask me then. Hike up to the water tanks, Pat? Go ahead, say that."

"Hikup waduh tahnk . . ." a pause, ". . . Paht."

"Good! Very, very good, Mike!" I had been prepared to break the words up as I'd always done before, assuming that Mike wouldn't be able to put them together on his own. Now I realized that, even though his pronunciation was odd, the language was certainly there and available for development. It was a distinctly pleasant surprise, and all the more so because this was also the first time Mike had called me by name. I gave his scarecrow hair a rub. "And that was especially good because you said my name. What's my name, Mike?"

"Paht."

"Pat, Mike, say 'Pat,' not 'Pot.' "

"Paht."

"Pat. Say 'at.' Paaaat."

"Paht."

"Well okay, Mike," I sighed. I guessed I could get used to being called "Pot," although it had a certain questionable connotation. "Close enough, and an extra scoop of chocolate ice cream for you today."

So that afternoon we climbed to the water tanks. They were enormous, and once we had ascertained that there were no handles, Mike set about exploring the network of interlocking pipes that ran just above ground level between the two tanks. The water mains were huge two-foot-wide pipes and I quickly climbed one and tightroped across it. Mike watched me, open-mouthed. Interspersed among the several mains was a series of smaller pipes and when I began balancing on them, he could restrain himself no longer. In moments he had scrambled up beside me and, when I hung by my knees and swung, his reaction was instantaneous.

"Me, me do! Paht, ME!"

"All right, sit like this." I slid off and put my hands on his legs to steady him. "It's okay now, I have you, just keep your legs curled around the pipe. There you go."

And there was Mike, hanging upside down, gently swinging. We spent the next hour clambering among the pipes, which made a nifty jungle gym. When we returned to the cottage and I asked Mike to draw a picture of the tanks, he jotted one right off. After that, the tanks became a regular destination—and the subject of many drawings.

Over the months, Mike's pictures had multiplied exponentially, and Jody suggested that he display some of them on the bulletin board near the nursing station. Soon it was filled and someone else prevailed upon Mike to transfer his efforts to his own room. That appealed to him, and he began to tape favorites to the cement block walls above his bed.

After a few trips to the water tanks, I decided to try to capitalize on Mike's affinity for water by describing the filtration plant, located on the other side of the hospital grounds. We were walking through the parking lot and, after arousing his curiosity, I concluded with, "Lots of splashing water!" and spread my arms like the big circling aluminum booms. I stopped by my car. "Would you like to go to the water plant, Mike?"

He agreeably fell in with the plan. "Go waduh . . ." was as far as he got.

"Come over here, Mike." I knelt down in front of him. "Try this. Watch my lips. Water—"

"Waduh."

"No, try once more. Wa-*ter*."

Mike's expression was earnest and he was really trying, but although we went over this several more times, the "ter" sound was just too difficult for him.

"Okay. Now plant."

"Pwahnt."

"Close, try it again. Plant."

"Pwahnt."

I gave up; this was beyond him, too. Most of Mike's vowels were distorted, particularly "a," which usually came out "ah." "Okay, now try it together. Water plant."

"Waduh pwahnt."

"Good, buddy, that's close enough. Now we have only one other problem."

Mike picked up on my tone immediately and glanced sharply at me.

"We have to take my car. It's too far away to hike. How do you feel about going for a car ride with me, Mike?"

It had probably been years since he had been in one and I wasn't sure how he'd react to this. He looked apprehensive, so I walked over to the car and opened the door.

"C'mon, Mike. A ride will be fun for you. We can go lots of places in the car. Especially the water plant. To see all the splashing water."

I got in and slid across to the driver's seat and then beckoned to Mike. He approached tentatively so I started the engine. "Last one in's a monkey's uncle, Mike!" I said, patting the seat beside me.

"Munng-key uhnn-koe."

"Right, come on."

After a brief hesitation, Mike climbed in and sat back stiffly against the seat. His head came barely to the bottom of the window so I told him to sit forward where he could see better. By the time we reached the main hospital grounds, Mike was craning his neck.

When we got to the filtration plant, I opened the door and he bounced out, eyes going wide as he spotted the water gushing out of the booms and cascading over the rocks. We walked around the massive pools and then climbed the catwalk that led to the plant. Stopping in front of a large control panel, Mike stared at the gauges, handles, and different colored lights.

A plant maintenance worker came over and, noticing Mike's interest, asked if he wanted to learn how to regulate the flow of water. Mike had moved closer to me as the man approached, but after I encouraged him he cautiously gripped the large wheel and rotated it slowly. When he grasped the connection between what he was doing and the increased water flow, he became euphoric. Spinning the wheel enthusiastically to the maximum output, he soon had the water splashing out of the pool.

"Waduh, waduh!!" he squealed.

The maintenance man moved in to shut the flow a bit. But Mike had a death grip on the wheel—he was in control and reveling in it.

"Easy, Mike," I counseled. "You're getting a little carried away. Turn it back down now."

But Mike wasn't having any of that, so I finally stepped over and cut the torrent to an acceptable level. Mike was acting goofy. His eyes dancing, he jumped up and down while holding tightly onto the wheel. I let him enjoy the ecstasy for a few moments, then said, "Okay, let the engineer take over, Mike, it's his turn."

I waited anxiously to see if he could relinquish his new acquisition. It was a struggle for him, but he finally backed away.

More comfortable now, the man said, "I'm going to give you a job here, Mike. Have to get you a hardhat like this." He took off his yellow hat and put it on Mike's head. "You like that?"

Mike nodded. This was almost more excitement than he could take.

"We'd better be going, Mike," I said.

"Come back anytime, Mike," urged the man. "My name is Ned. You can come and turn the valves and help me whenever you like."

Mike leaped at this offer. "Okay, come bahk tumawah!" he said emphatically, jumping again and clenching his fists into tight balls.

"Uhhh, Mike, slow down. Give Ned back his hat and let's go." Turning, I thanked Ned for his patience; he couldn't have known how much this had meant to Mike.

As we headed for the car, Mike looked reluctantly over his shoulder at the splashing, rotating booms. He talked of little else for the next few days and later that week we returned.

With experiences like these, Mike's innate appetite for discovery began to flourish. Once opened, the curiosity and wonderment so typical of normal children spilled out as forcefully as the flow of that favorite industrial water valve. For the next couple of months we explored the entire hospital complex, thoroughly investigating every nook and cranny, all the little-known buildings, trails, and roads. There was also the hospital farm, which provided all the milk and eggs along with part of the meat for the hospital population. Initially frightened of the animals, Mike gradually learned to pet the cows and feed the chickens from his hand, yipping boisterously as they pecked his fingers.

And I continued to blend in teaching with our jaunts. The narrow road that led to the farm was lined with green pepper trees and an occasional gray- and titian-colored eucalyptus. I commented on the contrast one day and Mike pulled up, his attention caught by the unusual names. Pointing to a tree, he asked:

"Wha' tha' twee name?"

"That one's a pepper tree, Mike."

"Wha' tha' one ovuh deh?"

"That's a eucalyptus."

"Ah whaaat?!"

"Sit down for a second, Mike," I said, motioning him toward the curb. "Now watch my lips and say it after me. You—"

"Youuu—"

"Ca—"

135

"Caaaah—"

"Lip—"

"Wippp—" Mike was still having trouble pronouncing the "l" sound. And he tended to drop the ends of words; I purposely exaggerated the sound so he wouldn't swallow the last syllable."

"Tus!"

"Tisss!"

"Okay, now try it with me. Eu-ca-lip-tus."

"Eu-cah—"

"That's right, Mike. Eu-ca-lip-tus."

"Eu-ca-wip-tiss."

"Fine, good. Let's hear you say it by yourself now."

"Eucawip-tissss!"

"Very good, but we'll have to work some more on 'l'—luh—won't we? You know, this is a good idea, Mike. We'll start working on pronouncing words, maybe even while we're climbing on Dogface. Watch my lips again, Mike. Dog—"

"Dug—"

"Dauuuuuuugh, Mike. Open your mouth more and at the end say, 'gah!' Try it."

"Dooooooogah—"

"Close. Good, try it again. Open wider. Like this. Dauuuuuuugah—"

"Dauuuuuuu-gah!"

"Fine! That's perfect! Now say, 'fayyysss' —whistle the 's' between your teeth. Fayyysss—"

"Faaahs—"

"Fayeeees—"

"Faaahs."

"Good. Pretty close. Now put them together. Dogface."

"Dog-fahs!"

"Excellent, Mike." Half right, anyway. "Very good—you're getting it! That deserves a double-dip chocolate ice cream cone!"

He was excited when we reached the canteen and bounced up and down in front of the ice cream freezer considering other flavors before settling on his favorite. The rest of the afternoon was punctuated with Mike's intermittent chanting of the new sounds. Learning new words and their pronunciations was a game he liked and shortly thereafter I began taking a magazine along on our hikes. Whenever it was time for a rest, we would sit together and leaf through the pages, identifying pictures and practicing diction. The words retained a bizarre quality because of Mike's peculiar intonations and manner of delivery, but gradually his speech was becoming easier to understand.

There was no doubt that the severity of Mike's illness had left its residual marks. But unlike mental retardation, where intellectual development is constitutionally limited—and thus arrested at some level—schizophrenia poses no such boundaries. The only question was, how well would the psychological wounds heal? That and only that would determine how much Mike could achieve. One point was in his favor, though: everything to date seemed to indicate that he was a pretty bright kid.

As the months went by Mike became increasingly aware of what the other children were doing, what they did when they went on home visits—indeed, what home visits were—and what kinds of things they brought back. Soon Mike was asking me to bring him some of those goodies: a box of animal crackers, his own crayons, a baseball cap.

Slowly the pathological behaviors dropped out. It was apparent that Mike's acknowledgment that all people were looking the other way had been a key turning point. With that behind him, he began to accept the fact that some of us cared about him.

Cecile enthusiastically reported that he was more alert and beginning to take an interest in some of the classroom doings. And this new receptiveness was also carrying over to the cottage. Mike was calling Chuck "Chahk," and relating to others on the staff as well, asking a question here and there, coming closer, and generally testing the risky waters of relationships.

His solitary dance—the repetitive steps and ritualized syncopation—occurred much less frequently, then virtually disappeared. And so, the bud began to open. Gradually the silent Little Shadow began to explore a whole new world—a world in which he had existed but had never understood.

chapter ten

My phone was buzzing. Insistently. That was unusual because I was seeing a family in therapy and the secretary generally didn't interrupt. But she did now.

"Chuck from Mike's cottage is on line two—needs to talk to you. Says it's urgent . . ."

"Okay, thanks." I punched the button, a queasy feeling in the pit of my stomach. Had something happened to Mike? Was he hurt? "Yes, Chuck. McGarry here."

"Doc, we got problems. Mike's dad showed up a little while ago. He's acting pretty strange, says Mike's a lot better so he wants to take him to church. Like right now. The minister wants to see Mike and pray over him. To get the demons out or something like that. Mr. Harris won't take no for an answer. Insists we sign Mike out to him right now. I told him we got to talk with you first."

"Okay, I'll be over as soon as I finish up here."

"Uh, Doc . . ." Chuck's voice sounded huskier.

"Yeh?"

"Better get here as soon as you can. And brace yourself. The old man's really been pressuring Mike and the little guy don't look so good. He's getting that spacey look again . . ."

"Okay, Chuck. Be right there. Thanks for warning me." As I hung up the phone I thought, Oh God, Mike, you sure didn't need this! Turning to the family, I explained that an emergency had arisen and that we would have to cut our session short. They were still nodding somberly as I raced from my office.

I had my key ready forty feet from the cottage, but Chuck was waiting, swinging the door open as I came up the walk.

"They're down in the dayroom." He closed the door and caught up with me. "It's gotten worse since I called."

I glanced at him questioningly.

"He's a different kinda guy."

"That's an understatement. What's he up to?"

"Seems to have a bug to take up where he left off four years ago. I don't know what in hell is going on with him. He just showed up, leaned on the buzzer 'til I let him in, and then when he saw Mike and how much better he seemed to be, he started telling him about all the things they were going to be doing together from now on. And first off is a visit to the minister, so he can pray for him! Now he's trying to get him to . . . well, you'll see for yourself. You won't believe it . . ."

By this time we were at the dayroom and I eased quietly through the door. Mike was crouched in the far corner, his eyes vacant. There was no recognition at all when I came in. He was scrunched down as if attempting to make the smallest possible target. His entire body was tensed for escape. What the hell *was* going on?

My eyes slowly left Mike and came to rest on Mr. Harris. He was down on both knees halfway across the room, his arms raised beseechingly toward Mike. He was so caught up in the fervor of his pleas that he didn't even see us come in.

"Tell Daddy you love him. Tell Daddy you love him, Michael; come here now, give me a big kiss and tell Daddy you love him. Please, Michael, tell Daddy . . ."

Chuck's whisper came over my shoulder. "That's what he's been doing for the last few minutes; nothing more about church. I think the guy's nuts."

Mike was staring vaguely in my direction and I tried to tell him with my eyes to hang on, I'd get him out of this fix. I was afraid of what was going on inside his mind. There was an unmistakably psychotic flavor to his expression; I hoped he wasn't retreating all the way back again. I approached his father and put my hand on his shoulder.

"Hello, Mr. Harris. Do you remember me? Patrick McGarry. Could we go to my office and talk, please?"

Silenced momentarily, he glanced back at my hand and then up at my face. There were tears trailing down both pasty white cheeks and his dazed eyes took a minute to focus on me. "He's my son," he said pleadingly.

"Yes, I know, Mr. Harris, but Mike isn't ready for this. It's too much, too fast. Now please, come with me."

He shook his head, turned away, and began to crawl toward Mike, resuming his appeal.

"Michael, tell Daddy you love him; please Michael, tell Daddy you love him—"

"Mr. Harris, stop it *right now!* This is very upsetting for Mike—he's not really able to tell you he loves you. Now I want you to get hold of yourself and come with me. *Immediately.*" My best authoritative tone was invoked. And ignored.

"Michael, come to Daddy, tell me you love me. Tell Daddy you care, you forgive him. Please Mikey, *tell me you love me!*" Mr. Harris's voice had become shrill, almost crackling with intensity.

There was something very wrong with him

today; he was completely different from the man I had met several months earlier. That day he had at least been fairly rational, if hostile. A sudden thought froze me: maybe he's had a psychotic break, too. That'd make it three for three. I turned to Jody, who had just come into the room.

"See if you can reach Scott, or Conable. Quickly."

"Right." Jody took one look, nodded, and disappeared.

Mike remained crouched in the corner, but now he began to rock back and forth, his eyes closed, a staccato chatter emanating from deep in his throat. I didn't like the sound of that at all.

Hastily I stepped around Mr. Harris and bent over Mike. "Mike? It's Pat. I'm here now, it's okay."

No response.

I edged a bit closer. "Mike, it's okay now, there's nothing to be afraid of. Can you hear me, Mike?"

The rocking gait changed slightly, but that was all.

Suddenly Mr. Harris began to shout, "MICHAEL ... TELL DADDY YOU LOVE HIM ... TELL DADDY—"

Abruptly the chattering stopped. Mike's eyes opened wide in terror, his mouth making grotesque soundless movements and then, from his very depths, came a reverberating, chilling shriek. Mike screamed and screamed and when I moved to go near him he jumped away, hitting his head on a window handle. Blood began streaming down his face, into his eyes and around his mouth, but Mike was unaware of it. He just continued shrieking, clawing at himself, and leaving great welts on his cheeks.

Jody was back at my side again.

"I called Dr. Conable, he'll be up in a minute. We'll have to sedate Mike. That gash looks like it'll need stitches."

I nodded numbly, glancing at Mr. Harris. I couldn't believe everything had been dismantled so quickly by this screwball. The dumb son of a bitch! What in hell was he thinking? Appearing out of the blue and pulling all this stuff on his son—after he'd abandoned him for four years!

Jody must have been reading my mind. "Be cool," she said softly.

"Yeh, sure," but my voice was tight. It was a fight for control.

Moments later, Conable and an entourage of aides joined us. As the aides moved in to assist, he was on their heels, pointing a mean-looking syringe in the air.

"Hold him still," he said and the aides closed in, but they weren't really needed. Jody had edged in ahead of them, speaking soothingly as she reached out and took Mike's arm. His eyes were tightly closed, as if he were expecting to be struck. He flinched when she touched him, but astonishingly made no attempt to get away. Still talking reassuringly, Jody unbuckled Mike's pants and bared a buttock. He scarcely moved as the needle penetrated and in less than a minute he slumped into her waiting arms. Almost immediately she was applying pressure to his head, blotting the blood with a piece of gauze, consoling Mike even after he was knocked out by the powerful sedative.

I was standing by, a bit in shock, and feeling totally helpless.

Conable looked over at me. "Why don't you see what you can do for him." He nodded toward Mike's father, and I could tell by his tone that he wasn't too pleased about all this, either.

Mr. Harris was still on his knees, leaning on a nearby stool, his head and shoulders sagging.

"Come with me please, Mr. Harris." This time I wasn't about to be ignored, but he offered no resistance. I lifted him to his feet and steered him down the hall and into the small anteroom behind the nursing station. Dazed and remote himself, he sat silently, tears streaming down his cheeks.

Then he began praying, softly at first. "Dear God, I just don't understand any of this. Whatever went wrong with my son is absolutely beyond me. I'll never understand why you did this to us—we never hurt nobody, we've led good Christian lives. What did we ever do to be punished like this? My only son ... only *child* ... and I don't even know him." He shook his head. "I've *never* known him. Oh God, why have you forsaken us like this? Why, why?"

Abruptly he began to sob, and all I could do was sit and listen to his grief spill out. In a sense he was right; it was almost as if the family *had* been cursed. Sorrow, sickness, and pain had certainly riddled their lives. My anger at what he had done began to abate. He was a person in deep trouble himself, another of life's walking wounded. Finally, the sobbing subsided and, his eyes avoiding mine, his voice hesitant, he began again.

"Mikey seemed so much better to me today. But I'll bet you're going to say I've ruined everything now ..."

"Well, we'll just have to wait and see, Mr. Harris. But in any event, you should have checked with us before coming up here so that we could have prepared Mike for your visit. It's been a few years, after all."

Mike's father recoiled, perhaps realizing for the first time how long it had been. He seemed compelled to justify his absence.

"Well, since your visit a while back, Mike has been very much in our thoughts—and in our prayers. But like I told you, when we brought him here he wouldn't even come near us, talk to us. It just hurt so bad, having a child who was a stranger to us. It was more than either my wife or I could handle. Especially my wife. It was all just too much for her." He ran a hand anxiously over his forehead and cleared his throat. "I took her to the mental health center like you suggested. She had the worst spell ever . . . came home and found her like in a trance or something . . . just staring at the TV—but it wasn't on. And she didn't even recognize me. That scared me plenty I can tell you. . . . She's better now since we've been going to the clinic twice a month. They put her on some sort of medicine."

"I'm glad to hear that, Mr. Harris."

"We've talked to them about Mike, too. It hasn't been easy. Have you any idea how you feel about yourself when your own son has to be shut up in a mental hospital?"

I shook my head. After a moment, I asked, "What made you decide to come out today?"

"Well, like I say, we've been praying for Mike every day now. Ever since you dropped by. Praying that he'll recover and be released. And we talk regularly with our minister and the social worker. But we have a new minister now, and he suggested that maybe we should bring Mike to church so that the devils that are inside him could be cast out. They're the ones—Satan, that is—who've done this to him. He's demon-possessed, you know!" Suddenly Mr. Harris's expression began to harden again, his voice becoming more charged, his eyes burning. It was the fanatical Mr. Harris threatening to emerge. But then he caught himself and looked sharply at me.

"I know you prob'ly don't believe in demon possession. You think I'm a crackpot, but that's what's happened to our little Mikey, and nobody is going to tell me *any different!*" His fist hit with a *whap* against his open palm to emphasize the point. Mr. Harris was cranking up again.

I raised my hand. "You're certainly entitled to your beliefs—"

"It doesn't matter," he interrupted, cutting me off. "Anyway, I came up to see Mike by myself, to see if I could take him to church. I thought it'd be too hard on Mother, she'd get too upset, so I came alone. And then when I saw how much better Mikey was when I got here, that he didn't run away like he used to, that he even talked to me—I thought he was cured, the demons had finally been driven out after all these years. It seemed like a miracle, a sign. I thought Satan had finally been beaten. And I rejoiced and thanked God . . .

"But then when I wanted to pray with Mike, to embrace him, he ran into the corner and no matter how hard I tried to tell him I love him, he wouldn't speak to me again or let me near him. Just like before. When he began screaming and hitting himself again—" Mr. Harris's voice caught, choked, and he sighed, "I guess I was wrong, it was too much to expect. I just don't get it, how he can change so quickly. One second he's fine and the next . . ."

"Would you like to begin trying to understand, Mr. Harris? And help Mike, too?"

He looked up sharply. "What do you mean?"

"I simply mean that Mike is," I paused, correcting myself, "*was* making real progress, and I hope he will again. But what would help immeasurably would be if he had a mother and father who would love him, show him that love, and at the same time gain some understanding of the serious emotional problems he has."

"Well of course we love him," Mr. Harris broke in. "We care about him very much, he knows that! We've told him enough."

"But because of his illness," I suggested carefully, "he just hasn't been in a position to accept or return that love. And still isn't, although he was getting better. But it'll take time before he'll be able to do that. I would suggest, though, that you and your wife continue in counseling and come up here occasionally, meet with me, visit with Mike, and perhaps in time Mike may once again be the child you love and have prayed for."

Mr. Harris stared at his hands and said nothing. So I went on:

"I guess we all want the same thing—to see Mike get better and be able to leave the hospital. Maybe we can combine our forces toward that end?"

I thought I detected a trace of interest. I was throwing Mr. Harris a rope and he couldn't decide whether to grab it or not.

"I'll consider your suggestion, but let me ask you a couple of questions."

I nodded. "Shoot."

"Are you a Christain? Do you read the Bible every day? Or are you one of those educated liberals who've destroyed the faith in what used to be a God-fearing country?"

"Well, Mr. Harris, I don't want to seem evasive, but my religious beliefs really have nothing to do with my work. All I'm concerned about is seeing that Mike and kids like him get the kind of treatment they need so they can leave here and get along on the outside and, with a little luck, lead fairly happy and healthy lives. That's the main thing. Isn't that what all of us are interested in?"

"Yeh, I suppose it is. But your religious background is mighty important. Don't ever underestimate how it influences your entire life, and the lives of everybody you come in contact with. The Lord is all-powerful, merciful to His flock, but you must repent your sins and accept Him as your Savior." His voice had taken on the cadence of a television evangelist.

"That may be true for you," I conceded. "I think I'm a deeply religious person, although I don't identify with any particular belief or church—Christianity, Judaism, or even Buddhism, for that matter. I guess I believe in parts of all of them."

Mr. Harris's eyebrows shot up. "Even Buddhism?" He pronounced it "Budism."

"Yes, especially Buddhism," I went on, undaunted. "And I couldn't tell you the last time I read the Bible because I honestly don't remember, but I *can* tell you that I don't think it's as important that a person read the Bible every day as it is that he abides by its principles." I met his scorching eyes straight on. "If you insist on categorizing me, I guess I'd be considered a humanist. My concern is for people, their welfare, their well-being. Especially those with psychological disorders. If you equate being liberal with making people's lives better, I'm all for it—but I certainly don't consider humanism, or liberalism for that matter, responsible for the problems our country is having—"

"So, you're not a God-fearing man?" Mr. Harris seemed to be pressing for some kind of surrender.

"No, I'm not, Mr. Harris. I can't relate to a God who would put demons in people—especially little boys—or punish them and inflict them with pain and suffering. People do that to people, nature makes mistakes, bad karma intervenes— there are all kinds of ways of explaining the illnesses, the suffering in this world. But I don't hold God responsible. So for what it's worth, I am a believer in God. I just don't fear Him. I fear destructive human qualities far more— greed, hatred, prejudice, cruelty . . ."

Mr. Harris's expression did not soften.

"Well, do I pass the test, Mr. Harris?"

"I'll think it over, what you suggested. We'll see, but I'm not promising anything."

"Fine. As long as you're willing to consider becoming more involved with Mike, that's all he, or I, could ask. Maybe we can combine the best of both our beliefs."

For that rejoinder I got a sharp, frank look.

"Well," Mr. Harris finally relented a bit, "I don't have much of an education, but I know you're trying to help Mike. Could you let me and the Mrs. know how he is from time to time?"

"Sure, Mr. Harris, I'll be glad to."

Later on that afternoon, I walked back over to Mike's cottage. A couple of nurses were conversing in the nursing station and both turned as I approached. I didn't even have to ask.

"Dr. Conable was up a little while ago and ordered another shot for Mike. Wants him knocked out for a while, hoping it'll minimize the aftereffects."

"Probably a good idea. I guess I'll just go down and see him for a few minutes."

"If there's anything we can do—"

"No, thanks anyway. Nothing anyone can do until we see how Mike comes out of this."

When I reached his room Mike was lying on his back, the deep regular breathing of sedation broken by an occasional tiny snore that made me smile. His cut had been bandaged, the white gauze encircling his head, his lopped-off blond hair protruding here and there in clumps. I tried to read from his expression what might happen, but without seeing his eyes, knowing whether they would be averted or not, it was impossible to tell anything. So I just sat on the edge of the bed and, in the half-light, tried to come to terms with the events of the day, and why such things had to happen to those least able to defend themselves. It all seemed terribly unfair.

Mike's leg began to twitch under the blanket, as if he were trying to run, and I rested my hand on it, giving it a few pats. Involuntarily, I spoke what I was thinking:

"You're going to be okay, little buddy. We've come too far together to let anything separate us now. I promise you, Mike, we'll work this out, too. You can count on it." Mike stirred, and the twitching stopped. Then the deep measured breathing resumed. Tucking the blanket up around his neck, I murmured, "See you tomorrow, Monkey's Uncle."

In the parking lot I ran into Scott. He had

been conducting a workshop down on the main grounds all day, so I hadn't seen him since early morning. But I could sense his concern as he came up to me.

"Heard about what happened. Pretty grim, huh?"

"Yeh. Very." I didn't feel very much like talking about it just yet.

"How did Harris know where Mike was?"

"One of the kids told him, so he just bypassed us."

"Ahhh, yes. That figures. Did you have a chance to talk with him?"

"Sort of. He's really an unstable guy. Anything bad that can't be explained is the work of the devil. But at least they've been getting some counseling since I saw him last. And he says Mrs. Harris is on medication now."

"Hmmm. How's Mike?"

"Not good, Scott, not good at all."

Aware of my reluctance to go into it, Scott said, "Well, we'll talk about it tomorrow. Anything I can do now?" he offered.

"Not really. Thanks anyway. I guess this sort of thing just comes with the territory. Under the circumstances, all you can do is keep your fingers crossed and hope for the best. Right?"

Scott nodded. "I'm afraid so. There's always going to be that element of uncertainty. You've done what you can and now you have to wait and see what develops. You have to learn to deal with situations like this."

"Yeh . . ."

"Take it easy now, Pat. Go on home and relax. We'll talk about it tomorrow."

—————— *chapter eleven* ——————

That night I gave some hard thought to my chosen profession. It was amazing how tangled up you could get with a kid. It was almost as if Mike had become my own child, but I hadn't realized until now just how much of an emotional investment I had in him. Now I was suddenly, acutely, aware of it.

I wondered if my attachment were impairing— would impair—the effectiveness of my work. A therapist inevitably has an emotional stake in his patients, particularly those he works with for any length of time. But he also has to remain objective and relatively detached. And yet with kids it just seemed so much more difficult not to become overinvolved. Where did you draw the line? It was something I needed to discuss with Scott.

I lay in bed, the events of the day on replay in my mind. I kept wondering if there were anything I could have, should have, done differently. And wondering, too, what the outcome would be.

It wasn't until after midnight that I finally fell asleep, and even then, as tired as I was, I slept badly. Finally, at half-past five, I gave it up. I needed to get out to the hospital and see what was going on.

By the time I arrived at the cottage, the ward personnel were waking the children and herding them down the corridor to the bathroom. It was by far the earliest I'd ever been there. This was a part of hospital routine I'd missed. I paused outside Mike's room and listened for any sounds from within, but I could hear nothing. Then, pushing the door slightly, I stepped inside. Mike was lying on his side, staring at the wall.

"Mike? Hi, how're you doing?"

There was no response from him, not even a slight movement. The vacant eyes were fastened to the cement block wall. I started to move toward the bed, but then stopped when Mike began curling up into a little ball, drawing the blanket over his head.

"Mike? It's Pat—your buddy."

A small hand clenched the blanket even more

tightly. It was all I could see; the rest of him was a motionless lump.

"Mike, are you okay? Can we talk about it, buddy? I won't come near if you don't want me to, but try and talk with me, okay?"

There was no reaction.

I pulled up the only chair and sat quietly for a while, thinking it would be better if I didn't push him right now. He'd been pushed enough yesterday. But after ten minutes of silence, I decided to try for some response, even just a tiny one. So that I'd know everything we'd worked so hard for wasn't irretrievably lost.

"Mike, I'm going to leave now. But do me one favor? Just stick out your finger and wiggle it a little. I need to know that my buddy's okay. Would you do that for me? Just wiggle a finger, Mike . . ."

Nothing. No movement at all. I waited several more minutes, but he remained rigidly still.

I sighed. "I'll be back in a while, Mike. You rest up some more and take it easy. See you later."

I walked back to the nursing station and wrote a brief note, detailing Mike's behavior. I asked the duty nurse to let him stay in bed for the time being, but if he did get up, or say anything, to track me down right away. Then I slowly wended my way to my office. Scott's secretary was just getting in and I asked her when he would have some time.

"Not till 11:30 at the earliest, I'm afraid."

"Okay, put me down."

I was busy myself all morning, but toward eleven the phone buzzed.

"McGarry."

"Jody here. I've got some good news . . . and some bad news . . ."

"Give me the good first."

"Mike's up, and he had something to eat. *But,* he won't get dressed, won't let anyone near him, won't speak to anyone, and—" Jody paused and sighed, "he's back to the stork steps, all the magical rituals and stuff again."

"Damn." My worst fears were confirmed. "Okay, thanks, Jody. Keep me posted, will you please?"

"Sure. Sorry, Pat, I guess we start over now."

After I hung up, I did some of my own staring out the window, trying to bring some understanding to it all. The gains Mike had made had been extraordinary, but there really hadn't been the opportunity to integrate them before the old man showed up. What timing!

Scott interrupted my reverie as he paused outside my door. "Bring your cup and come next door for a bit, huh?" he suggested. "You look like a man who could use some therapy . . ."

"I heard how Mike is—now tell me how you are."

"Not bad, I guess, all things considered. Spent

a lot of time last night, though, wondering if there were anything I could have done differently—wishing that I had just picked Harris up and booted him out the door . . ."

"But he *is* Mike's father—"

"Yeh, I know . . . some father. Mike was doing fine without him."

"I gather you were pretty angry with him?"

"Understatement of the year, but a good counseling reflection anyway!" I laughed. Scott looked a bit sheepish at being called on one of his therapeutic gambits. "Yeh, I was mad as hell at him. Still am. I lay awake most of last night thinking about it. Does this kind of thing happen very often, Scott?"

"Setbacks? Monkey wrenches in the works? Unfortunately, yes. It's one of the more common problems, especially when you work with children. You have to be very careful—particularly with the parents. Sometimes the whole family is locked into a scapegoating action; they've targeted one person—perhaps the most independent child—and everybody unloads on the kid. It's the therapist's job to help the family see that, and it's easy to get caught in the middle. Then, of course, the family dumps on you. Or worse yet, as the kid gets better, the parents, or the family, undercut you."

"Do you think that's what's happening with Mike's father? Is he going to try and sandbag us as Mike gets better?"

"It's hard to say. I don't think so; people don't consciously plan such sabotage. But he's been out of the picture so long it may be difficult for him to cope with Mike's improvement. Things like that do happen."

I was making little church steeples with my fingers, probably in deference to Mr. Harris. I couldn't quite voice what I was thinking and we sat in silence for a few moments. It was a hard thing for me to talk about, to put into words. Finally I began,

"You know, last night I really had trouble with this. To paraphrase one of our famous predecessors, I know I was never promised a rose garden, but I really feel terrible about Mike. I've been brooding over everything from his tenuous hold on reality to my equally tenuous hold on being a competent psychotherapist. And now, after yesterday, the futility of it all. I don't know, it's a hell of a time to find this out, but I think I get too caught up—overinvolved—and then, when the disappointment hits, the bottom drops out. Do you know what I mean?"

All I could read in Scott's expression was support; he didn't seem appalled by what I felt was a crushing admission. He nodded and then reached for his favorite briar. It took him a few seconds to get it stoked, and then he said, "Well, Pat . . . I can't give you the answer to that. No one can. My experience has been that each therapist has to work this out—for himself, or herself.

It's part of the price we pay for being in the trenches. And you can imagine what happens when you're following two dozen or more patients in therapy. The responsibilities are very demanding, and put fantastic pressure on you. You're involved, concerned, taking risks with depressed and suicidal patients, violence-prone ones, you name it. Last week when I let Amy go on a home visit, I worried all weekend, jumped every time the phone rang . . ."

Amy was a twelve-year-old who had seriously tried to kill herself a half-dozen times, the last one with rat poison. It had burned away much of her stomach, leaving what remained ulcerated and constantly painful. It was a miracle she'd survived.

"But we can't just lock her up in Merrick for the rest of her life," Scott went on. "I had to take a chance sometime, hope that I understood her and the family well enough to know that she had improved to the point that I could risk it. But," he sighed, "that didn't make it any easier."

"So you never really do learn to live with the pressure?"

"Oh, I think you come to terms with it. But being a psychotherapist *is* a high-risk job, and some times are worse than others. As we've talked about, people are not exactly predictable. They'll make demands, sometimes excessive ones, and you have to deal with it. Other times, a person seems to be doing exceptionally well and then all of a sudden everything falls apart. An unexpected psychotic break, a suicide attempt, maybe even successful, and everything crashes around you. That's why you have to learn to be tough-minded—and yet retain your sensitivity. Otherwise," Scott paused and drew hard on his pipe, "otherwise, you don't last, You burn out. Become indifferent to the plight of your patients or perhaps shield yourself with a harsh, no-nonsense style of therapy. Or—as some psychiatrists have been known to do—you become a pill-pusher, keeping the patient in a chemical straitjacket, so you never have to get around to doing deep, intensive psychotherapy. There are all kinds of escapes. Some people just opt out, become administrators or program directors, which cuts down their exposure to patients. The trend now is to try and spread yourself out a bit, maybe do some teaching, a little consulting, along with a therapy practice. The trick is to find a balance that suits you."

He leaned forward, tapping his pipe against the side of an ashtray. "But you see, Pat, situations like what occurred yesterday, and worse, are bound to happen, perhaps make you question the steps you took or whether there wasn't something else you could have done. We come back to the experience variable: knowing as much as you can about how human beings behave in certain situations, making the best professional judgment you can at the time, evaluating it afterward, and filing it away for future reference."

We sat in silence for a while. One other disturbing thought kept recurring, but I couldn't bring myself to say it aloud. Scott was watching me, an almost mellow softness to his expression; the concern for his star pupil was genuine and I knew it.

"Say it," he urged gently.

"Say what?"

"What you're thinking."

"Oh, Jesus, Scott. You damn psychologists, always reading people's minds."

Scott waited patiently.

"I don't know if I can express it or not. It's very difficult for me to admit."

"Try."

"Well, . . . you know what's going through my mind with all this. I mean, . . . maybe I'm just not cut out to be a psychotherapist. Maybe I'm not strong enough to ride the cutting edge, shoulder all the responsibilities, the disappointments, the upsets, the setups, the setbacks, you name it. God, I don't know what in hell I'd do if a patient ever suicided on me. Here I am coming unglued over Mike, but what would happen if someone in my care *killed* himself? If I were seeing a kid like Amy and she did herself in and it was my responsibility . . . God, that'd be hard to live with. . . ."

"All we can do is try, Pat. But you know, we don't have control over people's lives. Responsibility, yes—to a point. We do what we can to help others, but we can go just so far. The choice for what they do is theirs. Even suicide. If someone is determined to kill himself, there may be nothing we or anyone else can do to prevent it. But although we may feel a sense of responsibility when that happens—and agonize over whether we might have been able to turn things around if we'd just been more alert, more sensitive . . . in the end what it comes down to is that each person bears the ultimate responsibility for his own actions."

"I can accept that rationally, Scott. But how to deal with the *feelings* inside is the problem. . . . I just don't know. . . ."

Scott leaned back in his chair. "I guess the key is time. And with time comes experience. That will bring a certain measure of objectivity that allows you to monitor your feelings, your empathy. So that you'll know when to detach yourself, and pull back."

"Well, to be honest with you, I'm seriously questioning whether I'll ever be able to do that."

"There's only one way to find out, though, and you're doing it. You'll have doubts—the most natural thing in the world. There'd be something wrong with you if you didn't. But don't hold yourself accountable for too much. Just give yourself time, step back, keep your perspective, and use me. That's what I'm here for."

"Thanks, Scott." The weight of self-doubt had begun to lift and I felt almost cheerful. I couldn't believe it. "You know, you're a hell of a therapist!"

Scott shrugged, still serious. "Promise me one thing, though?"

"Sure."

"When you get into tough situations—and I can guarantee you that you will—use your colleagues. They're your friends. They'll understand the turmoil, the confusion, because they've experienced it, too. And you may have to help a few of them at times; it's reciprocal. As I said before, this is a high-risk business. There's a lot of stress—that's why we play up the team treatment concept. It's mutually supportive—we lean on each other. It diffuses things a bit when we know we can reach out to someone else if we have to, that there's no need for us to bear the whole weight ourselves. No one really can, you know."

"Yeh. This is quite a profession we're in."

"Nothing like it. It's not for everyone. But someone has to take care of the Amys, the Mikes, the Dannys of the world. As rough as it is sometimes, *someone* has to do it. . . ."

Later, sitting in my cubbyhole office, I was staring out the window, my mind idling in neutral, when I noticed Mike's folder at the top of the stack. The secretary must have left it there. A progress note was due. Good timing; I'd have a mouthful for this dictation.

Picking up the file, I leafed through the pages, smiling ironically as I read the frustration that flowed from between the lines of my earlier notes. The Good Old Days. Or were they so good? Actually, they had been pretty grim. Back then I hadn't seen a sign of anything encouraging. I was surprised all over again by how much progress Mike had made and how much there now was to build on. What the hell was I getting so discouraged for? Impulsively, I picked up the phone and dialed.

"Cottage 4, Fletcher."

"Jody, Pat here. When you have a chance, would you tell Mike I'll be up in a little while for our hike on Dogface. Even if he doesn't seem to hear you, say it to him a number of times."

"Okay, I'll tell him. But he's still out of it. No change."

"Yeah, I know, but I've got to try something."

"Okay."

Shortly after two o'clock that afternoon, I took a seat on a low table in the dayroom across from the hunched form near the window. Mike had his back to me. He still had his pajamas on.

"Mike, this is a special occasion. It's a beautiful day, and I'm ready for a hike up Dogface.

How about you? You don't have to draw any pictures or even ask for the hike. This is your day. Whatever you want to do, buddy, we'll do . . ."

There was no movement, just the rhythmic breathing reflected through the back of his thin pajama top.

"C'mon, Mike, get dressed, put on your hiking boots, and let's get out of this old cottage for a while. It's a nice day and I'll bet the views are great at the top of Dogface. Maybe we could stop for some pop or a chocolate ice cream cone on the way back if you want. It's your day!"

I tried a few more times to engage him, but there was no response at all and gradually my hopes for a speedy remission dwindled. It was going to be a long way home.

I pulled up a chair across the room, where I thought Mike's peripheral vision would include me. Then we sat quietly, listening to the rhythm of the cottage: periodic loudspeaker pagings, the occasional peal of a child's laughter, screams, or shouts that drifted into the room. There were some things that I thought needed saying; I'd just gamble that he would be tuned in enough to hear some of them.

"Mike, let me try and explain a little bit about what happened yesterday. First of all, I think your father felt very bad about how hard he pushed you and about what he caused. He just didn't understand what you've been through, how difficult it's been for you. And I guess when he first saw you, he wanted to believe that everything was all right, that somehow or other all the problems of the past had just gone away. He didn't realize how you've been struggling with things, trying to understand yourself and other people. Or how sometimes things hurt inside. Yesterday, you saw your father confused by it all. Like you have been at times. You've been trying to understand new words, new things, and it's been confusing for you, and very scary. Right?"

Mike continued to gaze blankly out the window. I had no idea whether he heard what I was saying. But I pressed on.

"I don't know what you're feeling inside right now, Mike, but let me guess. Yesterday, when your father asked you to do things you just couldn't do, you must have been really frightened. And then when you saw him getting so upset, it was even more scary for you. So now you're afraid of all of us again, afraid that we'll be expecting you to say or do things that you're not ready for yet. And the only way you have of protecting yourself is to close us out again. But everyone—especially your father—is truly sorry for what happened. We all feel very bad about it, especially because you've been trying so hard lately to understand yourself and all those scary feelings inside. We can't change what happened, but I want you to know that we won't ask you to do anything until you feel ready for it. So the next step is up to you. But we're hoping you'll give us another chance, Mike. Okay?"

I stayed with him for over an hour, but I might as well have been by myself. He had pulled way back again. The wall, which had so spectacularly toppled during the last few months, had been as spectacularly rebuilt overnight.

The next day, and the day after that, I went up to the cottage to sit with Mike, occasionally saying something to him, but generally just sharing the minutes of heavy, portentous silence. Usually he was in the dayroom rocking or moving to the synchronized beat of his solitary dance, his eyes empty, unseeing. When meals were called, the beat would stop and Mike marched mechanically out of the cottage and down the path, staying as far away from the other kids as possible, scrupulously inspecting each step to the dining hall. Apart from this, he showed absolutely no interest in leaving the cottage, much less hiking on Dogface or going to the canteen. He had become a thoroughly remote figure once again—even more so than before—and the staff, respecting his plight, made allowances.

I went up to see him every day that week. Friday was a particularly beautiful day, and I tried to tempt him with a hike, or a trip to the water plant, even a short walk. But it was all for naught. His mind was turned away and whatever recesses he had taken refuge in were not open to my pleas. He was on a totally different wavelength.

Nothing changed the following week. Each afternoon I prepped myself for another inspirational message to Mike, trod the path to the cottage, delivered my speech, sat in prolonged silence, and finally departed. I could sense the frustration creeping in, the edginess returning, the doubts resurfacing. I kept telling myself, I got through before, I can do it again. There's got to be an answer, there's got to be a way to reach him. But what is it? Where is it?

A few weeks later, I had a flareup with Dr. Conable. He had been switching and adjusting Mike's medications in an attempt to stabilize him but it hadn't made any difference and the staff had reluctantly agreed that Mike had regressed back to his former state. I hadn't contributed much during the review meeting, but just as I was about to urge that the staff should be patient and not assume the worst, to give Mike a bit more time, Conable closed Mike's metal chart with a snap.

"I'm afraid Mike Harris is beyond reach. There's nothing else I can think of in the way of chemotherapy. Maybe a shock treatment or two would do something. It might be worth a try. After all, he's practically catatonic."

An uneasy silence settled over the room.

Conable glanced up from the next chart he had opened, sensing that something was wrong. His eyes fell warily on me.

"That's bullshit!" I exploded. "That would drive Mike so far back in he'd *never* come out!" I could sense that my face had flushed.

No one spoke and an uncomfortable silence stretched out. It was Debbie Shaw who came to the rescue. "I think Pat is right. Shock treatments are pretty extreme. We have other options before we consider anything like that."

Several others quickly voiced their agreement.

"Well, we can wait," Conable said in a more conciliatory tone. He obviously had not expected such a strong reaction from me or so much resistance from the staff. "That's the absolute last resort, of course, and not something we'd ordinarily do with a child. But it may eventually come to that. . . ."

Someone hastily brought up another youngster who had been causing problems lately and the discussion moved on. From across the room, I shot a look of gratitude at Debbie and she smiled back. I owed her one.

After the meeting Conable and I apologized to each other. He admitted that his judgment was premature and, in any event, bad form when someone else's patient was involved. I grudgingly acknowledged that there might be some validity to his remark that Mike was beyond reach. At this point, I wasn't being terribly objective.

* * *

When I got back to my apartment late that afternoon, I made a nice, very-limey gimlet and, adding the makings for another to the frosty shaker, headed for the deck. Savoring that tangy first sip, rolling it around while my mouth puckered, I nestled into the chaise and considered the upcoming weekend. Tomorrow I'd go down to the beach and do a little surfing. That always cleared my head. Maybe catch a movie in the evening; some diversion might help. I watched the sun sink slowly into the ocean, waiting for the merciful withdrawal of the tension sword that had been embedded between my shoulder blades all week.

————— *chapter twelve* —————

Another week passed, which made five since Mr. Harris's visit. I hadn't heard from him, but then I really didn't expect him to reappear; he'd probably fade away again. Often during this time my mind would replay the whole incident. Mike's face—his total reversion—would fill the screen, and the anger toward Mr. Harris for what he had done would burn a little deeper. Finally, late one morning I rolled the chair back from my desk and said aloud, "The hell with it. I've got to get out of this nuthouse for a while."

I changed into my Levi's and hiking boots, which I hadn't bothered to wear for the last few weeks, grabbed my lunch, and took to the hills. On my way, I decided to stop at the cottage and give Mike the chance to go with me. He was in the dayroom he preferred, doing his rocking routine, so engrossed that he didn't notice me. Nor did he slow when I spoke.

"I need a break and I'm going to hike up Dogface, Mike. You've been cooped up here for over a month now, and so have I. If you'd like to come along, you're wlecome to. I'm leaving right now and since no one else is here, the door will be open for a few minutes if you decide you want to go with me."

Without waiting to see what, if anything, he'd do, I turned and walked down the corridor to the outside door and opened it. Fortunately, most of the kids were off having lunch and the ward was virtually deserted. I asked Chuck to watch for Mike and lock the door again if it didn't look as if he were going to leave. When I reached the hole, I peered out from behind the bushes. The door to Cottage 4 was shut again and there was no sign of Mike on the quad.

As I approached the foothills, my mood began to clear. Following a side trail, I decided to detour around by the old riverbed, laboring through the sand for a quarter of a mile before climbing up the clay walls to find a game path that led toward Dogface.

Periodically shifting my brown-bag lunch between my perspiring hands, I stopped every now and then to sniff the pungent aroma of the manzanita bushes that thrived in the rocky soil.

The undergrowth dwindled as I gained elevation and came at last to the familiar trail, the one that led to the lemon orchard. Soon the fragrant trees came into sight and a short time later I reached the grove. Crossing through it, I paused on the far side and leaned against a boulder to catch my breath before beginning the ascent up Dogface.

I was mopping my brow when, beyond the orchard and down along the brush line, a movement caught my eye. Maybe it was a deer; Mike and I had glimpsed them on occasion and once we had even seen the swift flash of a red fox. I watched the spot intently, hoping to catch sight of the creature.

And then a flapping checkered shirt darted out from a line of scrub. Moments later a slight figure entered the grove, head down, moving purposefully. He glanced briefly at a nearby lemon tree, but then came directly toward me.

It was Mike! Quickly I wheeled and began hiking swiftly up the trail, away from him. As I climbed, I marveled and exulted. He must have sneaked out of the cottage and hidden behind the building until I'd gone through the fence, because there wouldn't have been anywhere for him to hide once he cut across the quad. And he had caught up with me now because he'd taken our usual trail, the quickest way to the top. Maybe, just maybe, the lure of Dogface was going to start opening Mike up again. It was difficult to resist the urge to turn around to see how far back he was. But the voice of reason and caution rose inside me, counseling: Stay cool, don't get your hopes up! Push on ahead, let things develop as they will, let Mike call the shots.

I could feel the exhilaration when I reached the crest of Dogface and settled on the rock that had become my regular perch. One idea chased another through my mind as I rested there. Maybe Mike was back to his shadowing days, when he had followed people from a distance. But even that would be a vast improvement over his recent exile—the chance for another beginning. From the slope behind me came the sound of his boots scraping against the rocks and loose gravel. I tensed, but continued to gaze out over the valley while the anticipation roiled around inside me. And then Mike was striding past me not five feet away, his face set in firm resolution as I greeted him.

"Hey, Mike, you decided to come along after all."

He halted, head down, intent on arranging some pebbles with the toe of his boot. His stock monotone, with its equally familiar refrain, announced, "Hike up Dogfahs." Then Mike turned and marched over to his rock, seated himself and, taking a deep breath, assumed his all-encompassing ritual surveillance across the misty valleys toward the silvery ocean in the distance.

I said nothing more. The cool sea breezes were sweeping up the foothills today and farther north, along the coast, a fog bank seemed set on recapturing the shoreline. It was enough just to sit together for a while and let the beautiful vista do its own form of healing. That might be the kind of therapy Mike needed most now. I was determined to be patient, let him make the next move, and just be there if he needed me. Gradually, his expression softened and the harsh, guarded, crazy quality subsided.

Suddenly it occurred to me that I was hungry and I remembered my lunch. Mike certainly hadn't had time to eat, either. The bag rustled as I opened it and unwrapped a bologna sandwich. Tearing it in half, I looked up to see Mike staring at it.

"Would you like part of my sandwich, Mike? Hikers have to eat well. Here . . ." and I stretched the bigger half toward him, hoping the light breeze would give him a good whiff.

It did and Mike couldn't resist. He fairly leaped off the rock, grabbed the sandwich from my hand, and began wolfing it down.

"Hey, easy there, Mike. Nobody's going to take it away from you. Haven't they been feeding you?"

Mike continued to devour it noisily, his eyes

following my movements as I poured some iced tea from the thermos into its cap.

"Want something to drink?"

He nodded eagerly, but never stopped chewing as he took the cup from my hand. Downing the tea in huge loud gulps, he thrust the cup back at me.

I laughed and shook my head. "More tea? It's good, huh?"

He nodded absently, intent on the sandwich again as I poured him a second cup of tea. When my half of the sandwich was almost gone, I said, "You want my last bite? It's a little present for being such a good friend and coming up here today."

Mike took the sandwich remnant and half of the orange I had peeled.

"Tastes good when we can sit on Dogface and have a picnic, doesn't it, Mike? We should do it again. Would you like that?"

An emphatic nod.

"Good, we'll do it again real soon. And Mike . . . it's really great to have my hiking buddy with me again. I want you to know that. I missed you."

Mike glanced over at me and our eyes met. I saw the trust. We relaxed for a while then before it was time for me to get back. Eventually, I wadded up the paper sack and said, "Mike, time for me to go. If you want to stay up here, you can. But I have to start back."

I made a project of retying my boot laces to let him think it over, and then got up to set off down the trail. Mike arose, too, and as we began the descent he stayed right with me, picking his way down the rocky terrain. When we reached the lemon orchard, I pulled up and asked him if he wanted a lemon. Shaking his head, he said, "Nuh," and we continued on down the trail, through the fence, and up to the cottage. I unlocked the door and held it as Mike squeezed in and headed for his room.

"See you tomorrow, buddy," I said.

Chuck and Jody, along with several others, were waiting for me at the nursing station, brimming with questions. It turned out that about twenty minutes after I left, Jody had opened the door for a group of children returning from the food service building. In the midst of the rush Mike had darted out, and Jody had had to catch herself from calling him back as she saw him tearing off for the fence.

There was a quiet satisfaction all around now, and when I stopped at Mike's room as I was leaving, there was another upbeat moment when he answered my question about what he wanted to do the next day.

"Hike up Dogfahs tumawah."

After collecting Mike the next day, we stopped at the school to draw. I was anxious to see what, if anything, his pictures would reveal of the last several weeks. He set to work at once and soon, without any prompting, he produced two drawings. The first he identified as a "twee."

It was a picture he had drawn before, but this time, significantly, there were no people. Ground and horizon lines ran across the page, tightly enclosing the landscape, meager as it was—barren limbs and a branchlike network that looked like bars. No leaves. I guessed that this was representative of Mike's regression, his attempts to reduce his world to a manageable level. And that meant keeping it simple, and without people.

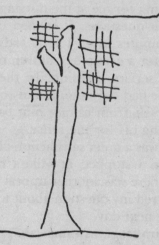

The next drawing was his conventional cottage scene. But again, there were no people outside, just one solitary stick person in the window whom I took to be Mike. The tiny figure was disproportionate to the size of the building, perhaps indicating that, once again, Mike saw himself as powerless, easily overwhelmed by outside forces beyond his control. And perhaps it was also significant that—as Mike so often did—the person was observing the world from the relative safety of his cottage.

I didn't question him, because the pictures told me all that was going to be expressed—I was hanging onto Mike's psyche by my fingertips.

I played it cozy for the next month, letting Mike set the tone. Gradually, he resumed his participation in school and became more communicative with the cottage staff. And we took up our twice-weekly hikes again, with Mike taking my hand for an occasional pull up and, in turn, helping me when I asked. Finally, some two and a half months after his father's appearance, Mike seemed to reveal, by his drawing of the two of us hiking on Dogface, that he was back to where he was before his father's visit.

I studied the picture a moment. Mike, unaccustomed to not receiving an immediate "Good," looked up and met my eyes.

"That's a really nice picture, Mike . . . I'm so glad to see us hiking together again. . . ."

I let out a big sigh in Scott's office. "Well, we've turned the corner. But it was a close call."

"Yes, it was," Scott agreed. "And not just for

Mike. There were moments back there when I thought you were going to bring in the Irish Mafia and put out a contract on Mike's dad."

"Yeh. I was resentful, frustrated—and angry. But I learned a lot. I just wish the exercise hadn't been at Mike's expense."

"But Mike bounced back," Scott retorted. "That's the important thing. And it also points up something else."

"What's that?"

"That Mike *can* bounce back, can cope. You're not the only one who learned something—Mike learned a lot about *himself* during that little interlude. He's got strengths that he didn't even know he had, and he was able to draw on them. He also discovered that there's somebody he trusts. And that, my young colleague, dictates the next step."

"Play therapy."

"Right. It should tell us whether Mike can move up another notch or two."

—————— chapter thirteen ——————

The room we used for play therapy at Merrick looked more like a recycled laundry room than quarters for doing psychotherapy. A light green tiled floor with the tiles continuing halfway up the wall made for easy cleanup and an occasional hosing down; a shallow sink was in one corner and next to it was a sturdy wooden cabinet filled with a variety of toys and games. There were latex hand puppets, some of which resembled a family—including grandparents, a father, mother, brothers, and sisters—plus a fierce alligator, a one-eyed wolf, a friendly but unidentifiable mutt, and a dragon with a well-chewed tail. Also available were building blocks, simple wooden toys, checkerboards, watercolor paints and crayons, modeling clay, cap pistols, and a decommissioned beebee gun.

In one corner was a small sandbox, and to the side stood a four-foot plastic Bobo clown that was stuffed with foam rubber. His feet were weighted, and thus he always managed to regain them, and his dignity, no matter how malevolent the assault. His head was cocked where it had been taped back on after countless decapitations, which gave him an understandably perplexed look, and here and there spongy rubber protruded. But no matter how often he was bombarded and mutilated, his cheerfully composed features remained the same. Which was not always the case with the therapist.

To one side of a long, low table was an easel with sheets of shiny paper ready for drawing or finger painting, and to the left was the one-way window that looked like a mirror from inside the play area. It was covered with a wire screen that had numerous and sundry dents, but the window itself had somehow survived, although traces of paint and a few globs of clay had penetrated the screen. Children liked to make faces and grimace into the mirror, little realizing that there was often an observer on the other side making notes, or recording the proceedings on videotape for later study and evaluation.

Children's play is often viewed as frivolous, wasted time, an activity that is uncomplicated, lacking in direction, and simply a fringe benefit of childhood to be enjoyed before the oars of responsibility are lowered. To someone casually watching a group of children it may appear that way, but in actuality, play is vitally important to a child's development. In fact, an inability to mix and play with other children or by oneself is often an important symptom.

In play children not only express themselves but also learn about social interactions—getting along with others, rehearsing the fine points of asserting oneself, channeling aggression through competition, and of particular importance, providing the first linking up with members of the opposite sex. Play is far more complex than we imply by the phrase "child's play."

There is another equally significant dimension of play. When confronted by bewildering notions, worrisome or frightening feelings, or explosively hostile impulses, the young child senses that fantasy play is the safest way to release them. The greatest advantage is that the youngster is in control. If monsters get too scary, they can be dismissed with a mere shift of attention. Frustration and anger can be dissipated with a stern monologue accompanied by the crashing of toys.

On one occasion at the university clinic, I'd had a play therapy session with a four-year-old boy who carefully piled blocks one on top of another until he had built an elaborate tower.

As he added the last block the tower began to sway, and abruptly the peaceful activity was transformed into a destructive tirade. Kicking and scattering the blocks around the room, he sternly addressed them: "Naughty blocks! Naughty, naughty, NAUGHTY! Don't you ever do that again or I'll send you to your room. Without supper! You won't have supper for a week! *Do you hear me?!*" His tone carried a strong parental inflection. Then, seemingly satisfied, he gathered up the errant blocks and quietly, painstakingly, began to rebuild.

Since play is one of the most important ways in which children declare themselves, it is that ongoing declaration that play therapy attempts to build upon, by setting up special conditions for the disturbed child. Oftentimes the youngster's choice of toys—what he does with them or has them say during play—reveals deep-seated conflicts, frightening fantasies, and occasionally, traumatic experiences. Thus, the antagonistic forces such as beset the child with his blocks are acted out and dispersed.

But first and foremost, play therapy is freedom. Freedom to explore, to test, to express feelings without fear of judgments being rendered or directions being dictated. And in this freedom the child, with the support of the therapist, has the opportunity to gain confidence in his or her own judgment of the way things are—and how one might go about changing what needs to be changed, or accept what can't be changed. Hence, the young child learns to work through the maze of negative emotions toward the parents—from ambivalence to fear, resentment, and anger. Later on, when others frustrate and anger him, this learning will carry over and the child will deal with the situation in ways that mirror a growing maturity.

It would be a real step up for Mike if he could participate in play therapy. The odds were against us, though. The severity of his disorder, the early onset, the apparent total lack of play in his life experience, all bespoke a poor prognosis. Still, Mike had improved significantly and this would be one way to find out just how far he could go.

I had begun preparing Mike for the shifts in treatment strategy just before our second Thanksgiving, wanting to give him enough time to make the adjustment. I brought it up first when we were seated on the summit of Dogface. He looked over at me quizzically when I mentioned that some new activities would be starting for him shortly. Two weeks later, just after his tenth birthday, we started play therapy.

Mike was already familiar with the playroom; we had used it now and then to escape inclement weather and still have somewhere to ourselves to draw some pictures or leaf through magazines. What had struck me was the fact that he had never shown the slightest interest in the toys in the room. But that, I hoped, was more a consequence of his preoccupation than an indication of his inability to engage in healthy fantasy and play.

Scott, who had agreed to observe these crucial first sessions, was already in the adjacent observation room when Mike and I entered the playroom. Pulling up one of the child-sized chairs, I gingerly seated myself; with my knees in my line of vision, I always felt like a squatting Indian. Once again, I went over what we would be doing.

"Mike, this is where we'll be coming twice a week. You've been doing very well and now I want to try some new things to see if they can help you even more. But we'll still go on our hikes. Can't miss those, can we?"

An emphatic shake of the head.

"Right, but what we're going to be doing in here is playing—with the toys over there if you like, or painting a picture, or building things in the sandbox if you want. You can play with anything in here, Mike." And then I paused, as I remembered a time some months before when we had been drawing pictures here. I had stepped out briefly and returned to find the water in the pint-sized sink running full-blast and a mesmerized Mike regarding it with relish.

He had the same thought I did. He swiveled his head in the direction of the sink.

I had to smile. "You remember the sink, I bet!"

"Mikoe wun waduh, go aw ovuh fwooah!!" came out excitedly.

"That's right, we had a bit of mopping up to do, didn't we?"

He nodded enthusiastically. He remembered well; the sink had overflowed quickly, and by the time I returned water was sloshing in torrential sheets over the sides. Fortunately, the large drain in the middle of the floor had handled most of the deluge. Mike continued to nod vigorously, the pleasure of it all rekindled. "Wun waduh . . ."

"Well, you can run the water again—but for using it in the sandbox over there, or for painting." And then, as gently as I could because I didn't want to establish any inhibitions, I added teasingly, "And no staring at the water. . ."

His head bobbed again, and he sneaked a last longing look at the beloved sink and faucet before surveying the room. But he wouldn't leave his chair. I sat watching him in silence for a while and then tried to encourage him to explore.

"There are a lot of toys in the cabinet, Mike. Remember, you can do anything you want in here. The toys are there for you to play with. And there's paper and crayons if you want to draw, and Bobo the clown over in the corner."

Mike got up slowly, paused, and then hesitated by the cabinet. I had opened the doors earlier and he bent over, cautiously scrutinizing the different toys. Then he moved on to the sandbox. But he only looked. He seemed very concerned about not touching anything.

He approached each part of the room this way—the painting easel, Bobo, the sink, even the mirror. Sometimes, after inspecting an object for a few moments, he would turn and look at me with a tentative expression. I wasn't sure if he was uncertain as to where to start first, or if he was having difficulty making the connection between the activity of play and the various objects. So each time he turned I smiled and nodded. He would watch me, seemingly trying to read something in my expression, and then resume his circuit. After twenty minutes or so of this, I realized that it was simply going to take time for Mike to feel comfortable enough to initiate anything resembling play.

Again I reassured him that this was his hour and he could spend it any way he chose, and by the end of our forty-five-minute session, it seemed as if Mike had done about three hundred laps around the room. I was almost dizzy, but I had also stayed patient and supportive, visualizing Scott's reaction in the observation room as he watched "Quick Results McGarry" exercise a little self-control.

Later, Scott complimented me on my forbearance. He also said that he hadn't really expected anything much different from how Mike behaved. Any real spontaneity would have been highly unusual.

The next two sessions were simply repeats of the first, with Mike continuing his tentative explorations around the room. On a few of his revolutions he would reach out slowly and touch Bobo the Clown, or place his hand hesitantly on the cool sand before quickly looking at me, his expression revealing wonderment. But the child's atavistic curiosity seemed to be consistently overriden by some urgent restraint.

For my part, it was difficult to sit quietly, awaiting Mike's first move. But in play therapy it is crucial that the therapist not direct, but rather allow spontaneous, uninhibited play. It is only in such an atmosphere that the child will feel assured enough to begin translating conflict into activity.

"It's hard to choose just what to play with first, isn't it?" I offered several times. But Mike would just glance blandly over and then continue his scrutiny.

In between sessions like this, we took our regular hikes on Dogface and then Mike was his usual inquisitive self, for that was a level of functioning that he had mastered. Finally, after the third meeting, Scott suggested I put paper and crayons on the table, articles Mike was comfortable with, and suggest that he draw if he wished.

I did so at the next session. Mike paced about the room for a bit and then came over and sat down by the crayons and paper. During the next few minutes he concentrated on his pictures. Mike seemed content to draw something and show it to me. Then we would examine the familiar scenes together. He was simply unable to make any exploratory gambits on his own.

Halfway through, I decided to provide more direction. This had gone on long enough. So, while he watched, I mixed paints and set them up in front of the easel; I took out the clay and molded a few crude animal shapes, leaving the rest on the table; I piled some of the blocks into a small arch and pushed a toy car through the opening. I even gave Bobo a couple of bops and Mike was entranced as the clown bounced up again.

"These are all things you can do too, Mike. You can play with any of the toys in here, do anything you want—paint, build blocks, play with Bobo, whatever . . ."

Mike inched over to where I was leaning against the toy cabinet.

"Wha' this?" he asked, picking up a soft, well-worn object with a red checkered shirt.

"A doll, Mike. Raggedy Andy is his name . . ."

Mike laid it gently back on the counter and picked up a small piece of pink modeling clay. He rolled it into a little ball and held it between his fingers while he passed it under his nose. I restrained myself from saying anything when his tongue flicked out and tasted it. At last, the examination complete, he laid the clay back down on the table. Taking several steps away from me, he reached his hand out toward the rubber dragon, then paused, withdrew it, and retreated back near me.

Mike just wasn't catching on and Scott and I spent considerable time discussing what to do about it. Finally, Scott backed my decision to become even more active. More and more I was coming to feel that I was going to have to teach Mike how to play. If that were possible.

I started our next session with the hand puppets, placing one on each hand and carrying on a conversation between them in which they expressed the hope that Mike would play with them. He watched attentively as the alligator and the dog discussed the situation, looking from one to the other as each said something, and then at me. He seemed intrigued, so I handed the mutt to Mike, showing him how to slip it over his hand. Then the alligator began talking again.

"Hi, Dog!" The alligator bobbed his head, but the dog remained motionless and silent.

"Hey Dog, I said 'hi'! Can't you say 'hi' back to me? Hi there."

But Mike was struck dumb.

I persisted. "Dog, what's your name?"

No response.

The alligator tried again. "Oh, I bet I know where you're from. You live on Dogface, that mountain out in back where Mike and Pat like to climb. Right?"

Mike looked up at me, pleased with the recognition of his favorite spot.

"Hey Dog, talk to me. Are you from Dogface?"

But no matter how I coached Mike, he couldn't make the transition from himself to playing a hand-puppet character.

"Well," concluded the alligator at last, "you don't have much to say, do you? I'm getting hoarse, doing all the talking. Just shake your head 'no' so I'll at least know you heard me!"

Mike sat looking at the dog, waiting patiently for it to shake its head. Finally, I reached over and rotated his wrist and the dog's head moved.

"Now *that's better!*" cheered the alligator.

Not much, I thought. Scott agreed with me.

———— *chapter fourteen* ————

The Christmas holidays always brought about a magical transformation within the children's cottages. Instead of the usual institutional pallor, doors, walls and even the ceilings were trimmed in shiny tinsel and red and green crepe paper. Christmas carols played bravely through the static of the speaker system and sprigs of holly and berries added touches of color here and there. In Mike's cottage, a tall artificial Christmas tree stood near the nursing station, where its ornaments and lights could be properly supervised. And brightly wrapped presents cascaded from under the shimmering tree. Some of the kids didn't respond at all to the sudden change in the cottage surroundings and routine; they wandered about as if sleepwalking and, perhaps, ventured to taste the plastic poinsettias. But others became increasingly euphoric with each passing day.

The day before Christmas, school was canceled and shortly after noon the exuberant children were escorted to the dining hall, where they hastily gulped their sandwiches. Before long, the room was abuzz with anticipation. Then suddenly sleigh bells jingled from the adjoining corridor as Santa Claus arrived. A naturally overstuffed psychiatric aide savored the yearly role. Within minutes he had the youngsters singing Christmas carols. Most of the kids hummed off-key and mouthed their own lyrics, while the rest stared out remotely. Staff members circulated throughout the room, gently trying to involve the more disturbed children in the festivities.

As I moved among the youngsters myself, I would occasionally catch Mike's roving eye. He had never learned Christmas carols, of course, and now he seemed fidgety and uncomfortable. I realized with a twinge of sadness that, as with so many children here, Santa Claus and Christmas didn't mean a thing to him. But at least he was here; last year he had stayed in his room. . . . Finally, I went over and sat beside him.

"Isn't this fun, Mike? Having Santa here and eating cookies and ice cream?"

Mike looked up from the second helping of ice cream that he had just polished off, searching for more. Quite a bit of it had missed his mouth. "Mo'chok-let, Paht." He pushed the bowl at me.

"Enough ice cream for now, Mike." I took a napkin and, wetting it, tried to scrub some of the chcolate remnants from his face, while he squirmed away. Then, putting my hands on his shoulders, I pivoted him toward the center of the room, where some of the kids had clustered around Santa. "Watch now, Santa Claus is going to be handing out presents pretty soon. See, he's picking up his bag now."

Mike glanced about listlessly as Santa began moving up and down the aisles between the tables, dispensing multi-colored packages. Sounds of ripping and tearing followed in his wake, punctuated by staccato yelps of pleasure. Teachers, aides, and nurses continued to mingle with the youngsters, encouraging the less able to open their gifts, sometimes taking a child's inert hands and helping to untie the bow and part the paper. Finally, Santa worked his way down our aisle and spied Mike. He came closer.

"Well, well, here's a young man who certainly deserves a surprise today. I'm glad you came this year, Mike."

I could feel Mike's shoulders tense as Santa moved in, so I whispered in his ear, "It's all right, he just wants to give you a Christmas present. It's okay—I'm right here."

Slowly, Santa knelt down beside him. "Mike, I

understand you've learned to draw pictures and even ask for things. My, my ... that's very, *very* good, and here's a nice present for you!" Reaching into his sack, he withdrew a large package covered with smiling snowmen and reindeer. "Merry Christmas, Mike."

Mike hesitatingly took the gift from Santa's outstretched arms and turned slowly toward me. He was plainly confused by the whole transaction. He glanced uncertainly from me to the box and back toward Santa, who was continuing his turbulent journey down the aisle. Then Mike focused his attention on the bow, giving it a tentative poke. When nothing happened, he eyed it suspiciously.

"Go ahead, open it. See what's inside," I encouraged. "It's for you."

But Mike didn't understand and finally I had to show him how to work his way through the ribbon and paper. I pulled away the last of it to reveal the carton with a shiny red truck showing through the cellophane wrapping. Removing it carefully from the box, I handed it to him. He seemed captivated, turning it over and over, observing it in minute detail.

"Wow, that sure is a beautiful truck, isn't it, Mike? Santa must think you're someone pretty special!"

Mike still didn't fully comprehend what was going on, but he was unmistakably interested.

"Trahk?"

"Truck, Mike," I intoned the drawn-out sound. "A toy truck just like the big one that delivers food up to the unit here. Now you have a truck of your own to play with."

Just then another child cruised by, spotted the sleek new truck, and pounced, trying to grab it away. In a flash, Mike's arms surrounded it and he yanked back, covering it protectively.

"Trahk . . ." he whispered softly, verbally caressing his new treasure.

At last, after all the gifts had been distributed, Santa asked everyone to join him in singing "Silent Night." By this time most of the children were staring impatiently around the room, checking out what others had received and already, predictably, a few altercations had erupted. The kids were becoming increasingly restless after two hours in the dining hall. Santa gathered up his bag and waved himself out the door; in the ensuing commotion, the staff began separating the youngsters for the walk back to the cottages. Parents would be arriving soon.

Mike and I took the long way back to his cottage, and I could sense his uneasiness diminish as we left the party behind. I still hadn't heard a word from the Harrises so, for Mike, this Christmas would be like all the others. He would stay here. It was probably just as well.

The next couple of hours were hectic ones. The parking lot soon filled to overflowing as families arrived to pick up their kids. Paper bags stuffed with clothing and marked with each child's name were handed to the parents, along with small brown envelopes containing enough medication to cover the long weekend.

By late afternoon, a strangely unfamiliar silence had fallen over Cottage 4. I walked down the long corridor to Mike's room, carrying the Christmas present that I'd brought up earlier from my office. Tapping on the door, I asked, "Mike, can I come in?"

No answer.

Pushing against the door lightly, I stepped partially inside. Mike was sitting in his chair, holding the truck on his lap and gazing out the window. I wondered if he had been watching the tableau in the parking lot, seeing all the other kids leaving with their parents. But if he had been, there was no outward sign.

I moved over to the bed and sat down, placing the gift beside me. "Did you have a good time this afternoon at the Christmas party? And seeing Santa Claus?"

He nodded absently, still watching out the window. There was no one out there that I could see.

"And your truck? Are you happy with the present Santa brought you?"

Another slight nod. He was off somewhere in a different world again. Something elusive was going on inside, but all I could do was try to pull him back.

"Mike, look at me."

His head rotated cautiously in my direction, but his eyes remained glazed and remote.

"Mike, are you okay? What's wrong?"

Another blank stare.

"Hey, are you with me, buddy? Are you here in this world?"

The only response was some rapid blinking. I peered intently at the somber little boy, baffled by the sudden change in his behavior. What on earth was going on behind that inscrutable mask? Whatever it was, though, he evidently couldn't bring himself to express it.

"Mike, why don't you come over here and sit next to me? Okay?" I patted the bed.

Still, there was no response. Seeing him walled off again was eerie. He hadn't been like this since the crisis of his father's visit. All I could do was wait. At last, Mike wrapped an arm securely around his truck, got up slowly, and shuffled over to the edge of the bed. He had not yet noticed the present.

I put my hand on his shoulder and for some time we sat quietly in the semidarkness of the settling dusk and listened to faint strains of Christmas music.

"Are you sad, Mike?"

A slight stiffening of the shoulders.

"It's all right to be sad. It's part of living—hopefully, a small part. But sometimes things make you feel sad, and that can hurt. And when that happens, there's nothing wrong with getting help from other people. I'd like to help you, Mike. Will you let me?"

Mike sat rigid and immobile, immersed in his thoughts. Finally, after another stretched-out silence, he looked down at his new possession.

"Trahk," he murmured faintly. Wherever he had been, he seemed to have returned.

"Mike, it's almost Christmas and that's a time when people share gifts with their friends. It's a way of saying thank you for being such a nice person and good friend. So I brought my best friend and hiking buddy a present." Moving the package closer to him, I asked, "Want to open it?"

Mike glanced up at me quizzically, as if he had just realized I was there. Then, falteringly, he reached out to touch the box, carefully running his hand over the top, feeling the design in the paper. Again he needed help and together we untied the rather incompetent bow I had managed to produce. Then we folded the paper back to expose a black-and-white-checkered carton, but this time there was no hint as to its contents. Taking his hands in mine, we removed the lid and laid it beside the box, uncovering a layer of bright green tissue paper. Nudging it a couple of times, he seemed reluctant, almost afraid, to discover what lay beneath, until at last he pulled the paper away and peeked inside the box. His eyes got very big as he saw a pair of brand-new hiking boots and realized what they were meant to be used for.

"Hikin' boats . . ." he whispered.

"Merry Christmas, Mike." I could sense my own feelings surging up and I cleared my throat. "They may be a bit big for you now. You may have to wear a couple pairs of socks at first, but the way you're growing, they should fit you in no time. Like to try them on?"

Mike still appeared somewhat dazed, his eyes like saucers, but he nodded a vigorous "Yes!" Seating himself hastily on the floor, he yanked off his old worn-out boots and pulled on the stiff new ones. Without even bothering to lace them up tight, he stomped around the room, all at once happy as a clam with something he finally understood. On his fiftieth orbit, he halted abruptly by the door, puffing as he stood poised in mid-step.

"Shall we go show Chuck your new boots, Mike?"

He nodded eagerly. "Yes! Show Chahk!" he said. Picking up his truck, he bounded out into the hall and down to the nursing station, where he received many compliments on his new "boats" and his "trahk." I smiled when I saw Jody loading the truck with Christmas cookies for him.

But it soon became apparent that all the excitement and activities of the afternoon had left Mike exhausted. I sent him back to his room to put on his pajamas.

As he stared after the retreating figure, Chuck said, "You know, this is the first time Mike's ever really reacted to Christmas ... at all. Before, he's always just withdrawn and avoided everybody." He shook his head. "Imagine, ten years old, and just experiencing his first Christmas ..."

—————— chapter fifteen ——————

I had been at Merrick for a year and a half now. My dissertation was going well and I hoped to finish it and receive my doctorate during the summer. I was amazed at how fast the time had gone, but nothing brought that home to me more than how Mike was shooting up and stretching out. There was usually a gap of leg between the hiking boot top and the cuff of his pants, and it seemed that at least once a month we had to go down to the Clothes Corner to pick out some bigger blue jeans or a larger shirt.

His speech had greatly improved, too. Once Mike began to attempt verbal communication, I couldn't believe how rapidly he put words together. Although he hadn't spoken intelligibly for several years, he must have had a good grasp of language before he sealed over. Now, after slightly more than a year of talking, much of his pronunciation, though not all, approximated normal speech. Perhaps the distortion was simply garbling that had occurred when Mike had internalized his language and shut out any feedback from others. But now he proved yet again that he was certainly not retarded—though I had never had any doubts about that. Once he became more receptive, he learned quickly, which was fortunate. We had no speech therapists at Merrick, so we usually just improvised.

Mike's dramatic improvement had created a ground swell of interest on the unit, and for some time now we had been planning similarly structured programs for some of the other youngsters. I sat in on these sessions as a consultant, gratified that I had made a contribution. Through sheer serendipity, of course.

After one such meeting, Chuck came over and we got to talking about Mike. "You know," he confided, shaking his head, "in all honesty I've got to admit it—I never thought you'd get *anywhere* with him. But it's incredible how much he's changed, and continues to change!"

It was nice to hear the admiration in Chuck's voice, but it also embarrassed me. "There wasn't any secret formula. Just a lot of luck," I shrugged. "Scott, of course, kept me hanging in there. He set me up, to begin with, by getting me so intrigued with Mike that I had to give it a try. And then he played my stubborn streak beautifully. Wouldn't let me quit. And you guys all encouraged me to stick with Mike, too."

"Yeah, but like I say, I never expected you to actually *get* anywhere with him! And I don't think too many others did, either. But he's really kicking up his heels. He identifies with you, imitates how you walk. And today, would you believe, I caught him saying, 'dammit'!"

"You're kidding. I can't imagine where he could have learned that—"

"Me neither." Chuck grinned. "But this morning I was going by his room and I heard a loud 'dommit.' Took a moment to register, so I stuck my head in the door and there's Mike, struggling with his jacket zipper. It was caught and he was yanking on it. Evidently he just got so frustrated he had to let it out, but he looked a bit sheepish when he realized I'd heard him. I told him it was okay, though—reinforced it, as you say—and said it was better for him to do that than hold it inside." Chuck paused and laughed. "It just about cracked me up on the spot, though, hearing him swear like that!"

Chuck's comments corroborated my own observations that Mike did seem to be moving into a new developmental phase. I had first noticed it a week before. We had just left the cottage for a play therapy session and were headed down the walkway when Billy, whose room was next to Mike's, came wheeling around the corner on a bike and yelled, "Hi!"

"Hi, Bil-*ee*," came right back from Mike and even Billy looked back over his shoulder in astonishment. It was the first time Mike had ever greeted him. Or, as far as I knew, any of the other children. And he had called him by name.

I stopped and stared at Mike while the impact of that spontaneous reply sank in. "Hey, that was really neat of you to say 'hi' to Billy like that. I'm proud of you!"

Mike was self-consciously studying the pavement, so I didn't press it, just gave him a squeeze on the back of the neck and left my arm resting lightly on his shoulder as we continued on down to the administration building.

Then, a couple of days after that incident, I saw Mike with Danny, the youngster who was so obsessed with his mathematical formulas and repetitious numbers. We hadn't had any success with Danny, but seeing the two boys together made me pause. Mike was intently studying the sheaf of papers Danny always pulled out. Then he said something, Danny pocketed his notes, and they both walked off in the direction of the riverbed.

Scott and I were talking in his office the next day when I glanced out the window and saw Mike and Danny together again. I called it to Scott's attention and we both got up and watched.

Danny was evidently having one of his rougher days; he seemed to be hallucinating, stopping every few yards and speaking up into the empty sky. Mike kept urging him along the walk, retrieved him twice when he began wandering away, and refused to be put off by the bizarre behavior. Scott made a note to ask Conable about checking Danny's meds.

"Can't seem to get Danny stabilized. But look at Mike—boy, that's great to see. Do you know if he's relating to any of the other kids, Pat?"

"From what I hear, he is. It's interesting, Mike is usually with kids like himself—the sensitive, reticent ones. Kindred souls, I guess. He avoids those who probably bullied and teased him in the past. He must have had his own private accounting system during his noncommunicative years, and now he knows which kids he wants for friends."

"What about the staff? Anybody else noticing any changes?"

"Pretty much everyone at the cottage has reported the same. Chuck and Jody both say he's relating well to the nursing staff."

"Well, that sounds great. But still nothing much going on in play therapy?"

"No. It's been almost two months now, but Mike just can't initiate much activity on his own. I'm trying to encourage him, but haven't been very successful. Why don't you observe again soon, see what you think. I need a second opinion."

"Okay. It's hard to know if he's just not ready for it yet, or if he can't do it. Maybe it's going to be beyond his capabilities, Pat. You'd better start preparing yourself for that eventuality."

"Yeh, I know, Scott. I know, I know . . ."

Scott's glance was perceptive. "Back off a bit, remember?"

I saluted. "Aye, aye, Captain."

Later that afternoon when Mike and I were in the play therapy room, I told him what Scott and I had observed earlier.

"We saw you and Danny today, Mike. You were really helping him, and being very thoughtful and considerate."

Mike, embarrassed by my compliment, hunched down so I had to bend over to see his face.

"Thoughtful and considerate—do you know what those words mean?"

Mike shook his head and continued to avoid my eyes.

"Well, that means you're being a good friend to Danny. You spend time with him, watch out for him when he's having problems, don't let him wander off by himself. That's what friends do for each other—help each other when they need it. That's why I said you're being such a good friend to Danny. And that means you must like him and feel for him and care what happens to him. How does that make you feel?"

"I few good."

"Great, Mike. That's exactly what should

happen. You know, when you do something nice for someone else, then you feel good about yourself, too."

Mike looked up at me. Then he said, as if it were so obvious that it hardly needed mentioning, "He my friend, I tichin' him ta hike, ahn' climb, ahn' name trees. About workin' togethuh, hikin'."

"Good. Working together is very important— we've learned that, haven't we? And sharing, being friends. Like we are, like you and Danny, Chuck and Jody, and Cecile, too."

Mike was twitching, eager to begin drawing.

"You like Chuck and Jody a lot, don't you?"

He nodded self-consciously.

"That's okay, Mike. They're both very nice people who care about you, just as I do. Those are the nice feelings we have about someone who is very special to us. That's why we say that we love people when we care a great deal for them. When we want to share things with them, feel pleasure when we're with them, and sometimes feel lonesome when we're away from them."

Mike had taken a crayon and was idly twisting it in his fingers, pulling at the paper covering.

"You know, not everyone can share his feelings with others, Mike. So that makes you someone very special. Because you give, and you don't hold back anymore when you want to do something to help someone else. Many of us here—Jody, Chuck, me—we care a great deal about you, even love you. Did you know that?"

Mike's head snapped up and he stared at me, open-mouthed. "You *wuv* me?"

"Yes, I love you, Mike. And it's a very special kind of love, because I'm a doctor who cares very much about you, and wants to see you get much better. Just as Jody and Chuck do—all the staff people, really. They love you, too. Does that surprise you?"

Mike nodded, again self-conscious. This was all rather confusing for him. Not the easiest thing in the world to understand—or explain, for that matter.

"What I'm trying to say, Mike, is that you're going to feel good when you care for people, when you help someone like Danny, because he's your friend. And you're going to love people, too, and care about what happens to them. I want you to know how proud I am of what a good friend you are, sharing your feelings with others and doing nice things for them to make them feel good and, more important, make you feel good, too."

Mike was sitting very still; he'd dropped the crayon in his lap and was staring at his hands.

"I guess in all fairness, though, Mike, we should also talk about the fact that sometimes things will happen that hurt, make you feel bad. We may do something and feel sorry about it later, or somebody may say something that hurts us, makes us feel bad inside. Like when your dad came that day. But if we learn to understand what we're feeling, to know that the hurt will go away, then it becomes a little easier to take."

Mike seemed to be memorizing the lines on his hands. This was a tough area, especially for him. But it was one that needed to be dealt with. For Mike, handling his feelings was going to involve a great deal of new learning and other accompanying adjustments. So much of what he had previously acquired had been covered with a shroud of fear. And there were still so many experiences and emotions that remained unknown to him.

But there was no doubt about it. More and more Mike was asking questions about what went on around him, and usually spontaneously. On one occasion when we saw a recently admitted child having a temper outburst, Mike showed a marked curiosity. I explained about anger, reminding him of times when he had felt frustrated, and how that led to feelings of anger and the actions—like stomping off—that he had taken.

Another time we came upon a young girl sobbing uncontrollably and, after comforting her and finding a psychiatric aide to help her back to her cottage, we talked about it. When Mike asked, "Why she cry?" it meant everything from what does crying mean—how is it possible for someone to cry both when he's happy and when he's sad—to how does a person cry, or stop crying? I tried to help him grasp the concept of emotional expression by interpreting what we observed and helping him to identify his own feelings.

In this context, we often talked about physical affection and how it was demonstrated by holding hands, hugging, and kissing. The nature of his questions indicated that some serious reasoning was taking place. Mike could not remember anyone ever expressing affection to him; until relatively recently, he hadn't given anyone much of a chance to. So he was very uncertain about hugs and kisses. But holding hands seemed to be okay, and with increasing frequency he began to take mine. Soon he was doing it automatically. Wherever we went—to the farm, the water tanks or filtration plant, the canteen, even up into the hills—we held hands. There seemed to be basic reassurance and stability in that very simple act.

But giving a person a hug seemed unsettling and scary to him, and not something he could initiate himself. Mike had his ways, usually very subtle, of conveying when something was beyond his reach. I had sensed this constraint and so, one day as we were lacing up our boots for another assault on Dogface, I proposed a new requirement:

"Mike, before we take off today, I'd like to give you a big hug and I'd like you to give me a big hug back. Would you do that for me?"

Mike looked up sharply, then bent back down to adjust the laces of his hiking boots.

"Mike?"

He was scared, but moved slowly in front of me, eyes averted.

"One big hug for each other, then we'll be off for Dogface."

I leaned over and put my arms around him, giving him a squeeze. Tentatively, his arms went around my neck, but he remained stiff and uncertain.

"Good, Mike. That's a great start. Wasn't so bad after all, was it?"

Mike shook his head mutely; he still couldn't bring himself to look at me.

"Okay?" I said, reaching for his hand. "Ready for Dogface?"

Mike raised his head, squinting in the direction of his favorite spot, and said, "Yes, we go hike Dogfahs."

From then on I required Mike to give me a hug each time I came to get him and whenever we parted. Gradually, he relaxed and allowed himself to enoy the physical contact and affection. And in time, he even began to hug first, without being asked. Still, although touching and the burgeoning friendships were signs of significant growth, the underlying psychological situation was more mixed. There continued to be very little emotional expression. Despite the happiness I could sense just beneath the surface, Mike had yet to laugh spontaneously, or get overtly angry, or cry. These emotional outlets were still capped. Perhaps such feelings would come eventually; and then again, as Scott had warned me, there was the possibility that they might never emerge at all.

At times it seemed as if things were falling into place, but then a drawing would seem to indicate the opposite. I guessed that it was all part of Mike's working through the trauma of his early years. One afternoon he drew this rather austere picture of a house:

The severe, cold characterization depicted a formidable door, dark and out of proportion, with a large doorstop at its base. The three windows were tiny and devoid of curtains. At its worst, Mike's world seemed to be confined to that dreary institutional cottage. It *was* a very depressing place, I had to admit. Mike's choice of colors—deep purple and black—demonstrated that and, I presumed, accurately reflected his mood.

These occasional black periods seemed to be holding actions, providing Mike with an interval to consolidate his gains. But each time I held my breath, wondering if he had reached the level that would prove to be his developmental limit.

——— *chapter sixteen* ———

"We do somethin' diff'rent today."

"All right . . ." Such a statement was a new wrinkle, and I was somewhat taken aback. "What would you like to do, Mike?"

Without answering, he marched purposefully to the toy cabinet. I could feel my neck tingling as he reached inside, drew out the hand puppets, and carefully lined them up in a row on the table. He poked at the rubber faces, watching each sink in and then pop out when he released his finger. Mike seemed to be talking under his breath; then he broke off to share his conclusions.

"This dahdee, this mommy, this girl, this babee, this dog, this—" and he stopped, looking puzzled.

"That's a dragon, Mike," I offered.

"This drah-gun," he finished, and turned to see my reaction.

"Very good, Mike, you named all of them. That's very, very good!"

He gave an emphatic nod and spent the remainder of the session pulling toys out of the cabinet and asking what they were. When we were through, I gazed about the cluttered room. Everything that could possibly have been extracted from the cabinet lay strewn about everywhere. As Mike reexamined first one object and then another, naming each of them again, I felt nothing but gratitude for the mess.

We were back the next day. Mike went immediately to the cupboard and gathered up several toys. He had brought his truck with him this time and, climbing into the sandbox, he proceeded to push it and a train caboose through the sand. I had asked Scott to observe again today and, although I couldn't see him, I smiled through the one-way mirror. I knew he'd be enjoying this new development as much as I was.

For the next several weeks, Mike actively played with many of the toys. I encouraged him to explore freely, and once again, I was amazed by the speed with which he grasped ideas. The pattern that evolved was interesting to follow. Mike was like a shopper, tentatively testing the watercolors until he felt at ease, then moving on to clay, then more toys, and finally games. He was particularly taken with the wire slinky, which he "walked" down a series of wooden boxes. He would become totally absorbed as the wire spring wiggled and jiggled down the "steps," quickly making adjustments in the position of the boxes whenever the slithering toy altered course.

The hour of play went too fast as far as he was concerned, and I began to get a plaintive, "Stay a liduh longuh, Paht? Please, Paht ... jus' a liduh longuh?"

How could anyone say no to that? I certainly couldn't.

Mike's momentum was building. One afternoon when we were scheduled to hike on Dogface, he asked if we could go to the playroom to draw instead. Again I was surprised. Usually he dashed off his pictures in the dayroom or outside under a tree. I went along with him, wondering why he was postponing his hike; it wasn't like him. When we got to the playroom, he quickly collected some paper and the crayons.

"All set? Ready to draw your pictures, Mike?"

He nodded, working busily. He was quietly occupied for some time and I was absently pushing some modeling clay when I became aware that Mike was standing next to me.

"Hi, Monkey's Uncle. What's up—you got something for me?"

He nodded shyly, looking down at the floor as he handed me a piece of paper. I scanned it thoughtfully, feeling a surge of elation as I realized what it conveyed:

Two hikers stood together on Dogface, hand in hand, each one smiling broadly . . .

I couldn't believe it. Finally, after literally hundreds of drawings of people without faces, here were two individuals who were *not* looking the other way! The figures were still crude, the features consisting merely of dots for eyes and nose and a curved line for a smile—*but the faces were there!* And the figures were holding hands!

"Mike—" I began, and then my throat caught and all I could do was look at him and shake my head. "That super picture deserves a big hug, don't you think?"

Mike smiled bashfully—actually *smiled!* His first real smile! And yelped a little when I squeezed too tight.

"That's really a great picture, Mike. This must be you here, right?" I pointed to the figure with the bigger grin. "And this is me—the one with the big head? We look pretty happy, don't we?"

Mike nodded self-consciously, squirming slightly as I continued to admire his drawing.

"Do you suppose you could draw another picture just like this one for me to keep? I know you'll want to put this one above your bed, but I'd sure like to have one of my own. What do you think—would you do that for me?"

His head bobbed agreeably and he bounded back to the table, grabbing a crayon to begin another masterpiece.

Later that afternoon I recounted the incident at the review meeting, and after the picture had been passed around and the chatter abated, I asked the team to be alert for more new developments. It turned out to be another significant stride. Soon reports were coming in from aides and nurses that Mike was becoming more sociable, acknowledging more people, calling everyone by name. He was even getting into a bit of mischief at school. Cecile laughingly told me that she had allowed Danny and Mike to sit together in class, but that she had had to gently reprimand them a number of times for goofing around.

"It was all I could do to keep a straight face, because actually I was just delighted to see them acting like a couple of normal cutups! And they're so good for each other. Both boys have started collecting rocks and cactuses and they're building a classroom garden together. It was their own idea. I couldn't be more pleased. In many ways, Mike's having far more success with Danny than any of us have!"

As Mike began to assume the lead, I was only too willing to relinquish it. Scott had been preparing me for this transition. Months ago he had told me, "With someone as deeply withdrawn and out of touch as Mike is, extraordinary measures are required. Sometimes when these individuals need to lean on you psychologically, you virtually move into their psychological space and take over. But once they're going under their own steam, the therapist has to sense at what point to begin stepping back, allowing the patient to resume control once again—at his or her own pace, of course. It's a slow, difficult process, but this is the time when the self theorists, with their commitment to providing psychological support and backing, are at their best.

"Watch Mike carefully. Give him the opportunity to test, to explore, to reach out. And expect to be amazed; kids can be so responsive and unpredictable. But remember, Mike's still a very, very disturbed youngster, and whether or not he can ever make up for all that lost time and trauma remains to be seen. Your responsibility is to take him as far as he can—and wants to—go. Okay?"

At the time I'd nodded, sobered by the consideration that it was, indeed, quite possible that complete recovery and discharge from the hospital might not be a part of Mike's future. But the thought of his having to spend his whole life at Merrick was so abhorrent that I quickly shoved it out of my mind.

That summer was marked by accomplishments for both Mike and me. I successfully defended my dissertation and was at last awarded my doctorate. I was relieved to have finished up, but after eight years of grinding study, the degree was almost an anticlimax. What I thoroughly savored, though, was the new title that preceded my name. Every time the paging system crackled, "Dr. McGarry, dial 296," I was inwardly thrilled—"Hey, that's *me!*"

And Mike kept progressing. He became noticeably bolder, willing to take chances and risks. Not long after Cecile reported the classroom misbehavior, Mike ventured into that great childhood pastime—testing the limits. It was mid-June, but already the weather was unbearably hot and sticky.

One Wednesday afternoon, Mike and I drove down to the canteen, forsaking our hike. The breeze through the open car windows provided only minor relief and we were both anticipating the air-conditioned snack bar. I slid my old Ford into a parking space next to a shiny new Cadillac, casually commenting on the disparity between the two vehicles. Mike looked over and then, apparently unimpressed, opened the door, bumping it against the side of the Cadillac.

I had started to get out, but paused when I heard the thud. "Be careful, Mike. Don't open the door into another car."

He sat there, holding the door, and a kind of impishness crossed his face. Then he pushed the door into the side of the car again, even harder this time.

"Mike—don't do that again!"

I had visions of an irate Cadillac owner bearing down on us, and the weather would definitely not be in our favor. Mike seemed to be measuring my resolve; then, rearing back swiftly, he subjected the Cadillac to another solid thump.

That did it. I reached across the seat, grabbing his arm and pulling him toward me.

"Mike, that's enough! I want you out of this car *right now,* and don't you touch that door again!"

Suddenly Mike was frightened; he knew he had gone too far. He was very subdued as he slid across the seat, climbed out, and slunk around the car, eyes focused on the ground.

A quick inspection revealed no damage to the Cadillac and also provided a few moments for me to consider how best to handle the incident. I closed Mike's door and then approached him, kneeling down so he would have to look at me. But before I could say anything, Mike said very softly, "Mik'l won't bahng the cah doah again—" His voice quavered; he was a very scared little boy.

"Mike—" I began, and then stopped as I saw that tears were beginning to stream down his cheeks. How long had it been since he had cried? Gently I put my arm around his shoulders and guided him to a nearby bench. He sat quietly, scrunched down, awaiting some kind of punishment.

"Mike, I want you to understand what just happened here. I was disappointed and irritated with what you did, but I also know why you did it. You wanted to see if I would still like you even if you were naughty and did something bad. You were really just testing me—and that's okay. But I also want you to know that if I get irritated or even angry with you, it doesn't mean I don't love you anymore, because I do. It just means that at the moment when you did something you weren't supposed to do—and *knew* you weren't supposed to do—I was angry. But I still love you and we can certainly talk about it, like we are now."

Mike watched me intently, listening carefully, and as I finished he was sobbing quietly. I put my arms around him and held him tightly as he buried his face in my shoulder, the accumulation of hurt and disappointment and fear pouring out. Perhaps, too, the tears expressed sheer disbelief that—at last—someone truly cared for him, no matter what he did. He was beginning to reach some of those agonizing, long-stifled feelings, and they were terrifying for him.

For some time after he stopped crying we sat and talked. Then, when I was certain he was feeling better, I gently led him back to the incident.

"Do you remember what you were thinking and feeling when I told you not to bang the door again, Mike?"

He looked thoughtful, a slight frown wrinkling his forehead. "I do' know. It jus' hahpen, the doah jus' hit the cah. Then I jus' did it again."

I believed him. It seemed like the kind of confronting, impulsive behavior that pops out of children, with no rhyme or reason. Or, if there is some motive, it's buried.

"Then you saw me, your friend, getting angry. What did you feel then, do you remember?"

Again Mike thought, at last looking up at me. "Scahred?"

"Okay, what did scared feel like, Mike?"

"It hurt—heah—" and he rubbed his stomach, "ahn' heah—" Mike's hand clutched his chest. "I afwaid . . . ahn' scahred, few bahd aw ovuh."

"And unhappy?" I asked.

"Unhahppy, too." Mike looked dismal as he recalled it.

"All right, Mike, so unhappy is feeling bad, the opposite of happy, like when we do something fun and enjoy it. I'm sorry that you had to feel hurt and scared and unhappy. But it's good that you felt those feelings, knew what they were, and most important, shared them, talked about them with your friend. Do you know why that's good?"

He shook his head, picking at strings on a blue jean patch.

"How do you feel now?"

Again, the self-examination. "Okay."

"Do you know why you feel better now?"

"Nuh."

"Because you talked about the feelings, could tell me what they were and how they made you feel. So the unhappy or bad feelings have been let out by talking about them and not keeping them inside you. Now when something happens that makes you feel like that, you know what to do, don't you?"

"Talk!" Mike said emphatically.

This was another milestone and a particularly meaningful one. Scott cautioned me that the limit testing would more than likely recur; Mike needed to become better acquainted with his rebellious, misbehaving side. What it amounted to was more catch-up childhood behavior.

One afternoon Mike took me to the school and proudly showed me the rock garden he and Danny were building. Then, spotting some paper and crayons, he flopped down at his desk and began drawing. I was leafing through a large atlas when it struck me how quiet it was—*too* quiet. I looked up to see Mike standing next to a heavily crayoned wall, the scribbling hand dropping in mid-line as he became aware of my attention. He turned slowly, awaiting my reaction.

Saying nothing, I glanced at the sink where the soap and sponge lay. Mike followed my gaze, then proceeded to draw another few lines before again turning to watch me, a nervous twitch tugging at the corners of his mouth as he continued to push for a reaction.

Finally, when none was forthcoming, he sighed deeply and said, "Mik'l not draw on the wall. I few bahd, unhahppy. Not do it again."

Then he walked over to the sink, wet the sponge and soap under the tap, and began to scrub the crayon marks off the wall. When he had finished, I asked him to come over and sit by me. He slumped down, repeating his earlier admonition to himself that he wouldn't draw on the wall again.

I spelled out for him the parallel between the car-door incident and drawing on the wall, once more reassuring Mike that we were still the best of friends, and that there was nothing he could do that would have an effect on how much I cared for him. I particularly stressed that things like this happened to all boys and girls as a part of growing up.

Mike listened solemnly.

"Okay, buddy, ready to go hiking now?"

He bounded out of his chair, the misbehavior immediately forgotten. I could only shake my head ruefully; he really was getting to be like other kids.

A couple of weeks later, Mike produced this picture after we had splashed around in the hospital pool. I interpreted it as an indication that Mike was still unsure of himself and of our relationship. He identified me as the one with the blank face.

Then, the following week, came a picture of us hiking on Dogface, the hues more vivid and varied as Mike expanded his repertoire from blues and browns to brighter, happier colors. And he had given me a smiling face again.

A few days after that, we were driving around the hospital grounds, content to enjoy the lovely day. Instigating our identification game, I pointed to a eucalyptus tree on the side of the road.

"What kind of tree, Mike?"

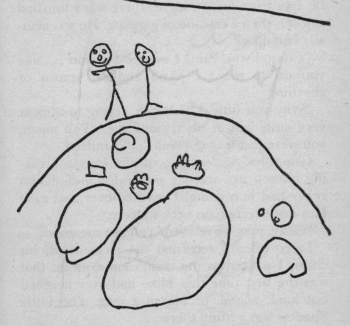

"Pep-puh—pep-puh tree," came back.

"Huh? C'mon, Mike, you know better than that. What's that one coming up?" There was a row of eucalyptus lining the roadway.

"Pep-puh—they all peppuh trees."

I pulled over to the edge of the pavement. This was an unexpected turn of events and I didn't know quite what to make of it. Mike had identified these same trees many times before.

"Hey, what's going on? You know a eucalyptus tree when you see one, Mike."

He was looking out the window, concealing his face from me. Suddenly there was a muffled snicker, then a cascade of giggling. He was actually laughing!

"I fuood you, Paht! I was tee-zun you . . . like you do to me . . ." And another spasm of chortling.

"Why you little—" I began, trying to appear very indignant at his tricking me. "You mean, you were just *teasing?* Well . . ." I huffed.

Gale-force giggles followed this. He was breaking himself up, and my pretended indignation really had him going. I reached over and gave him my affectionate neck squeeze.

"Okay, now we're even. You got me good!"

Later when I recorded the incident on his chart, I paused as the realization sank in: that was the first time that Mike had ever laughed out loud, teased, or played a joke. The Little Shadow was getting there . . .

That was the first time, but it certainly wasn't the last. Mike delighted in teasing me about the tree names, and my feigned indignation always broke him up—another game had evolved. Reports started to come back from the cottage, and the classroom too, that Mike was kidding around, laughing, and beginning to behave like a little kid.

Mike's sense of humor carried over into his drawings, too, and he began to present me

236

with put-ons like upside-down faces, which he would hand me with great seriousness, and then snicker gleefully when my eyes widened at the absurdity.

Gasping and guffawing, he would confide, "Mik'l tee-zun Paht—put mouf on *top* head!!"

Such responsiveness built momentum, and soon I was prodding Mike to make his pictures more representational, more complex. Following my prompting for details like clothes, fingers, and shoes, he produced this drawing of the two of us at the water tanks. The runged ladders had made quite an impression.

One day he sneaked up behind me and tried to tickle me in the ribs. He was giggling and there was mischief in his eyes. So, unmercifully, I pulled the oldest trick in the book:

"Look out, Monkey—there's someone behind you. He's gonna get you . . ."

Mike spun around to look and in that instant I caught him, picked him up off the ground, and tickled the daylights out of him. He loved it, laughing and squealing and gasping for breath. Finally, though, Mike wore me down. I think he probably could have survived, even thrived on, several consecutive hours of tickling—after all, there were so many years to make up for.

From then on we spent a lot of time just horsing around. An odd kind of therapy perhaps, but as Scott had said, "If it works, do it!"

—————— *chapter seventeen* ——————

When I called for Mike a few days later, he caught me off guard again by not asking for a hike. Readily taking my hand, he accompanied me to the administrative cottage and, once in the playroom, followed his usual routine, inspecting the toys thoroughly before deciding which one he wanted. After twenty minutes or so, he settled down with the mother and father hand puppets. Some kind of involved conversation seemed to be going on, but his voice was so low that I could make out only an occasional word. Abruptly, Mike removed the puppets from his hands and laid them side by side on the table, staring at them pensively. Then he gave a deep, extended sigh. I watched him closely; something significant was happening.

"What are the mommy and daddy doing, Mike?" I asked.

A pause. "Sleepin' . . ."

"Sleeping, huh. Where are they sleeping?"

"Ah hoome . . ."

"Oh. Is it a nice home?"

"Uh huh."

"Are the mommy and daddy happy?"

"I do' know." Mike turned and looked at me. "Yes, hahppy."

"What's the mommy like, Mike?"

A shrug. "Do' know."

"And the daddy, do you know what he's like?"

Mike picked up the father puppet and studied it. "Dahdee nice."

He put it back down, and I thought, what a beautiful example of a child's capacity to forgive.

"So, it's a nice house and a nice daddy, but you're not too sure about the mommy? Would you like to know more about the mommy, Mike? Your mommy?"

Another shrug. He looked down, then murmured, "Yes."

"You haven't seen her in a long time, have you?"

Mike shook his head.

"And you miss her? Would you like to see her again?"

"Yes." A long silence. Then, his gaze still fastened on the puppets, he said, "Mik'l go un hoome bisit, Paht?"

"You'd like to see your mom and dad? And go on a home visit?"

A vigorous nod.

"Well, I can write to them. You know, though, that for a long time your mother wasn't well. Maybe she's better now. But Mike . . ."

"What?"

"Maybe it would be better if we ask them if they'd like to come and visit you here first. That way you could take them around, show them your room and all your drawings. Plus the cactus-rock garden that you and Danny made. That would be fun. Would that be okay?"

"Yes, thaht be okay. Then we go—"

"Then maybe after they've come here a few times, we could talk about a home visit."

"Okay."

The remainder of that session was spent talking about Mike's separation from his parents. I tried to tell him, in words he could understand, about the nature of severe emotional problems, putting my explanation in a context of withdrawal, not having any friends, and feeling bad all the time. And why it was sometimes necessary for a person to come to a hospital for care and treatment. Mike sat across from me, his chin cupped in his hands, and nodded from time to time. When I asked if he had any questions, he just shook his head and went over to the sandbox.

Later that afternoon, I wrote a letter to the Harrises telling them of Mike's request. Would they please call or write me at the earliest opportunity. I added a paragraph saying how much Mike had improved and that a visit at this point was particularly important to him. And, just for insurance, I stressed that since certain arrangements would have to be made for this meeting, they should let me know when they could come. I hadn't a clue whether they'd respond or not. If I didn't hear from them within a few weeks, I'd make another house call.

But a week later a hastily scrawled postcard arrived. The Harrises would like to see Mike, and they asked if I would call them. A number was at the bottom; Mr. Harris had finally relented and they now had a telephone. Before I left the hospital that day, I spoke briefly with Mrs. Harris, who sounded much better. As we were talking, her husband came home and she went outside to get him.

Mr. Harris wasn't used to the telephone. He shouted into it, and I had to hold the receiver at arm's length while we settled on a day. They would come the following Friday, meet with me for a while, and then spend some time with Mike.

"I'll see you at the administrative cottage at one o'clock, Mr. Harris," I concluded.

"One o'clock Saturday," yelled Mr. Harris. "See you then."

"Friday, Mr. Harris. One o'clock *Friday*. I'm not here Saturday." I caught myself shouting back at him, afraid he'd hang up.

"Oh, Friday you say? Right, see you then." Crash went the receiver in my ear.

When I told Mike about the impending visit, his response was immediate and unrestrained.

"Mommy, dahdee come *here?!* Come see Mik'l?!" He began jumping around, waving his arms and chattering. "My dahdee ahn' mommy come see Mik'l. Come take Mik'l hoome. Cahn we hike Dogfahs now ahn' go to cahn-teen for ice creemcone? Paht? Okay, Paht?"

I smiled down at the barrage of questioning.

"Hey, take it easy. One question at a time, old buddy. This is just going to be a visit. They're not going to take you anywhere this time. But they want to come and see you, Mike, so they're coming on Friday. If we hurry now, we can sneak in an ice cream cone before my next appointment. Let's go."

Mike was so exuberant that I took the opportunity to raise another important matter. It was the umpteenth time I had broached the issue. "Mike, with both your mother and father coming to see you, wouldn't you like to look your best?"

A suspicious scowl—he knew instantly what I was getting at.

"Well, you do want to look nice for your mother, don't you, Mike? And there's nothing to worry about. I'll be right there, holding your hand. In fact, we could get haircuts together. And then we'd both be ready to meet your folks. Okay? How does that sound?"

It was a most difficult decision for Mike, but he finally acquiesced without enthusiasm.

"Paht, you be with Mik'l *all the time*—not let them *hurt* me?"

"I promise, Mike, I'll be with you—right beside you—the whole time. Nobody's going to hurt my hiking buddy."

The next morning I talked with one of the hospital barbers, thoroughly preparing him so as to avoid any mishaps. Then, a little while later, with Mike still vacillating, we went over to the barbershop together.

But once we arrived, there were no problems. Initially Mike was skittish, holding the mirror with one hand and me with the other. He watched the proceedings intently, but slowly a smile crept over his face as he relaxed and felt safer.

"How's that look, Mike?" asked the barber.

Mike carefully examined his hair, running his hand over the evened-out surfaces.

"It look nice!"

"What do you say to the barber, Mike?"

"Tonk you, Mista Bahbah, fuh haah-cut."

"You're welcome, Mike. Come see me again."

"Okay." He turned to me with alacrity. "Now you, Paht. *You* get haah-cut!"

As I climbed into the barber's chair for the institutional haircut I had had some second thoughts about, I reflected wryly that there was certainly nothing wrong with Mike's memory.

On Friday, the rusty Cadillac Fleetwood came pop-popping into the parking area a half-hour late. I escorted the Harrises directly to my office. I was reassured to see that both of them seemed fairly stable—Mr. Harris a bit more subdued and friendly, Mrs. Harris far more intact and alert.

But they were both rather uncomfortable and I spent some time making small talk—about the unseasonable weather, the coming election—in an attempt to put them at ease. Remembering Mrs. Harris's fear of the hospital, I was particularly concerned about her. I asked if they still went to the mental health center and Mrs. Harris was quick to nod yes, volunteering the information that she was regularly taking medication. The drug she mentioned was a well-known antipsychotic, and it was evident that it was doing its job. The hallucinations, the psychotic withdrawal had receded. Though still shy and reticent, Mrs. Harris was a different person from the woman I had met that day in Reidsville.

Finally I began filling them in on Mike's progress, stressing that he was relating much better, had some friends, could express affection, hold hands, hug—in short, that he had come a long way. And then I asked them about Mike's earlier years, explaining how little we know about schizophrenia and its development. Besides, I was curious about how they saw Mike's problems, and I wanted to hear their side of the story. I wondered how it would mesh with the original records.

"Can you recall how it all started?"

After several moments of silence, Mike's father sighed. "It was never easy. Michael was . . . always difficult. The slightest thing would upset him, 'specially if it was something different. Then he'd fuss. And whenever we wanted him to do something, he'd get *really* upset. Like, we'd ask him to pray with us. Instead, he'd throw the most unbelievable temper tantrums—worse than you could ever imagine. Lots worse than that time I came out here. . . . Or when I'd try to quiet him down or take something away from him—or even try to get him to play with one of his toys instead—he'd run away from me screaming and holding his hands over his ears. We knew there was something wrong, we just didn't know what to do . . ."

Mike's mother had been nodding from time to

time as he spoke, and when he stopped, she haltingly began.

"Dr. McGarry, I've never mentioned this to anyone before—" she glanced nervously at her husband before continuing, "because Gerald has always felt so responsible. But I've always thought ... well, that the problems started because of the hard time I had when Mikey was born and then all the sickness he had at the beginning. It was a very long labor—and he was a blue baby, too, and very tiny, weighed only four pounds. They had to keep him at the hospital for several weeks. . . . After he came home, he never slept, just cried and cried and cried. I couldn't take it. . . . I got sick, too. Pretty soon the doctor was coming to see both Mikey and me. He gave Mikey shots and I could tell how Mikey just *hated* them. And—as young as he was—I just *knew* that Mikey . . . hated *me* . . . blamed *me* for causing him all that . . ." Her voice caught and she shook her head morosely.

"I don't think Mike ever hated you, Mrs. Harris," I said, "or even blamed you. But it was certainly a tough way for him to be introduced to the world, wasn't it?"

Mrs. Harris was weeping, and her husband reached over and cradled her hand between his two ruddy ones. He looked at me. "The social worker at the mental health center said that we should ask you about Mike—whether you think we can take care of him if he comes for a home visit. We were also wondering ... what will happen to him now that he's getting older." .

"Well, that brings up some points we need to discuss. The serious mental problems he's had are in remission now. That means that he's not doing the things that were so distressing for you—throwing tantrums, lighting fires, running away. But there's no getting around the fact that Mike is way behind, and there's a very good chance that he'll always need some care and help. On the other hand, I don't believe that he'll have to spend the rest of his life in a hospital. I think it's quite possible that in time Mike could make a good adjustment to a group home.

"But what you'll have to prepare yourselves for at the moment is this: even though Mike is now ten years old, and he's really grown—he's quite tall for his age—his stature is misleading. His mind is more like a child of five or so. The severity of the schizophrenia has caused him to miss an awful lot, and whether he'll ever be able to make it all up is questionable. His psychological makeup is still rather fragile—much stronger than when you came up here last time, Mr. Harris—but Mike will always be an extremely sensitive person, very much attuned to how others behave toward him."

Mr. Harris averted his eyes, and I paused to let that sink in before going on.

"But Mike is also a very giving, loving person.

He has a lot going for him, and a lot to share. He wants to spend time with his mother and father now. He's curious, sees all the other kids visited by their parents, going on home visits, doing things together. And he'd like to sample those experiences himself. Since Mike seems to be ready for this, I hope you folks will want to get to know your son again."

Both parents nodded agreeably, although Mrs. Harris still appeared somewhat apprehensive. I called the cottage to have Mike sent down, and then we talked a while longer as I answered more of their questions. At last Mrs. Harris's skepticism overcame her and she blurted,

"Is Mikey *really* doing that much better?"

"Well—" I began, but was interrupted by the familiar high-pitched voice wafting down the hall. "You'll see for yourself in about three seconds."

At that moment Mike burst through the door, his face flushed and jubilant.

"Dahdee, Mommy—I go for hoome bisit with you?"

I had to laugh at his directness. "Now wait a second, Mike," I cautioned. "How about sitting down for a few minutes and talking before you start asking to go home?"

As Mike began chattering, neither of his parents could remain indifferent to his enthusiasm. Jumping from one item of interest to another, he recounted details of trips to the canteen, the farm, the water tanks, and the small circus that had recently visited the Children's Unit for a special performance. As he rattled on, he looked eagerly from one to the other and it was obvious that, as far as Mike was concerned, the lonely years were over and he was ready at last to become a member of the family. There was nothing to indicate that he held anything against them.

Mike's parents were quiet, listening attentively, although they didn't have much choice—it would have been impossible for anyone to get a word in edgewise. Through it all, his mother watched him intently.

Finally I interrupted him.

"Mike evidently wants to share with you everything that's happened to him. Would you like to go for a walk around the grounds? Perhaps Mike could show you the cactus-rock garden he built with his friend Danny."

The Harrises readily agreed.

"Mike, after you've shown your folks around, will you bring them back here, please?"

"Okay. We go now, we *gooooooo!!*" Mike jumped up and stuck out his hand. "Heah, Mommy, take my hahnd. You too, Dahdee," and he thrust his hand into his father's.

As the three of them left, Mike eagerly pulling his parents along, both Mr. and Mrs. Harris looked back at me. They were smiling—joyful, but still disbelieving. A half-hour later they returned, looking rather harried, but happy.

"Mike, you say good-bye to your folks now. It's almost time for your meds, so you'd better skedaddle back up to the cottage. Why don't you give them a hug good-bye like you give me, Mike?"

He nodded vigorously and gave each of his parents a big hug, wrapping his arms around them and squeezing.

"G'bye Mommy, g'bye, Dahdee—when cahn I go for hoome bisit?"

"Let me talk with your parents now, Mike. We'll talk about a home visit later."

Mike's face squinched up in mild disapproval. Reluctantly, he backed out of the room and, after a few moments for a last look, he disappeared down the hall.

When he'd gone, I said, "It looks like Mike gave you quite a tour."

Both of them seemed overwhelmed, almost to the point of stupefaction. We sat in silence awhile, Mrs. Harris seemingly replaying the events in her mind because every now and then she shook her head. Finally Mr. Harris, obviously moved, cleared his throat.

"Well, Mikey *is* very different. Beats me how you did it!"

Over the next half-hour, I briefly outlined what had happened during the last two years.

When I mentioned the "hikers' rule" of helping each other, Mr. Harris nodded.

"So that's why Mike wanted me to climb up the bluff with him. We started to, but before long I was beginning to puff pretty good and I stopped. Mike had already gotten a ways up, but when he saw I'd stopped, he came back down the hill and said somethin' about that— hikers working together. Then he took my hand and started pulling me!"

"That's what a super guy he is, Mr. Harris. And that's why I'd like to see the two of you get more involved with him now. Of course, it's really up to you, but we'll be glad to work with you and help out in any way we can. Initially, maybe you could come up to see him a few more times, and then if that goes all right, eventually we could try a home visit." They seemed uncertain about that, so I added, "Just think about it, talk it over together, and let me know what you decide."

Mr. Harris looked at his wife and an understanding seemed to pass unspoken between them.

"Well, it'd be okay with us," he said. "If you doctors think he's ready. Then maybe we'll see about that home visit he wants so bad."

"Fine, we'll set up some times for you to come out, then."

I happened to be at Cottage 4 a week later when Mike came bounding in the door, towing his parents. He announced to all within earshot, "My Dahdee ahn' Mommy brought me *cahndee!*" He was holding a rumpled paper bag and his grin was laced with caramel and nuts. Quickly Mike opened the bag and offered me a piece. Then he spotted Jody.

"You want some, Jo-dee?"

She nodded, smiling, and with great ceremony Mike placed a selected piece in her palm. Then he clutched the sack to himself as if it were gold.

Chuck, coffee cup in hand, came down the corridor.

"I got cahndee, Chahk—you want some?" Mike opened the sack again and peered in with Chuck. "Those ah good—" he said.

"Okay, I'll try that one, Mike. Thank you."

"You welcahm, Chahk." Mike turned and grinned at me. That was something he had learned to say a month ago, and he rarely missed an opportunity to use it.

During this time, Mike's parents had stood to the side watching the scene unfold.

"I think your folks probably need to get back now, Mike," I said. "Are you going to hug them good-bye?"

"Okay." Mike swooped over to where they were waiting and, as each bent down, he curled his arms around them and embraced them. Then he stepped back.

"Didn't you forget to say something, Mike?" I asked.

He beamed. "Tonk you for comin' Mommy ahn' Dahdee. When cahn you come again?"

That was nearly too much for the Harrises; their eyes filled with tears as they said their good-byes. I left the cottage with them. As we reached the walk by the side of the building, a rattling from the dayroom window caused us to turn. There was Mike, his grinning face pressed up against the glass, waving vigorously. We all waved back.

Near the parking lot, Mr. and Mrs. Harris both stopped. They stood there, uncomfortably shifting their feet, apparently with something on their minds. Finally, Mr. Harris found his voice. Taking his wife's hand in his, he said, "Dr. McGarry, we both want to thank you, you've done a lot for Mike. He's really so much better. Long ago we'd given up hope that he could ever be like he is now . . ."

Then it was my turn to feel awkward. I have never been very adept at accepting compliments, so I mumbled something to the effect that it was actually the team, the staff who deserved the credit. And, of course, Mike. Embarrassed, we stood together, unable to put what we wanted to say into words. But then, there wasn't really any need to do so.

* * *

The hospital visits continued to go well and a month later Mike went on his first weekend trip home. It included a long car ride, a trip to the zoo, and a Walt Disney movie. Although Mike's parents admitted he was a handful, his energy leaving them exhausted, when they returned to the hospital on Sunday afternoon they were eager to make arrangements for another home visit. Mike couldn't have been happier.

chapter eighteen

Scott and I were just polishing off our morning coffee when his telephone rang. It was long-distance, so I went back to my own office. Twenty minutes later, he appeared in the doorway.

"That was a friend of mine in Wisconsin. Teaches there. Wanted to know if I knew of anyone who'd like a good job opportunity—it combines teaching with clinical practice with kids."

I shrugged. "Can't think of anyone offhand."

"Actually, I thought perhaps you might be interested."

"Me? Hey, what is this? You trying to get rid of me?"

Scott smiled and shook his head. "Just thought

I'd mention it. There're some fine clinicians in the group, good psychotherapists. They could teach you a bit, build up your professional credentials. It'd be a definite step up. But if you'd rather not . . ."

"Well, if I were looking for something else—which I'm not—Wisconsin wouldn't be my first choice, anyway. It's the boonies, isn't it?"

"Not really. I think you'd like the Midwest. It's a nice place to live; the people are the salt of the earth." He grinned. "I grew up there."

"But Scott, I'm happy here. And besides, there's Mike to consider."

"I know, it'd be rough for him at first."

"To say the least."

"But I think Mike is strong enough now to handle separation. We could work out a way to transfer him to someone else. In fact, this would be as good a time as any to do it. You've gotten awfully attached to each other, and actually it might be better for him in the long run if he had a different therapist before long. It would broaden his base, help him to adapt better to change. He's very dependent on you. And then, of course, some new experiences would be good for you, too."

"Well, I don't know—"

"Think about it, anyway. I wouldn't let your concern for Mike stand in the way. I certainly don't want to lose you, Pat, but this sounds like a strong group, a good program. Might be worth checking it out."

"Okay, Scott, I guess I can at least do that."

The next day I called Wisconsin and had a long conversation with the chief psychologist. By the time I hung up, I had agreed to go for an interview. No question about it—this was an impressive opportunity.

My main worry was the risk to Mike. Despite Scott's words, I was afraid that Mike might interpret my leaving as abandonment, as one more person—indeed, the very one who had promised never to do so—"looking the other way." At the same time, though, I had to admit that Scott was right. As attached as Mike was to me, he was also reaching out to the staff and the kids around him as well as forming a new, positive relationship with his parents. Perhaps it *was* time for me to move out of the center of his life and leave the space open for him to develop. If I did leave, however, I would have to be certain that Mike understood my reasons and plans, so that he wouldn't take my departure as rejection.

Two weeks later I flew to Wisconsin. The countryside was a picture right out of my fifth-grade geography book—red barns, black-and-white cows, crisp rivers, and placid lakes surrounded by lush greenery. They offered me the position, but I begged off letting them know immediately. I just wasn't sure, so I returned home to mull it over. Finally, at about the last moment, I decided to accept the appointment. Slightly over two months remained for me to prepare Mike.

As I thought about possible therapists, my mind kept returning to Debbie. She would be ideal. Not only was she a warm and caring person, she was also an avid backpacker. All of the kids thought the world of her. Even Mike had remarked about the fun they had had on a recent outing to the beach. When I mentioned the idea to Debbie, she agreed immediately, saying she liked Mike and would be happy to take over with him.

"After all," she grinned, "you've already done the hard part! And frankly, the chance to go hiking really appeals to me."

Scott supported the arrangement, pointing out the potential benefits for Mike of having first a male therapist and then a female therapist as role models. But everything depended on how Mike reacted to Debbie, whether he'd respond to her, accept her. The next time I went to Mike's cottage to pick him up, Debbie went with me.

He seemed surprised but pleased when I told him that Debbie wanted to go on a hike with us, and he readily agreed with my suggestion that he show her some of the more interesting places we'd discovered on Dogface. More than once I caught him looking at her out of the corner of his eye. Lithe and deeply tanned, with a quick engaging smile and long auburn hair worn free, Debbie was extremely attractive. And Mike had obviously noticed. He was, I thought to myself, getting to that age. I was sure that he had never seen a woman quite like her. The ones he was used to—primarily nurses—all dressed in white uniforms. And Cecile was an older woman who had grandchildren Mike's age.

Initially, he was very bashful around Debbie, but she adroitly put him at ease. Changing into her "grubbies"—faded Levi's and a T-shirt—and anchoring her hair with a blue paisley scarf before setting out, Debbie slid easily into the routine. Over the next several weeks the three of us thoroughly scoured Dogface, hiking up to the summit and returning to the canteen for refreshments. Mike took great pride in showing Debbie around the water filtration plant, the farm, the water tanks, even teaching her the names of the trees. He seemed more than happy to include her in all our activities, although he frequently walked next to me, holding my hand and positioning me between him and Debbie.

One day an incident occurred that really made me smile. We were coming back down the trail from the crest when Mike, clambering among the boulders, found himself overextended and stranded on a ledge leading to a drop of several feet. He needed assistance.

"Some-bahdy help me . . ."

Debbie, who was closer, stepped over near him.

"C'mon, Mike, you can climb down from there by yourself. It's not that high."

Mike stared down at her for several seconds, then drew himself up to his full, gangly height. Waggling his finger at Debbie, he said reproachfully, "Hikas hahfta work togethuh!"

Debbie looked at me, chagrin written clearly across her face. Then she began climbing up to where Mike was.

"You're absolutely right, Mike—hikers *do* have to work together. C'mon now, give me your hand."

He accepted readily and they scrambled down the short wall. Later, after we had returned to the administrative cottage, Debbie mentioned Mike's rebuke.

"He made me feel that high!" she winced.

"That's okay," I countered. "He's done that to me lots of times. Anyway, it was just a little testing for you. I suspect he knows he's breaking you in as his new therapist."

I figured Mike would surmise that I was leaving. After all, he was a very sensitive kid who didn't miss much—those little antennae were always out there waving around.

But with only five weeks left before my departure, it was time for me to have a talk with him. I had rehearsed in my mind a hundred different ways of telling him I was leaving, but none seemed any easier than the others. I was dreading the whole thing. The most harrowing fantasy was that perhaps he would immediately and irretrievably melt back into his shell. There was just no way of predicting how Mike would react. The longer I put off telling him, the more anxious I got about it. I couldn't delay any longer.

The following day Mike, Debbie, and I went for a short hike and then stopped at the canteen for ice cream cones. I had forewarned Debbie, so she excused herself early to return to the unit while Mike and I wandered down to some nearby trees along the dry creek bed to finish our ice cream. Settling comfortably under an old willow tree, I summoned up my courage as Mike scrambled in pursuit of a sunning lizard. After watching him for a few minutes, I said,

"Mike, I want to talk with you."

He paused and glanced quickly over at me. Something in my voice arrested him and, forgetting the lizard, he scuffed over to me, a serious look on his face.

"Sit down here beside me for a minute, okay?" I patted the nearby grass.

Mike flopped down cross-legged, leaning his back against the trunk of the willow.

"Mike, we've been good friends, hiking buddies, for quite a while now, haven't we?"

He nodded soberly.

"And you know that during this last year I

finally became a doctor—a doctor who is going to work with girls and boys like you who have problems and have to come to a hospital like this one."

Mike nodded again.

"Now Mike, I've been offered a position—a job—at a place far away from here. I can work with some people there who can teach me much more than I know now about helping kids. But to do that, Mike, I have to go away. I've thought about it a lot—believe me, it's been one of the hardest decisions I've ever had to make. But I feel I have to do it. Mike, I'm going to be going away . . ."

Up to this point Mike had been watching me, his eyes darting around nervously. Now as he finally heard me acknowledge my leaving, a look of desolation spread over his face. Almost immediately his eyes shifted away and gazed out at some point above my shoulder. I recognized the same expression I'd seen that afternoon on Dogface so long ago just before he made the decision to reach out and give me his hand, to trust me.

"Mike—" I began falteringly, "I do love you and we've been the best of buddies. But sometimes people have to go on to new things, different things. And sometimes that means they have to leave someone who's very special. It hurts a lot to have to separate, and I feel really bad because I know this is hurting you. Believe me, that's the last thing in the world I'd want to do to my hiking buddy. Can you understand that, Mike?"

His eyes shifted back to me, his face flushed and contorted as he tried not to cry.

"Mike—" I put my arms out, and with a little whimper his muffled sobs were buried in my shoulder.

And I cried right along with him, intensely sorry to have caused this pain, wondering whether I had indeed made the right decision. But at the same time, I was relieved that at last he knew.

After a few minutes we both sat quietly, my arm still around his shoulders. Finally he gazed up at me, his red-rimmed eyes and dirt-streaked face set, but his voice faltering a bit.

"Hike Dogfahs a liddo ways, Paht?"

Giving him another big hug, I said to him, "Sure, Mike. You know, you're one spunky kid!"

During the next few weeks, I took some time at each of our meetings to talk with him about my leaving. Debbie would always take off early while Mike and I walked slowly back to the cottage together. Other times we sat and talked in his room, surrounded by his pictures of our hikes and the other places we'd visited and things we'd done together. It was important that Mike fully understand that I was really going away. But it was even more vital that we talk about our relationship and how he felt about my departure. At first the discussions took a fairly predictable direction.

"But why do you hahfta go, Paht—don't you like it heah?" ... "Why cahn't you learn to be a betta docta heah?" ... "If you leaf, you cahn't hike up Dogfahs."

I tried to help Mike reach a balance, to understand the feelings he had toward me, and to recognize that there would always be an element of risk involved whenever he got close to someone. And Mike continued to astound me with his ability to grasp these concepts.

One day I told him, "You know, Mike, even grown-ups have trouble with all this—loving someone, caring deeply, and taking the risk of opening themselves up to others. That's scary because it's always possible that the other person may not return their affection or might someday leave them. It's a really tough thing to deal with."

Mike met my eyes with an intensely perceptive look. "You mean like when Debbie was—" he searched for the word, trying to grapple with something he didn't understand, "—when Debbie was dee-borse ahn' she was unhahppy . . ."

I just stared at him. Debbie's recent divorce was more or less a secret. In fact, most of the staff hadn't known what was going on.

"How did you find out about that, Mike? Do

you know what it means when you say she was divorced?"

He shrugged. "Nuh. But I saw Debbie—ahn' she was crying. I nevuh saw a grown-up cry. She few bahd?"

I shook my head, amazed by his forthright logic.

"Well yes, she felt bad. When two people have been married and they're not happy together, sometimes it's better for them to separate and not live together anymore. That's what divorce is, and it can be very painful. But there are also other kinds of separation that are difficult to adjust to. Like when someone dies and everyone feels sad inside and misses him. Or when people have to stay in the hospital for a long time like you have and they're away from their families. They miss their folks very much. I think your mother and father have missed you a lot all these years. It's been very hard for them."

Mike looked away for several moments, struggling to reconcile this jumble of ideas. At last he said, "Ah Mommy ahn' Dahdee go-ing to come ahn' get me ahn' take me hoome?"

"Well, Mike, I just don't know about that. Certainly they will take you on more home visits so all of you can spend some time together. Perhaps eventually it would be for good. Would you like to go and live at home?"

"Yes, I would—vewy much!"

"Well, we'll have to see about that. In the meantime, you just keep doing as great as you have been and maybe things will work out that way. Keep on drawing all those nice pictures, going to the playroom with Debbie, and learning in school. But especially, Mike, stay the super person you are, always doing things for other people and letting them do things for you—just being nice to them the way you are. You know, everyone really likes you a lot. Did you know that?"

He shook his head, squirming and blushing with embarrassment.

"Well, they do—very much. Because you're such a nice person. And you like them, too, don't you? That's what it's all about, isn't it?"

He nodded, still self-conscious and bashful.

There were many talks like this and gradually Mike seemed to begin to accept my leaving. One day in school, he showed Cecile a picture that he had just drawn, saying, "This is my friend, Paht, and this is me—Mik'l. Paht is go-ing fah away, ahn' he won't be able to hike with Mik'l on Dogfahs anymore . . . or go to cahnteen . . ."

An occasional report filtered back to me from the cottage, too. For instance, one evening a television program contained a tearful leave-taking, and as Mike made the connection an aide overhead him say softly to himself, "Paht is leaf-ing, too. Paht is my friend . . ."

* * *

One warm afternoon in late summer, over a month after we'd first included Debbie in our activities, she joined us again for a hike. We had climbed to Mike's favorite spot on Dogface and now we were relaxing on the crest, idly talking and joking, when Mike abruptly turned to Debbie with the candor only a child can muster.

"Once I saw you cry. On the baseball field"

Debbie looked surprised, then nodded.

"I saw you crying when you got dee-borse. You fewt bahd . . . it hurt you . . ." The statements were tentative, searching.

"Yes, it did, Mike. Whenever something like that happens, it hurts—a lot. You and Pat are feeling bad now because Pat's moving so far away. That hurts inside, too, because you're going to miss each other very much. Isn't that right?"

Mike nodded. He seemed lost in thought and Debbie and I exchanged concerned looks.

After a while we started back down the hill, in no particular hurry and somewhat reluctant to return to the hospital. Mike seemed oddly subdued; that wasn't like him and I wondered what was up. By the time we reached the quad, we were walking three abreast, Mike in the middle, and he was holding my hand.

Suddenly, with incredible enthusiasm, he exclaimed, "*I* know! *Debbie* cahn be my new friend!!"

Without breaking stride, he reached out and

clutched Debbie's hand, the ultimate gesture of acceptance. Over his head, Debbie and I smiled at each other.

"That sounds like a great idea, Mike," I said. Then all three of us stopped, looked from one to the other, and burst out laughing.

Debbie and I wondered aloud why *we* hadn't thought of such a fine idea, but Mike was impervious to such conjecture—he had found a solution to the problem all by himself. The rest of the way back to the cottage, Mike skipped along between us, holding both our hands.

As for me, I felt as though the entire weight of Dogface had suddenly been lifted from my shoulders. The reaction was, of course, exactly what we'd planned and hoped for, but it was significant that Mike had initiated the final choice on his own. The following days substantiated his decision as reports accumulated from those in contact with Mike that he was telling everyone who would listen, "Debbie is go-ing to be my new friend ahn' hike with me on Dogfahs ahn' take me to th' playroom. Debbie is my new friend . . ."

During our final meetings, I tended to become less involved as the relationship between Mike and Debbie began to flourish. And Mike slowly pulled back from me as he spent more time with his "new friend."

*　　*　　*

I was ready to leave. I had said my farewells to the staff at a going-away party on the unit and then Scott and I walked down to his office. I eased into the familiar red leather chair, stretching my legs out. "I've spent a few hours in this baby," I said.

Scott selected a pipe and proceeded with the established ritual. By mutual accord, we had grown accustomed to using that time to collect ourselves, and our thoughts. After those moments of preparation, Scott peered at me through the tangy smoke.

"How's the packing going?"

"Slowly."

"Still not too sure that you made the right decision?"

"No, I guess not, Scott."

We sat in silence.

"Mike?"

"He's doing fine so far. It's other things, too, I guess."

"Like . . ."

"Well, I don't know exactly where to begin. You know, Scott, it's like my life before coming here just flowed along and I never fully appreciated how lucky I am. I took so much for granted—my parents always being there, being supportive, caring, giving me the freedom to do whatever seemed right at the moment. Now I'm so much more aware of people and relationships. Of not taking anyone for granted. I look at my parents—they're getting older now, worried because I'll be living so far away—and I'm finally getting around to appreciating them, saying thank you. And, of course, they know what brought it all home ... literally. A goofy little kid who buzzed around this place and about drove me up the wall. It's been shock therapy for me."

Scott nodded, watching me closely.

"And my teachers—you, Warfield, and others —all of you set expectations for me. High ones. But what you really did was believe in me, in my ability to figure things out, excel at whatever I chose to do. And that helped me to believe in myself. Parts of me have been reached that I didn't know I had, and I'll never be the same ..."

Scott was examining his pipe in minute detail. Then he said, "It really works both ways, Pat. It's been rewarding for me, too, seeing you grow and mature. And that's where a major part of professional and personal satisfaction comes from—not only from helping the troubled, but also from enhancing the skills of someone like you who is entering the field. This power of understanding and caring, and certainly love, is of such significance I'm sure you'll carry it with you the rest of your life.

"And now you're off for more challenges. I'm sure there'll be many more professional successes like the one you've had with Mike. But I can tell you this—no matter how many people you help over the years as a psychotherapist, there'll always be one who will be very special, one who will always come to mind when you reflect upon your work. Because Mike was the very first—and a pretty tough customer—but you did it."

At last I went searching for Mike to say my final good-bye to him. We sat in his room under the myriad of Dogface pictures, neither of us wanting to resurrect the gearing-down of feelings and involvement that was occurring inside both of us. I made my farewell breif.

"Mike, you've been a very good buddy, and I want you to know how much I appreciate your willingness to share so much with me. We've both come a long way together . . ."

Mike sat on his bed, looking down at the floor. Slowly he reached behind him and handed me a rolled-up paper tied with a green ribbon. Shyly, he said, "This is fur you, Paht. From me—"

I slipped off the ribbon and unrolled the paper. "Thank you, Mike." My voice caught and "Mike" came out as a throaty whisper. I gave him a quick hug and moved to the door. "We'll see each other again, Mike. I promise . . ."

He nodded, glancing briefly at me, then lowered his head again and blinked back the tears. As I left he remained there, poised quietly on the edge of his bed, and once again I thought how special he was. I was sure he'd make it. Really, he'd made it already.

Out in the parking lot I gazed for a few moments at the silhouette of Dogface, set ablaze by the red-orange rays of the late afternoon sun. Then I picked up the picture Mike had given me and looked at it for a long time. It was a "cooperative" drawing we had done several months ago—started by me, finished by Mike.

I set it down on the seat beside me, shaking my head. Something momentous had happened to me here—something, as Scott had said, that would be a part of me for the rest of my life.

A movement caught my eye and I turned to see three small children making their way back from the riverbed. From this distance they looked like any other children, not the exceptional ones they were. I remembered that that had been my impression on my very first day at the hospital. The day I had spotted that little urchin scurrying along the wall.

What extraordinary experiences, and extraordinary people, I had met here. With a heavy sigh, I turned the key in the ignition and then retraced the winding road that would take me away from the hospital and halfway across the country.

—————— *chapter nineteen* ——————

Since I left California, Debbie has helped Mike write and draw picture-letters to me that relate his continuing activities. It's difficult to know just how complete his recovery will be. There is little doubt that the early and severe onset of schizophrenia arrested his development. Along with that handicap, the dimension of living in a hospital for many years can produce a large degree of dependence. It may be that Mike will always need a certain measure of professional help. But he's a fighter and, with time and treatment, he may just be able to put it all behind him.

For myself, I can now better understand why what happened between Mike and me was significant—not only for him, but for me as well. Each of us was ready for the other. My enthusiasm was genuine, if a bit misdirected at times. I had a lot of energy, fueled by idealism, and a good hunch that I could reach that forlorn kid. As a psychotherapist, I've learned to value that kind of intuition.

I also believe that very early in the game, Mike sensed all that in me. The layers of hurt and rejection ran deep, but underneath was a child—a tentative little creature who yearned only to be understood, cared for, loved. But until someone came along who could find a way to gain his trust, Mike had waited, like a dormant plant, for the warming winds of spring.

——A NOTE ABOUT THE AUTHOR——

A native Californian of maverick Irish extraction, Robert Lane has long been fascinated by human behavior. After receiving his Ph.D. from the University of Wisconsin, Madison, he worked as a clinical psychologist in various mental institutions and treatment centers in the Midwest. Dr. Lane is now on the faculty of the University of Wisconsin, Oshkosh. He and his wife, Mary, live on the shore of the legendary Lake Butte des Morts.

Ø

SIGNET Books of Related Interest

Buy them at your local
bookstore or use coupon
on next page for ordering.

Great Novels from SIGNET

(0451)

- [ ] **SECOND HEAVEN** by Judith Guest. (124995—$3.95)*
- [ ] **DANIEL MARTIN** by John Fowles. (122100—$4.50)†
- [ ] **THE EBONY TOWER** by John Fowles. (123549—$3.50)
- [ ] **THE FRENCH LIEUTENANT'S WOMAN** by John Fowles.
(110951—$3.50)*
- [ ] **BREAKFAST AT TIFFANY'S** by Truman Capote.
(120426—$2.50)*
- [ ] **THE GRASS HARP** and **TREE OF NIGHT** by Truman Capote.
(120434—$2.75)*
- [ ] **IN COLD BLOOD** by Truman Capote. (121988—$3.95)*
- [ ] **MUSIC FOR CHAMELEONS** by Truman Capote.
(099346—$3.50)*
- [ ] **OTHER VOICES, OTHER ROOMS** by Truman Capote.
(099613—$2.25)
- [ ] **THE ARMIES OF THE NIGHT** by Norman Mailer.
(123174—$3.95)
- [ ] **THE CHAPMAN REPORT** by Irving Wallace. (127102—$3.95)
- [ ] **THE PRIZE** by Irving Wallace. (123050—$2.95)
- [ ] **THE FABULOUS SHOWMAN** by Irving Wallace.
(113853—$2.95)
- [ ] **THE THREE SIRENS** by Irving Wallace. (125843—$3.95)*
- [ ] **THE SECOND LADY** by Irving Wallace. (125908—$1.95)
- [ ] **GOD'S LITTLE ACRE** by Erskine Caldwell. (121554—$2.95)
- [ ] **TOBACCO ROAD** by Erskine Caldwell. (121562—$2.95)*

*Prices slightly higher in Canada
†Not available in Canada